Alastair
Sawday's

Special Places
to Stay

British
Bed & Breakfast

"The best-selling guide to
British B&Bs... nothing quite
compares."
The Bookseller

Edited by Nicola Crosse

Alastair
Sawday's

Special Places

Pubs & Inns
of England & Wales

"...more selective than
its competitors."
The Bookseller

Edited by David Hancock

Alastair
Sawday's

Special Places
to Stay

Devon &
Cornwall

"When they say 'special'
that's exactly what you get."
Observer

Edited by Nicola Crosse

Alastair
Sawday's

Special Places
to Stay

Scotland

"Much-loved guidebooks."
The Guardian

Alastair
Sawday's

Special Places to Stay

Tenth edition
Copyright © 2008 Alastair Sawday
Publishing Co. Ltd
Published in October 2008
ISBN-13: 978-1-906136-06-2

Alastair Sawday Publishing Co. Ltd,
The Old Farmyard, Yanley Lane,
Long Ashton, Bristol BS41 9LR, UK
Tel: +44 (0)1275 395430
Email: info@sawdays.co.uk
Web: www.sawdays.co.uk

The Globe Pequot Press,
P. O. Box 480, Guilford,
Connecticut 06437, USA
Tel: +1 203 458 4500
Email: info@globepequot.com
Web: www.globepequot.com

Series Editor Alastair Sawday
Editor Tom Bell
Editorial Director Annie Shillito
Writing Tom Bell
Inspections Tom Bell
Accounts Bridget Bishop,
Christine Buxton
Editorial Sue Bourner,
Kate Ball, Jo Boissevain
Production Julia Richardson,
Rachel Coe, Tom Germain,
Anny Mortada
Sales & Marketing & PR
Rob Richardson,
Sarah Bolton, Thomas Caldwell
Web & IT Joe Green,
Chris Banks, Mike Peake,
Russell Wilkinson

We have made every effort to ensure the accuracy of the information in this book at the time of going to press. However, we cannot accept any responsibility for any loss, injury or inconvenience resulting from the use of information contained therein.

Alastair

Sawday's

Special Places
to Stay

British
Hotels & Inns

4　Contents

Front

Guide entries

The buildings

Beautiful as they were, our old offices leaked heat, used electricity to heat water and rooms, flooded spaces with light to illuminate one person, and were not ours to alter.

So in 2005 we created our own eco-offices by converting some old barns to create a low-emissions building. Heating and lighting the building, which houses over 30 employees, now produces only 0.28 tonnes of carbon dioxide per year. Not bad when you compare this with the 6 tonnes emitted by the average UK household. We achieved this through a variety of innovative and energy-saving building techniques, described below.

Insulation   We went to great lengths to ensure that very little heat will escape, by:
• laying insulating board 90mm thick immediately under the roof tiles and on the floor
• lining the whole of the inside of the building with plastic sheeting to ensure air-tightness
• fixing further insulation underneath the roof and between the rafters
• fixing insulated plaster-board to add another layer of insulation.
All this means we are insulated for the Arctic, and almost totally air-tight.

Heating   We installed a wood-pellet boiler from Austria, in order to be largely fossil-fuel free. The pellets are made from compressed sawdust, a waste product from timber mills that work only with sustainably managed forests. The heat is conveyed by water to all corners of the building via an under-floor system.

Water   We installed a 6000-litre tank to collect rainwater from the roofs. This is pumped back, via an ultra-violet filter, to the lavatories, showers and basins. There are two solar thermal panels on the roof providing heat to the one (massively insulated) hot-water cylinder.

Lighting   We have a carefully planned mix of low-energy lighting: task lighting and up-lighting. We also installed three sun-pipes — polished aluminium tubes that reflect the outside light down to chosen areas of the building.

Electricity   All our electricity has long come from the Good Energy Company and is 100% renewable.

Materials   Virtually all materials are non-toxic or natural. Our carpets, for example, are made from (80%) Herdwick sheep-wool from National Trust farms in the Lake District.

Doors and windows   Outside doors and new windows are wooden, double-glazed, beautifully constructed in Norway. Old windows have been double-glazed.

We have a building we are proud of, and architects and designers are fascinated by. But best of all, we are now in a better position to encourage our owners and readers to take sustainability more seriously.

Photo: Tom Germain

What we do

Besides moving the business to a low-carbon building, the company works in a number of ways to reduce its overall environmental footprint:

• all office travel is logged as part of a carbon sequestration programme, and money for compensatory tree-planting is dispatched to SCAD in India for a tree-planting and development project

• we avoid flying and take the train for business trips wherever possible; when we have to fly, we 'double offset'

• car-sharing and the use of a company pool car are part of company policy; recycled cooking oil is used in one car and LPG in the other

• organic and Fair Trade basic provisions are used in the staff kitchen and organic food is provided by the company at all in-house events

• green cleaning products are used throughout the office

• all kitchen waste is composted and used on the office organic allotment.

Our total 'operational' carbon footprint (including travel to and from work, plus all our trips to visit our Special Places to Stay) is just over 17 tonnes per year. We have come a long way, but we would like to get this figure as close to zero as possible.

For many years Alastair Sawday Publishing has been 'greening' the business in different ways. Our aim is to reduce our environmental footprint as far as possible – with almost everything we do we have the environmental implications in mind. (We once claimed to be the world's first carbon neutral publishing company, but are now wary of such claims). In recognition of our efforts we won a Business Commitment to the Environment Award in 2005, and in 2006 a Queen's Award for Enterprise in the Sustainable Development category. In that year Alastair was voted ITN's 'Eco Hero'.

We have created our own eco-offices by converting former barns to create a low-emissions building. Through a variety of innovative and energy-saving techniques this has reduced our carbon emissions by 35%.

Photo: Tom Germain

But becoming 'green' is a journey and, although we began long before most companies, we still have a long way to go.

In 2008 we won the Independent Publishers Guild Environmental Award. The judging panel were effusive in their praise, stating: "With green issues currently at the forefront of publishers' minds, Alastair Sawday Publishing was singled out in this category as a model for all independents to follow. Its efforts to reduce waste in its office and supply chain have reduced the company's environmental impact, and it works closely with staff to identify more areas of improvement. Here is a publisher who lives and breathes green. Alastair Sawday has all the right principles and is clearly committed to improving its practice further."

Our Fragile Earth series is a growing collection of campaigning books about the environment. Highlighting the perilous state of the world yet offering imaginative and radical solutions and some intriguing facts, these books will make you weep and smile. They will keep you up to date and well armed for the battle with apathy.

THE QUEEN'S AWARDS
FOR ENTERPRISE:
SUSTAINABLE DEVELOPMENT
2006

Thomas Jefferson wrote that he had "not observed men's honesty to increase with their riches". Indeed, and we have probably all noticed the same thing.

I wonder if the same might be said of men's commercial institutions — companies. It is a short hop from there to a reflection on the nature of large hotels and small ones. You probably believe, as we do, that small hotels are more honest, in general, than big ones — 'honest' in the fullest sense. They will recognise your own honesty and respond to it. If you make a mistake, they won't punish you. If you sound honest when explaining that you are going to be late, they may keep the restaurant open for you. There is, in short, a human relationship there, and it is that very humanity that allows for honesty, nuances, kindnesses and give-and-take.

So we are committed to the small hotels of Britain. They are going to have a tough year, with the credit crunch and emptier pockets. They work their socks off to keep going, bravely trying out new ideas and putting their creative heads over the parapet. Survival is fraught with cost. (We all know about staff costs, but think of what the Health and Safety people can do to a hotel!) The hotels in this book are, however, terrific value and Tom Bell has found and encouraged many places that make my heart sing: the unusual, the brave, those driven by aesthetics as much as by commercial need. He has paid attention,

Photo: Tom Germain

too, to the way hotels function within their communities; many here are powerful advocates of local food production and supporters of local vitality and diversity.

So the message is: the small hotels of Britain are thriving, as energetic as ever, filled with enterprising owners who will pull out the stops for you. Their enterprise is honest and decent, deserving your support. If you haven't tried a hotel for a while, now is the time — for we are in a creative and dynamic period. Perhaps the economic woes will encourage the best of us to do our best.

Alastair Sawday

What makes a special hotel? We all have different answers: a fabulous setting knee-deep in the country; stylish interiors that spoil you rotten; beds to-die-for wrapped in crisp linen; owners who go the extra mile.

My father would have had a simple answer – breakfast – and for anyone who has travelled a little, the following story may strike a chord. Last November, while touring Indo-China, I found myself in Saigon staying at an extremely smart hotel. At seven o'clock in the morning I took the lift to the 14th floor, for breakfast on the roof terrace. I found that I was not alone – 200 others had beaten me to it and I joined the bun fight somewhat reluctantly, running around frantically trying to scoop up whatever sustenance remained. Chaos reigned. Waiters were rushing about replenishing stocks, weaving past queuing guests with platters of fruit

held high in the air, while a couple of maître d's stood like traffic policemen at a busy road junction, directing new arrivals through the crush. The food was average – not what you hope for when paying $250 a night – the orange juice hot, the bacon cold, the coffee non-existent. My father would have been distinctly unimpressed, and as I sat stoically battling with the plastic seal of a tiny jam container, I conjured up happy memories of the sort of breakfast you will tuck into when staying at hotels in this book.

It was a nostalgic indulgence that made me smile and determined these words to be written. I thought of Arbroath smokies, venison sausages, black pudding from the local farm, hot porridge sprinkled with brown sugar, blueberry pancakes drenched in maple syrup, strawberry sorbet served with pink champagne. Over the last ten years I have nobly surrendered to duty, sacrificing my waistline to ensure hotels pass muster at breakfast, and I can humbly report that in my opinion no nation serves a better breakfast than the British. Sure, I like a good croissant and a stick of baguette, or freshly brewed coffee and tropical fruits, but I also enjoy Victorian sugar shakers and a menu of exotic teas, of which you will find several in this book. I like a little service, too – my newspaper waiting at the table, the waitress bringing a hot pot of tea and a quick chat about the weather or, as I eagerly received earlier this year, a good tip for the Grand National (it fell at the seventh!).

Photo right: Holm House, entry 270
Photo left: The George Hotel, entry 127

Breakfast in a good hotel is more than a meal: it is a daily ritual performed, one hopes, with elegance, kindness and attention to detail, a short piece of theatre which sets us up for the day. It is for residents only, the last meal we eat before leaving, the final impression we carry away, and the sight of a bright yellow egg yolk that was plucked from the hen house an hour before, or of cornflakes being ferried to the table in elegant blue china by a smartly dressed waiter, can lift the spirit just as effectively as discovering a travertine marble bathroom or a terrace that looks out to sea.

And so I commend to you a book of breakfasts and I ask you to dig in and test ᵔm for yourself. Should a hotel come up short, point out the virtues of hot toast, local produce, homemade marmalade and freshly-squeezed orange juice: after all, we have a tradition to uphold here and an orchestra of voices may persuade the owner of the benefits of change. Equally, when you experience a sublime moment, do let the waiter, the manager or the owner know. The effect on staff is greatly appreciated: it makes their day.

Tom Bell

It's simple. There are no rules, no boxes to tick. We choose places that we like and are fiercely subjective in our choices. We also recognise that one person's idea of special is not necessarily someone else's so there is a huge variety of places, and prices, in the book. Those who are familiar with our Special Places series know that we look for comfort, originality, authenticity, and reject the insincere, the anonymous and the banal. The way guests are treated comes as high on our list as the setting, the architecture, the atmosphere and the food.

We hope you enjoy these places. They all have something special to offer, whether it be fine views and great antiques, a fire in your bedroom (or bathroom!), food that is fresh as the day or a dazzling garden. The owners of these properties often go beyond the call of duty and strive to provide the best that they can.

Inspections

We visit every place in the guide to get a feel for how both house and owner tick. We don't take a clipboard and we don't have a list of what is acceptable and what is not. Instead, we chat for an hour or so with the owner or manager and look round. It's all very informal, but it gives us an excellent idea of who would enjoy staying there. If the visit happens to be the last of the day, we sometimes stay the night. Once in the book, properties are re-inspected every three to four years so that we can keep things fresh and accurate.

Photo right: Mill End, entry 74
Photo left: Plas Bodegroes, entry 272

Feedback

In between inspections we rely on feedback from our army of readers, as well as from staff members who are encouraged to visit properties across the series. This feedback is invaluable to us and we always follow up on comments.

So do tell us whether your stay has been a joy or not, if the atmosphere was great or stuffy, the owners and staff cheery or bored. The accuracy of the book depends on what you, and our inspectors, tell us. A lot of the new entries in each edition are recommended by our readers, so keep telling us about new places you've discovered too. Please use the forms on our website at www.sawdays.co.uk, or later in this book (page 375).

However, please do not tell us if your starter was cold, or the bedside light broken. Tell the owner, immediately, and get them to do something about it. Most owners, or staff, are more than happy to correct problems and will bend over backwards to help. Far better than bottling it up and then writing to us a week later!

Subscriptions

Owners pay to appear in this guide. Their fee goes towards the high costs of inspecting, of producing an all-colour book and of maintaining our website. We only include places that we find special for one reason or another, so it is not possible for anyone to buy their way onto these pages.

Nor is it possible for the owner to write their own description. We will say if the bedrooms are small, or if a main road is near. We do our best to avoid misleading people.

Disclaimer

We make no claims to pure objectivity in choosing these places. They are here simply because we like them. Our opinions and tastes are ours alone and this book is a statement of them; we hope you will share them. We have done our utmost to get our facts right but apologise unreservedly for any mistakes that may have crept in.

You should know that we don't check such things as fire alarms, swimming pool security or any other regulation with which owners of properties receiving paying guests should comply. This is the responsibility of the owners.

Photo: Cowley Manor, entry 108

Finding the right place for you

All these places are special in one way or another. All have been visited and then written about honestly so that you can take what you want and leave the rest. Those of you who swear by Sawday's books trust our write-ups precisely because we don't have a blanket standard; we include places simply because we like them. But we all have different priorities, so do read and choose carefully.

Maps

Each property is flagged with its entry number on the maps at the front. These maps are a great starting point for planning your trip, but please don't use them as anything other than a general guide – use a decent road map for real navigation. Most places will send you detailed instructions once you have booked your stay.

Ethical Collection

We're always keen to draw attention to owners who are striving to have a positive impact on the world, so you'll notice that some entries are flagged as being part of our "Ethical Collection". These places are working hard to reduce their environmental footprint, making significant contributions to their local community, or are passionate about serving local or organic food. Owners have had to fill in a very detailed questionnaire before becoming part of this Collection – read more on page 373. This doesn't mean that other places in the guide are not taking similar initiatives –

Photo: The Mill at Gordleton, entry 121

many are – but we may not yet know about them.

Sawday's Travel Club

We've recently launched a Travel Club, based around the Special Places to Stay series; you'll see a 📖 symbol on those places offering something extra to Club members, so to find out how to join see page 367.

Symbols

Below each entry you will see some symbols, which are explained at the very back of the book. They are based on the information given to us by the owners. However, things do change: bikes may be under repair or a new pool may have been put in. Please use the symbols as a guide rather than an absolute statement of fact and double-check anything that is important to you – owners occasionally bend their own rules, so it's worth asking if you may take your child or dog even if they don't have the symbol.

Wheelchair access – Some hotels are keen to accept wheelchair users into their hotels and have made provision for them. However, this does not mean that wheelchair users will always be met with a perfect landscape. You may encounter ramps, a shallow step, gravelled paths, alternative routes into some rooms, a bathroom (not a wet room), perhaps even a lift. In short, there may be the odd hindrance and we urge you to call and make sure you will get what you need.

Limited mobility – The limited mobility symbol 🏃 shows those places where at least one bedroom and bathroom is accessible without using stairs. The symbol is designed to satisfy those who walk slowly, with difficulty, or with the aid of a stick. A wheelchair may be able to navigate some areas, but in our opinion these places are not fully wheelchair friendly. If you use a chair for longer distances, but are not too bad over shorter distances, you'll probably be OK; again, please ring and ask. There may be a step or two, a bath or a shower with a tray in a cubicle, a good distance between the car park and your room, slippery flagstones or a tight turn.

Children – The 🧍 symbol shows places which are happy to accept children of all ages. This does not mean that they will necessarily have cots, high chairs, etc. Having said that, there are several places in this book that are ideal for families with young children. Many have huge swathes of lawn for running and tumbling, a swimming pool for fun and plenty of games and other things to do. Plenty of other children around means you won't be quite so embarrassed when your child has the loudest tantrum of its life in the dining room, and a newly found friend for your little dear can sometimes leave you time to read at least the first page of your novel. If you want to get out and about in the evenings, check when you book whether there are any babysitting services. Even very small places can sometimes organise this for you.

Pets – Our 🐕 symbol shows places which are happy to accept pets. It means they can sleep in the bedroom with you, but not on the bed. It's really important to get this one right before you arrive, as many places make you keep dogs in the car. Check carefully: Spot's emotional wellbeing may depend on it.

Owners' pets – The 🐈 symbol is given when the owners have their own pet on the premises. It may not be a cat! But it is there to warn you that you may be greeted by a dog, serenaded by a parrot, or indeed sat upon by a cat.

Photo: White House, entry 84

Types of places

Hotels can vary from huge, humming and slick to those with only a few rooms that are run by owners at their own pace. In some you may not get room service or have your bags carried in and out. In smaller hotels there may be a fixed menu for dinner with very little choice, so if you have dishes that leave you cold, it's important to say so when you book your meal. If you decide to stay at an inn remember that they can be noisy, especially at weekends. If these things are important to you, then do check when you book: a simple question or two can avoid regrettable misunderstandings.

Rooms

Bedrooms – these are described as double, twin, single, family or suite. A double may contain a bed which is anything from 135cm wide to 180cm wide. A twin will contain two single beds (usually 90cm wide). A suite will have a separate sitting area, but it may not be in a different room. Family rooms can vary in size, as can the number of beds they hold, so do ask. And do not assume that every bedroom has a TV.

Bathrooms – all bedrooms have their own bathrooms unless we say that they don't. Bath/shower means a bath with shower over; bath and shower means there is a separate shower unit. If you have your own bathroom but you have to leave the room to get to it we describe it as 'separate'. There are very few places in the book that have shared bathrooms and they are usually reserved for members of the same party. Again, we state this clearly.

Meals

Breakfast is included in the room price unless otherwise stated. If only a continental breakfast is offered, we let you know. Often you will feast on local sausage and bacon, eggs from resident hens, homemade breads and jams. In some you may have organic yogurts and beautifully presented fruit compotes.

A few places serve lunch, most do Sunday lunch (often very well-priced), the vast majority offer dinner. In some places you can content yourself with bar meals, in others you can feast on five courses. Most offer a three-course, fixed-price menu, for £25-£35 without wine. In many restaurants you can also eat à la carte. Very occasionally you eat communally – if you loathe making small talk with strangers avoid these places. Some large hotels (and some posh private houses) will bring dinner to your room if you prefer, or let you eat in the garden by candlelight. Always ask for what you want and sometimes, magically, it happens.

Prices and minimum stays

We quote the lowest price for two people in low season to the highest price in high season. Only a few places have designated single rooms; if no single rooms are listed, the price we quote refers to single occupancy of a double room. In many places prices rise even higher when local events bring people flooding to the area, a point worth remembering when heading to Cheltenham for the racing or Glyndebourne for the opera.

The half-board price quoted is per person per night and includes dinner, usually three courses. Mostly you're offered a table d'hôte menu. Occasionally you eat à la carte and find some dishes carry a small supplement. There are often great deals to be had, mostly mid-week in low season.

Booking and cancellation

Most places ask for a deposit at the time of booking, either by cheque or credit/debit card. If you cancel – depending on how much notice you give – you can lose all or part of this deposit unless your room is re-let.

It is reasonable for hotels to take a deposit to secure a booking; they have learnt that if they don't, the commitment of the guest wanes and they may fail to turn up.

Some cancellation policies are more stringent than others. It is also worth noting that some owners will take this deposit directly from your credit/debit card without contacting you to discuss it. So ask them to explain their cancellation policy clearly before booking so you understand exactly where you stand; it may well avoid a nasty surprise. And consider taking out travel insurance (with a cancellation clause) if you're concerned.

Weekends

Most small hotels do not accept one-night bookings at weekends. Small country hotels are rarely full during the week and the weekend trade keeps them going. If you ring in March for a Saturday night in July, you won't get it. If you ring at the last moment and they have a room, you will. Some places insist on three-night stays on bank holiday weekends.

Payment

Those places that do not accept credit or debit cards are marked with a cash/cheque symbol.

Arrivals and departures

Housekeeping is usually done by 2pm, and your room will usually be available by mid-afternoon. Normally you will have to wave goodbye to it between 10am and 11am. Sometimes one can pay to linger. Some inns are closed between 3pm and 6pm, so do try and agree an arrival time in advance or you may find nobody there.

Smoking

It is now illegal to smoke in public areas and no hotel in this guide permits smoking in bedrooms (you may be fined if you do). Bars, restaurants and sitting rooms have become smoke-free. Smokers must now make do with the garden.

Closed

When given in months this means for the whole of the month stated.

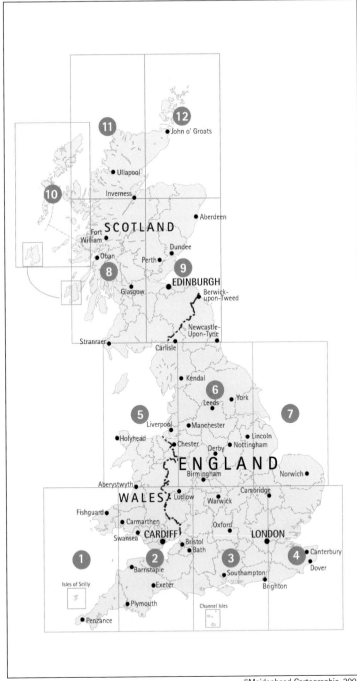

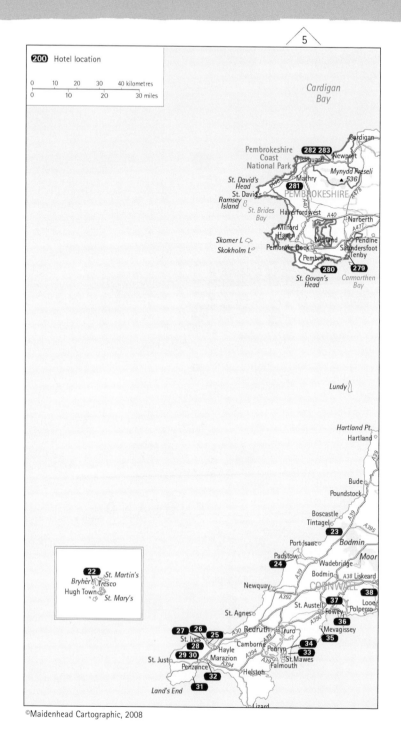

5

200 Hotel location

| 0 | 10 | 20 | 30 | 40 kilometres |
| 0 | | 10 | 20 | 30 miles |

Cardigan Bay

Pembrokeshire
Coast
National Park

282 283 Newport

Cardigan

Fishguard

Mynydd Preseli
▲ *536*

St. David's Head   **281**   Mathry

PEMBROKESHIRE

St. David's
Ramsey Island

St. Brides Bay   Haverfordwest

A40

Narberth

A477

Milford
Haven

Neyland

Pendine

Skomer I.

Skokholm I.

Pembroke Dock

Saundersfoot
Tenby

Pembroke

280   **279**

St. Govan's Head   *Carmarthen Bay*

Lundy

Hartland Pt.
Hartland

A39

Bude
Poundstock

Boscastle

A39

A395

Tintagel

23

Port Isaac   *Bodmin*

Padstow   Wadebridge   *Moor*

24   A39

Bodmin   A38 Liskeard

Newquay   CORNWALL

A392   **38**

St. Austell   Looe

37   Polperro

St. Agnes   Fowey

A390   **36**

Redruth   Truro   Mevagissey

27 26   A30   A39   **34**   **35**

28   **25**   Camborne   Penryn   **33**

St. Ives   A394   St. Mawes

29 30   Hayle   A39
Marazion   Falmouth

St. Just   A394   Helston

Penzance

32

Land's End   **31**

Lizard

22 St. Martin's

Bryher   *Tresco*

Hugh Town   *St. Mary's*

Map 2   21

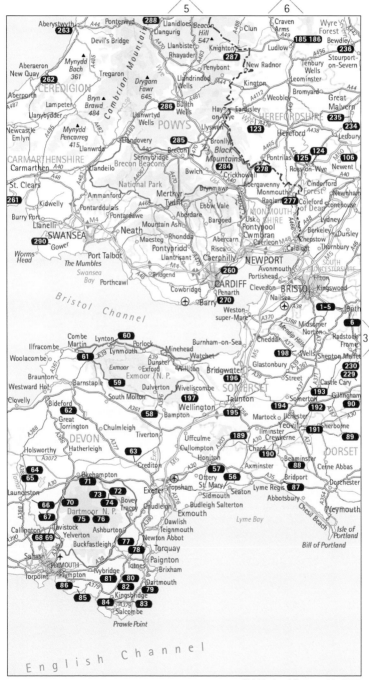

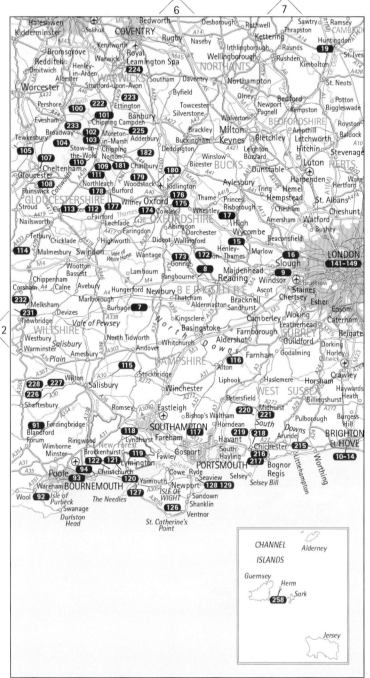

Map 4   23

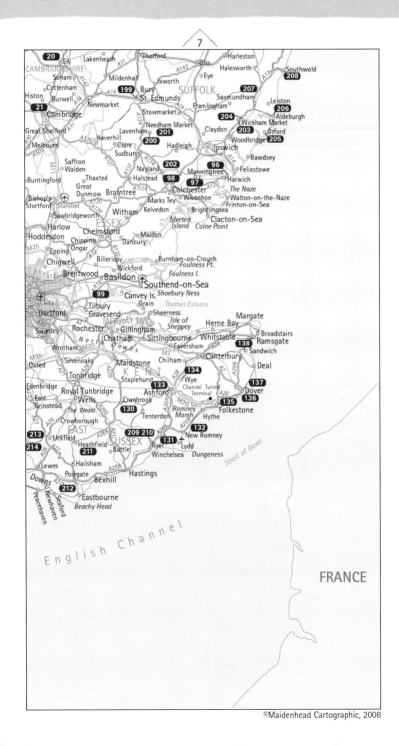

Map 6

25

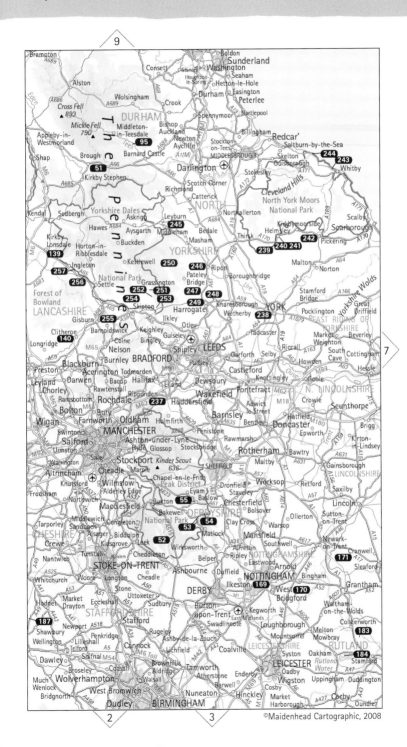

©Maidenhead Cartographic, 2008

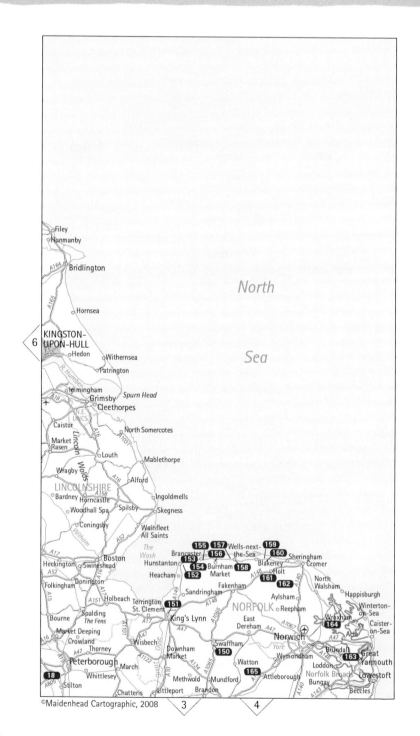

Map 8

27

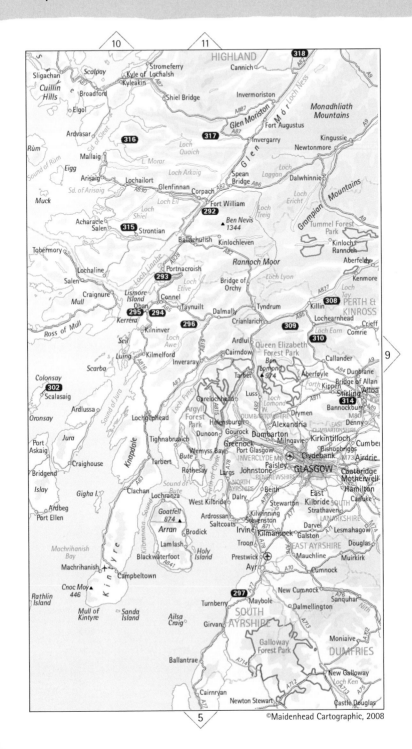

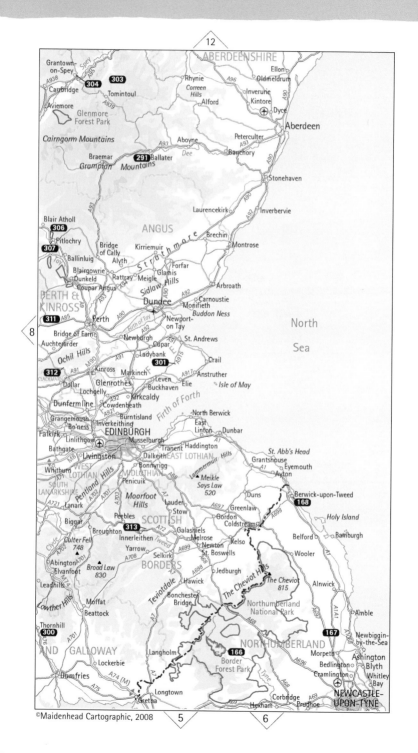

Map 10   29

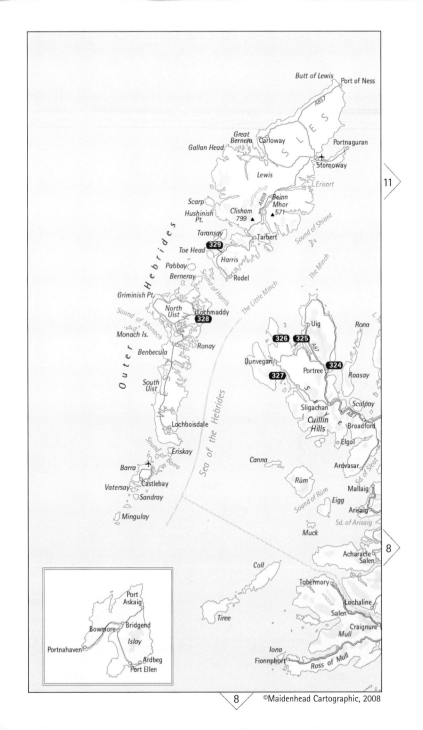

©Maidenhead Cartographic, 2008

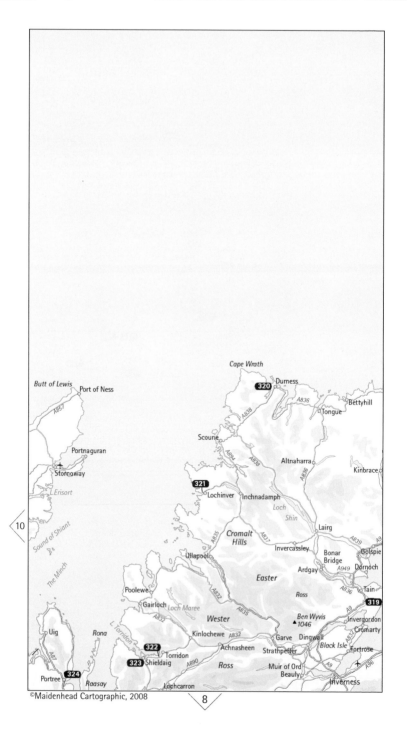

Cape Wrath
Durness **320**
A836
Bettyhill
A838
Tongue
Butt of Lewis Port of Ness
A857
Scourie
Altnaharra
A836
Kinbrace
Portnaguran
Stornoway
A894
A838
L.Erisort
321
Lochinver Inchnadamph
Loch
Shin
Sound of Shiant
Cromalt
Hills
Lairg
A839
A9
Invercassley
A837
Bonar
Bridge
Golspie
Ullapool
Ardgay
A949
Dornoch
The Minch
Easter
A836
Poolewe
Ross
Tain
Gairloch Loch Maree
A832
319
A832
Wester
A835
Ben Wyvis
▲1046
Invergordon
Uig
Rona
Kinlochewe A832
Garve Dingwall
Cromarty
L.Torridon
A890
Achnasheen Strathpeffer
Black Isle
Fortrose
A87
322
Torridon
Ross
Muir of Ord
A96
Portree **324**
323 Shieldaig
A890
Beauly
Inverness
Raasay
Lochcarron
A9

10

8

Map 12

31

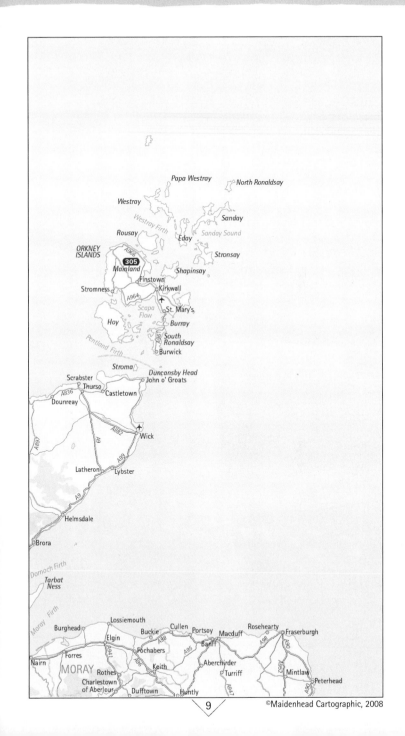

England

SACO Serviced Apartments, Bath

Fabulous Bath is England's loveliest city, Georgian to its bone. It's built of mellow golden stone, so wander its streets for elegant squares, beautiful gardens, pavement cafés, delicious delis and the imperious Roman Baths (there's a spa if you want to take a dip). Close to the river, bang in the middle of town, these serviced apartments bask behind a beautifully restored Regency façade – look out for the pillared entrances. Inside you find a collection of airy studios and apartments, all of which come with sparkling kitchens that are fully stocked with ovens, dishwashers, washer/dryers, microwaves, fridges, freezers if there's room. Some are small, some are big, and if you need a bolthole for a night or a cool pad for a week, you'll find one here. You get white walls, Italian designer furniture, flat-screen TVs, CD players and big fluffy towels in spotless bathrooms. There's a lift to whisk you up and away, 24-hour reception, and high-speed broadband connection throughout. Supermarkets are close, but there are masses of great restaurants on your doorstep, too. *Minimum stay two nights at weekends.*

Price	Studios: £61–£152; 1-bed apartment: £126–£203; 2-bed apartment: £208–£270.
Rooms	43 studios & apartments for 2 & 4.
Meals	Full kitchen facilities. Restaurants within 0.5 miles.
Closed	Never.
Directions	In centre of town, 5-minute walk from station. Full directions on booking.

Jo Redman
SACO House, St James Parade, Bath,
Bath & N.E. Somerset BA1 1UH
Tel   01225 486540
Fax   01225 480025
Email   bath@sacoapartments.co.uk
Web   www.apartmentsbath.co.uk

The Queensberry Hotel & Olive Tree Restaurant

You are in the architectural epicentre of Bath with the Assembly Rooms at the end of the road, the Circus a two-minute stroll and the centre of town all around. You couldn't hope for a better base. The hotel, built by John Wood in 1771 for the Marquis of Queensberry, occupies three grand houses in a sublime terraced street. Interiors elate, while grandly proportioned first-floor bedrooms are some of the best in town, high ceilings, magnificent windows and Georgian colours running throughout. The four-poster comes in ivory white (with a suede sofa in the bedroom and a chaise longue in the bathroom), but all rooms are luxurious with thick fabrics, crisp linen, sparkling bathrooms, perhaps a rosewood armoire or a vintage wallpaper. All have robes and hi-tech gadgetry; smaller rooms up in the eaves are just as lovely and have rooftop views. Downstairs are flowers in the sitting room, a fire in the bar and contemporary art in the candlelit restaurant, where super food waits: delicious duck, perfect venison, fabulous poached figs. Staff are delightful, too. *Minimum stay two nights at weekends.*

Price	£115–£230. Suites £235–£450.
Rooms	29: 26 twins/doubles, 1 four-poster, 2 suites.
Meals	Breakfast £10–£15. Lunch £16.50. Dinner, à la carte, about £35.
Closed	Never.
Directions	Into Bath on A4 London Rd to Paragon; 1st right into Lansdown; 2nd left into Bennett St; 1st right into Russel St.

Laurence & Helen Beere
Russel Street, Bath,
Bath & N.E. Somerset BA1 2QF

Tel	01225 447928
Fax	01225 446065
Email	reservations@thequeensberry.co.uk
Web	www.thequeensberry.co.uk

 Travel Club Offer: see page 367 for details.

The Bath Priory Hotel, Restaurant & Spa

An exquisite country-house hotel, with staff who greet you by your name when you step through the front door. Spin into the drawing room while porters see to your luggage, gaze at exceptional art, warm yourself in front of the fire, then throw open the French windows and explore the four-acre garden for swimming pool, croquet lawn, kitchen garden and an ancient cedar... colour bursts through in summer, and loungers flank the pool. Back inside a Michelin star in the dining room will keep a smile on your face and may offer roasted scallops marinated in lime, slow-poached saddle of fallow deer, nougatine leaves with manuka honey and a lavender-scented truffled goats' cheese. Plush bedrooms are as you'd expect with rich fabrics, warm colours, crisp linen and Roberts radios. Those at the back have garden views, there are shelves of books, proper armchairs, a sofa if there's room. Back downstairs, fresh flowers everywhere and a spa with indoor pool, sauna, steam room, gym and treatment suites. The city is on your doorstep: stroll through the park to the Roman Baths and Royal Crescent. *Minimum stay two nights at weekends.*

Price	£250–£400. Suites £435.
Rooms	31: 27 twins/doubles, 4 suites.
Meals	Lunch from £22. Dinner £60.
Closed	Never.
Directions	From centre of Bath follow red hospital signs west for a mile. Right at far end of Royal Victoria Park. Left at T-junction into Weston Road. Hotel on left.

Travel Club Offer: see page 367 for details.

Sue Williams
Weston Road, Bath,
Bath & N.E. Somerset BA1 2XT

Tel	01225 331922
Fax	01225 448276
Email	mail@thebathpriory.co.uk
Web	www.thebathpriory.co.uk

Bath Paradise House Hotel

You'll be hard pressed to find a better view in Bath. The views draw you out as soon as you enter the house: the magical 180-degree panorama from the garden is a dazzling advertisement for this World Heritage city. The Royal Crescent and the Abbey are floodlit at night and in summer, hot-air balloons float by low enough for you to hear the roar of the burners. Nearly all the rooms make full use of the view; the best have bay windows but all have a soft, luxurious country feel, with contemporary fabrics, wicker chairs and fabulous bathrooms. There are also two garden rooms in an extension that planners took years to approve; it's a remarkable achievement, in keeping with the original Bath stone house, and David is justly proud. The whole place has glass in all the right places, and the sitting room has lovely stone-arched French windows that pull in the light. In summer, don't miss afternoon tea in a half-acre walled garden, a perfect place to lose yourself in the vista. The occasional peal of bells comes for a nearby church. The Thermea Spa, newly opened, is a must. *Seven-minute walk down hill to centre.*

Price	£75–£175. Singles £65–£115.
Rooms	11: 4 doubles, 3 twins, 1 family, 3 four-posters.
Meals	Restaurants in Bath 0.5 miles.
Closed	24 & 25 December.
Directions	From train station one-way system to Churchill Bridge. A367 exit from r'bout up hill; 0.75 miles, left at Andrews estate agents. Left down hill into cul-de-sac; on left.

David & Annie Lanz
86–88 Holloway, Bath,
Bath & N.E. Somerset BA2 4PX

Tel	01225 317723
Fax	01225 482005
Email	info@paradise-house.co.uk
Web	www.paradise-house.co.uk

Dorian House

A smart Victorian townhouse owned by a musician with a love of interior design. Tim is the London Symphony Orchestra's principal cellist and was once taught by the late and great Jacqueline du Pré. When he's not on stage in town, he's in Bath overseeing the smooth running of Dorian House, where the feel is more home than hotel, and the mix of traditional and contemporary design makes for a very pleasant base in the city. Everything has been beautifully restored. Step into a tiled hallway with exquisite stained glass, sink into deep sofas in the sitting room, or pop open a bottle of champagne in super bedrooms named after cellists. No surprise that the most impressive – and the most secluded – is du Pré: its huge four-poster bed is reached up a flight of stairs. Every room is decorated with beautiful fabrics and Egyptian linen. Those on the first floor are traditional, those above have a funkier feel, three have fabulous travertine marble bathrooms. The owners' art collection is everywhere, gathered from their travels abroad. Relaxation assured, and maybe some music, too. *Minimum stay two nights at weekends.*

Price	£80–£160. Singles £60–£89.
Rooms	11: 3 twins/doubles, 4 doubles, 1 family, 3 four-posters.
Meals	Pubs & restaurants within walking distance.
Closed	Never.
Directions	From Bath centre, follow signs to Shepton Mallet to sausage-shaped r'bout, then A37 up hill, 1st right. House 3rd on left, signed.

Kathryn & Tim Hugh
One Upper Oldfield Park, Bath,
Bath & N.E. Somerset BA2 3JX

Tel	01225 426336
Fax	01225 444699
Email	info@dorianhouse.co.uk
Web	www.dorianhouse.co.uk

Wheelwrights Arms

A pub for all seasons. In winter, grab the table in front of the ancient fire where the wheelwright worked his magic; in summer, skip outside for a pint on the terrace. You're in the country, three miles from Bath, so drop down to the nearby Kennet & Avon canal and cycle or walk through glorious country into the city. The Wheelwrights dates to 1750. Inside, beautiful contemporary colours mix with soft stone walls and exposed timber frames. Logs are piled high in the alcoves, there's a wonderful snug, the daily papers are left on the bar and the food is delicious, perhaps chilli mussels, rack of lamb, banana crème brûlée; in summer you can eat in the garden illuminated by lights in the trees. Airy bedrooms in what was the wheelwright's annex come in fresh, original style. Expect dark wood floors, shuttered windows, old-style radiators, flat-screen TVs. Wooden beds are covered in immaculate linen, white bathrooms come with robes and L'Occitane potions. The inn holds two season tickets for Bath Rugby Club. Guests can take them at cost price, so book early. *Minimum stay two nights at weekends.*

Price	£100–£145. Singles from £80.
Rooms	7: 5 doubles, 1 twin, 1 single.
Meals	Lunch, 2 courses, £10.
	Dinner, 3 courses, about £25.
Closed	Never.
Directions	A36 south from Bath for 3 miles, then right, signed Monkton Combe. Over x-roads, into village, on left.

David Phillips-White
Church Lane, Monkton Combe, Bath,
Bath & N.E. Somerset BA2 7HB

Tel	01225 722287
Fax	01225 722259
Email	bookings@wheelwrightsarms.co.uk
Web	www.wheelwrightsarms.co.uk

Crown & Garter

An unreformed country local. On the night we stayed Gill was serving at the bar, her father was keeping an eye on the fire and her son was running through questions for the pub quiz. Gamekeepers and village footballers come for a pint and hearty food. In summer life spills onto a stone terrace and into the pretty garden, and cockerels crow in the fields. Inside you get wooden floors, red curtains and a huge settle by the fire. There's a small restaurant, so dig into spinach and mozzarella tart, spicy sausages with a chilli bean casserole, then sticky toffee pudding with caramel ice cream. Bedrooms are in a single-storey building that looks prettier in summer when the vine is out. Rooms, however, are big. Four have painted floorboards, all have voile wall hangings. Beds are brass or wooden, linen is crisp and white, there are quilted bedspreads, coloured rugs and floral curtains; two rooms interconnect. Piping hot water flows in super little bathrooms. You can walk from the front door, try your luck at Newbury Races or watch the early morning gallops at Lambourne. James II is said to have visited.

Price	£99. Singles £65.
Rooms	8: 6 doubles, 2 twins.
Meals	Lunch & dinner from £10. Not Mondays or Tuesday lunchtimes.
Closed	Rarely.
Directions	A4 for Hungerford. After 2 miles, left for Kintbury & Inkpen. In Kintbury, left at corner shop onto Inkpen Road; inn on left after 2 miles.

Gill Hern
Great Common, Inkpen, Hungerford,
Berkshire RG17 9QR

Tel	01488 668325
Email	gill.hern@btopenworld.com
Web	www.crownandgarter.com

The Elephant at Pangbourne

There are elephants everywhere – all benign, including those in the Ba-bar. This is a super hotel on the edge of town, renovated in unremitting style, with huge sofas in front of the fire, a tongue-and-groove bar for Sunday brunch, a cocktail lounge where candles flicker and an elegant restaurant that spills onto a terrace. It's a big hit with the locals, with much to draw them in: a supper club on Wednesday nights (good food and a glass of wine for £10), a cinema club on Sunday afternoons (£5 for a classic movie and popcorn). Eclectic bedrooms come fully loaded and spin you round the world in style: an Indian four-poster in 'Viceroy'; collage wallpaper in 'Charlestown'; colonial chic in 'Rangoon'. Beds are dressed in Egyptian cotton, there are flat-screen TVs, perhaps leather sofas, regal colours and rugs on stripped floors; bathrooms, most in charcoal grey, are delightful. Back downstairs eat informally in the bar (steak frites, smoked ham with free-range eggs) or in the restaurant for something fancier, perhaps ham hock terrine, fillet of beef, coconut panna cotta.

Price	£140. Singles from £100.
Rooms	22: 18 doubles, 2 twins, 2 singles.
Meals	Lunch from £8.95.
	Dinner, 3 courses, £30.
Closed	Never.
Directions	M4 junc. 12, A4 south; then A340 north. In village on left at roundabout.

Christoph Brooke
Church Road, Pangbourne,
Berkshire RG8 7AR

Tel	01189 842244
Fax	01189 767346
Email	reception@elephanthotel.co.uk
Web	www.elephanthotel.co.uk

The Christopher Hotel

The Christopher, an old coaching inn, sits quietly on Eton High Street, with the school running away to the north and Windsor Castle a short walk across the river. Many years ago the hotel stood opposite the school, but was politely asked to move as too many boys were popping in for refreshments; remarkably, it obliged. Recently a new broom has swept through, bringing with it colour and comfort in equal measure. A brasserie-style restaurant and a half-panelled bar stand either side of the coach arch and both come in similar vein with warm colours, stripped floors and big windows that look onto the street. In the restaurant you can stop for a bite, perhaps whitebait, wild boar sausages, lemon meringue pie; in the bar you'll find sofas, armchairs and champagne by the glass. Bedrooms – some in the main house, others stretching out at the back in motel-style – have comfy beds, padded heads, crisp white linen, a sofa if there's room. Those in the main house have the character, three are in the old magistrate's court, all have internet access and adequate bathrooms.

Price	£131–£200. Singles from £90.
Rooms	33: 24 twins/doubles, 9 singles.
Meals	Breakfast £8–£10.
	Lunch & dinner from £8.
Closed	Never.
Directions	M4 junc. 5, into Datchet, through to Eton & left onto High Street. On right.

 Travel Club Offer: see page 367 for details.

Janet Tregurtha
110 High Street, Eton,
Windsor, Berkshire SL4 6AN

Tel	01753 852359
Fax	01753 852359
Email	reservations@thechristopher.co.uk
Web	www.thechristopher.co.uk

Neo Hotel

A groovy bohemian bolthole one block up from the seafront. Steph, a stylist, has a great eye, and has poured love and colour into her boutique empire; exquisite vintage wallpapers by Ralph Lauren, Osborne & Little and Florence Broadhurst adorn most walls. The hotel – a listed Georgian townhouse – is small but sweet with a cool little bar that comes in deep pink and a breakfast room that doubles as an art gallery. Bedrooms over three floors – some snug in the eaves, others with high ceilings – have padded headboards, silky curtains, Egyptian linen and super-comfy beds. Black mosaic bathrooms, some compact, have mirrored walls, and there are kimonos instead of bathrobes. Sensational breakfasts – raspberry and banana smoothies, blueberry pancakes, the full cooked works – are served under a tear-drop chandelier while Billie Holiday and Ella Fitzgerald serenade you. Friendly staff steer you in the right direction for clubs, pubs, concerts and restaurants – pop down for a chilli chocolate martini before heading out for a night on the town. *Minimum stay two nights at weekends.*

Price	£95–£160.
Rooms	9: 5 doubles, 3 twins/doubles, 1 single.
Meals	Pubs/restaurants nearby.
Closed	Christmas.
Directions	A23 into Brighton. Down to seafront and right at pier. Pass Grand Hotel, Hilton Hotel and square on right, then 2nd right. Parking: £12 a day off-street.

	Steph Harding
	19 Oriental Place,
	Brighton BN1 2LL
Tel	01273 711104
Fax	01273 711105
Email	info@neohotel.com
Web	www.neohotel.com

Hotel Una

A double-fronted Regency townhouse that stands on one of Brighton's imperious seafront squares. Revolving doors spin you into a stylish world of cool interiors, where rustic wood abounds. Downstairs, huge bay windows flood grandly proportioned rooms with light. The sitting room/bar comes with stripped floors and funky art; the breakfast room shines with white leather banquettes and fairy lights on the wall. Excellent bedrooms come in contemporary style, and those at the front on the first floor are some of the best in town, with floor-to-ceiling windows that open onto balconies, free-standing baths at the end of low-slung beds, walls covered with golden art. Elsewhere, leather beds, varnished floors, fancy bathrooms and white walls to soak up the light. Two rooms have en suite saunas, all have Egyptian cotton, flat-screen TVs, DVD players and bathrobes. Smaller rooms have smaller prices, but the style doesn't waver. Breakfast can be brought to your room: freshly squeezed orange juice, organic yogurts, hot croissants, the full cooked works. The beach is on your doorstep. *Minimum stay two nights at weekends.*

Price	£110–£160. Suites £170–£270. Singles from £60.
Rooms	20: 7 doubles, 3 singles, 10 suites.
Meals	Bar snacks from £8.50. Restaurants nearby.
Closed	Never.
Directions	A23 into Brighton, right at pier for 0.5 miles. Regency Square on right, opp. old West Pier. Car park under square.

Travel Club Offer: see page 367 for details.

Alejandra Valencia
55-56 Regency Square,
Brighton BN1 2SS

Tel	01273 820464
Email	reservation@hotel-una.co.uk
Web	www.hotel-una.co.uk

Square Hotel

An über-cool pied-a-terre that stands a hundred metres up from Brighton's famous beach. This may be a listed Victorian townhouse on the outside, but inside, funky interiors prevail. Step into the bar to find flames rising from pebbles in the fireplace and a mosaic of Madonna hanging in a pink neon frame. There are stripped floors, leather sofas, a fridge jammed with champagne. Bedrooms go all the way with walls of fabric, iPod docks and lots of white leather. You get DVD players and flat-screen TVs, faux-fur throws, perhaps a chaise longue covered in suede. Some rooms have high ceilings, those at the front flood with light, all come with suitably cool bathrooms: black marble, white robes, walls of glass, power showers or double-ended baths. The basement suite has glass steps leading down and occupies the whole of the lower-ground floor. Outside, wander down to the pier, browse the Lanes, marvel at the Pavilion. There's great food, too. Try Riddle and Fyn's for tasty seafood, Havana for modern cooking and live piano, and the Ginger Man for the best food in town. *Minimum stay two nights at weekends.*

Price	£120-£230. Suite £320-£400.
Rooms	10: 9 doubles, 1 suite.
Meals	Restaurants nearby.
Closed	23-28 December.
Directions	M23/A23 into Brighton. At seafront, with pier in front, left up hill. 9th street on left. On-street parking only.

Brian Ferguson
4 New Steine,
Brighton BN2 1PB

Tel	01273 691777
Email	info@squarebrighton.com
Web	www.squarebrighton.com

Drakes

If you were to compile the definitive list of England's top ten boutique hotels, you'd include Drakes. It's small and intimate with a funky bar, a super restaurant and a heavyweight design that sets it apart from most. More than anything else, this is a hotel that stirs the adrenalin, that gives you the buzz of excitement you get when someone throws you the keys to their Ferrari and insists you drive. Bedrooms are exemplary. Eleven have free-standing baths in the room (you can gaze out to sea as you soak), while the list of must-haves is as long as your arm (flat-screen TVs, monsoon showers, waffle bathrobes, White Company oils). Yet what impresses most here is the detail and workmanship. Handmade beds rest on carpets that are changed every year, contemporary plaster mouldings curl around ceilings like mountain terraces, Vi-Spring mattresses come in the crispest cotton and are piled high with pillows. Don't worry if you can't afford the best rooms – all are fantastic, some are just bigger than others, and those in the attic are as cute as could be. Kylie loved hers. *Minimum stay two nights at weekends.*

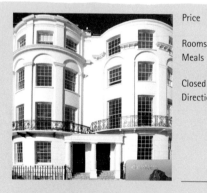

Price	£125–£325. Suite £375–£520. Singles £100–£130.
Rooms	20: 17 doubles, 2 singles, 1 suite.
Meals	Breakfast £7.50–£12.50. À la carte dinner about £35.
Closed	Never.
Directions	M23/A23 into Brighton. At seafront, with pier in front, left up hill. Hotel on left after 300 yds.

Richard Hayes
43-44 Marine Parade,
Brighton BN2 1PE

Tel	01273 696934
Email	info@drakesofbrighton.com
Web	www.drakesofbrighton.com

brightonwave

A small, friendly, boutique B&B hotel in the epicentre of trendy Brighton. The beach and the pier are a two-minute walk, the bars and restaurants of St James Street are around the corner. An open-plan sitting room/dining room comes in cool colours with big suede sofas, fairy lights in the fireplace and ever-changing art on the walls. Bedrooms at the front are big and fancy, with huge padded headboards that fill the wall and deluge showers in sandstone bathrooms. Those at the back have a simpler feel (sisal matting, muted colours, local art). They're smaller, but so is the price, and they come with spotless compact shower pods; if you're out more than in, why worry? All rooms have fat duvets, lush linen, flat-screen TVs and DVD/CD players (there's a library of films downstairs), and the lower-ground king-size has a private garden. Richard and Simon are easy-going and happy for guests to chill drinks in the kitchen (there are corkscrews in all the rooms). Breakfast, served late at weekends, offers pancakes, the full English or sautéed tarragon mushrooms on toast. *Minimum stay two nights at weekends.*

Price	£90–£175. Four-poster £130–£200. Singles from £80.
Rooms	8: 2 twins/doubles, 5 doubles, 1 four-poster.
Meals	Restaurants nearby.
Closed	Rarely.
Directions	A23 to Brighton Pier roundabout at seafront; left towards Marina; 5th street on left. On-street parking vouchers, £5 for 24 hours.

Richard Adams & Simon Throp
10 Madeira Place,
Brighton BN2 1TN

Tel	01273 676794
Email	info@brightonwave.co.uk
Web	www.brightonwave.co.uk

Travel Club Offer: see page 367 for details.

The Hand and Flowers

It's almost Shakespearean. Ludlow's claim to the culinary crown of England is under challenge from prosperous Marlow. Instead of arrows falling from the sky, Michelin stars are tumbling down. Chief instigator is Tom, whose incredible cooking has attracted great interest in only two years; locals now pack the place day and night. Step into these airy 18th-century cottages and find flagged floors under low beams – it's remarkably easy-going. There's no froth on the menu, no dress code in the restaurant, just ambrosial food that elates; make sure you book. Try perfectly cooked salmon with frozen horseradish, slow-cooked English veal with a succulent beetroot linguini, vanilla crème brûlée washed down by a honey-sweet beer chaser. Four stylish rooms stand 30 paces along the road in two refurbished cottages (expect a little noise). Beth, a sculptor, oversaw their creation; you get exposed beams, cow hide rugs, Egyptian cotton and flat-screen TVs. One room has a hot tub on a private terrace, another has a telescope and a window for star-gazing. The Thames is close for revitalising walks.

Price	£140–£190.
Rooms	4 doubles.
Meals	Lunch from £12.50. Dinner, 3 courses, about £30.
Closed	25 & 26 December.
Directions	M4 junc. 9; A404 north; into Marlow; A4155 towards Henley; on edge of town on right.

Tom & Beth Kerridge
126 West Street, Marlow,
Buckinghamshire SL7 2BP

Tel	01628 482277
Email	theoffice@thehandandflowers.co.uk
Web	www.thehandandflowers.co.uk

Stoke Park Club

James Bond played golf with Goldfinger here and nearly lost his head to Odd Job's bowler hat. Whether he stayed for a massage, a game of tennis, a swim in the pool or a meal in the Art Deco-style restaurant is not recorded, but if he didn't, he should have. Stoke Park is a Palladian-style mansion set in 350 acres on an estate that is noted in the Domesday Book. Matchless interiors thrill: Corinthian columns and a cupola dome in the Great Hall, the largest free-standing marble staircase in Europe, and a grand piano opposite a roaring fire. The Orangery, for late breakfasts, is also the members' clubhouse and buzzes with life (ladies in for a hand of bridge, old timers lamenting a missed putt). In summer, life spills onto a balustraded terrace for views across croquet lawn and golf course to the heritage gardens. Expect panelled bars, padded window seats, elaborate wall hangings, even a chapel. Bedrooms are the very best (Hugh Grant and Renée Zellweger stayed in *Bridget Jones's Diary*), with oak four-posters, big fat sofas and fabulous marble bathrooms. The health club, spa and golf club are yours to enjoy.

Price	£285-£345. Suites £400-£1,100. Half-board £180 p.p.
Rooms	49: 38 doubles, 11 suites.
Meals	Breakfast £15-£18. Lunch from £15. Dinner, 3 courses, £39.50
Closed	24-26 December & 1st week in January.
Directions	M4, junc. 6, A355 north, then right at 2nd r'about. On right after 1.25 miles.

Mark Fagan
Park Road, Stoke Poges,
Buckinghamshire SL2 4PG

Tel	01753 717171
Fax	01753 717181
Email	info@stokeparkclub.com
Web	www.stokeparkclub.com

Three Horseshoes Inn

London may only be an hour's drive, but you'll think you've washed up in the 1960s. Red kites circle a bowl of deep countryside, smoke curls from cottages that hug the hill. As for the Three Horseshoes, you find flagstones and an open fire in the tiny locals' bar, exposed timbers and pine settles in the airy restaurant. Simon, chef turned patron, has cooked in The Connaught, Chez Nico, Le Gavroche – all the best places – and dinner is a treat, the homemade piccalilli worth the trip alone. Come for lunch and dig into baked camembert with garlic and rosemary, stay for dinner and try tiger prawns, roasted sea bass and bread and butter pudding with marmalade ice cream. Guests have a private entrance, stairs lead to super-smart rooms. Expect silky quilts, goose-down pillows, funky furniture, Farrow & Ball paints. Also: flat-screen TVs, deluge showers and views of the Chilterns. Breakfast indulgently, hike in the hills, walk by the Thames, hop over to Windsor. There's jazz and tapas once a month and in summer you can eat in the garden while ducks circle a sunken phone box in the pond. Only in England.

Price	£95–£120. Suite £145.
Rooms	6: 2 doubles, 1 suite, 1 single, 2 garden rooms.
Meals	Lunch from £5. Dinner, 3 courses, £25–£30. Not Sunday night or Monday lunch.
Closed	Rarely. Tuesdays after bank holiday Mondays.
Directions	M40 junc. 5, A40 south thro' Stokenchurch, left for Radnage. After 2 miles, left to Bennett End. Sharp right, up hill, on left.

Simon Crawshaw
Bennett End, Radnage, High Wycombe,
Buckinghamshire HP14 4EB

Tel	01494 483273
Fax	01494 485464
Email	threehorseshoe@btconnect.com
Web	www.thethreehorseshoes.net

Crown Inn

A dreamy inn built of mellow stone that stands on the green in this gorgeous village. Paths lead out into open country, so follow the river up to Fotheringhay, where Mary Queen of Scots lost her head. Back at the pub, warm interiors mix style and tradition to great effect. You can eat wherever you want – in the bar, where a fire roars, in the airy snug with views of the green, or in the orangery, which opens onto a terrace. Wherever you end up, you'll eat well, perhaps langoustines with garlic and dill, saddle of venison with poached pear, Bramley apple and cinnamon crumble. In summer life spills onto the gravelled front, on May Day there's a hog roast for the village fete. Six hand pumps bring in the locals, as do quiz nights, live music and the odd game of rugby on the telly. Bedrooms are excellent. The two courtyard rooms are nice and quiet and come with padded bedheads, pretty art, lovely fabrics and flat-screen TVs; one has a magnificent bathroom. Those in the main house are above the bar and overlook the green. The small room has a four-poster, the big room is perfect for families.

Price	£90–£120. Singles from £60.
Rooms	4: 3 doubles, 1 twin/double.
Meals	Lunch & dinner £5–£30.
Closed	First 2 weeks in January.
Directions	A1(M), junc. 17, then A605 west for 3 miles. Right on B671 for Elton. In village, left, signed Nassington. On green.

Marcus & Rosalind Lamb
8 Duck Street, Elton, Peterborough,
Cambridgeshire PE8 6RQ

Tel	01832 280232
Email	inncrown@googlemail.com
Web	www.thecrowninn.org

The Old Bridge Hotel

A smart hotel – the best in town – with battalions of devoted locals who come for the food (delicious), the wines (exceptional) and the hugely comfortable interiors. Ladies lunch, business men chatter, all are happy. Order a glass of champagne at the bar, then sink into a winged armchair in front of the fire and study the menu. You can eat wherever you want, so lope into the murralled restaurant or grab a sofa in the lounge and feast on anything from sweet potato soup to rack of Cornish lamb (starters are available all day long). Breakfast is served in a panelled morning room with Buddha in the fireplace; in summer you decant to the terrace. Spotless bedrooms are scattered about, all in warm colours with rich fabrics, padded bedheads, crisp linen. One has a mirrored four-poster, another a sitting room/bathroom. Some overlook the river Ouse, all have spoiling extras: Molton Brown potions, Bang & Olufsen TVs, power showers and bathrobes. Kind, attentive staff deliver. As for John, he's a Master of Wine; browse and buy his stock. The A14 may pass to the front, but it doesn't matter a jot.

Price	£125–£190. Singles from £95. Half-board at weekends from £75 p.p.
Rooms	24: 13 doubles, 1 twin, 7 singles, 3 four-posters.
Meals	Lunch & dinner £7–£30.
Closed	Never.
Directions	A1, then A14 into Huntingdon. Hotel on southwest flank of one-way system that circles town.

Nina Beamond
1 High Street, Huntingdon,
Cambridgeshire PE29 3TQ

Tel	01480 424300
Fax	01480 411017
Email	oldbridge@huntsbridge.co.uk
Web	www.huntsbridge.com

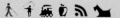

The Anchor Inn

A real find, a 1650 ale house on Chatteris Fen. The New Bedford river streams past outside. It was cut from the soil by the pub's first residents, Scottish prisoners of war brought in by Cromwell to dig the dykes that drain the fens. These days cosy luxury infuses every corner. There are low beamed ceilings, timber-framed walls, raw dark panelling and terracotta-tiled floors. A wood-burner warms the bar, so stop for a pint of cask ale, then feast on fresh local produce: hand-dressed crabs from Cromer in spring, asparagus and Bottisham smoked meats in summer, wild duck from the marshes in winter; breakfast is equally indulgent. Four spotless rooms above the restaurant fit the mood exactly (not posh, supremely comfy). Expect trim carpets, wicker chairs, crisp white duvets and Indian cotton throws. The suites each have a sofabed and three rooms have fen and river views. Footpaths flank the water; stroll down and you might see mallards or Hooper swans, even a seal (the river is tidal to the Wash). Don't miss Ely (the bishop comes to eat), Cambridge, and Welney for nesting swans by the thousand.

Price	£79.50–£99. Suites £129.50–£155. Singles from £59.50. Extra bed £20.
Rooms	4: 1 double, 1 twin, 2 suites.
Meals	Lunch, 2 courses, £11.95. Dinner, 3 courses, about £26.
Closed	Never.
Directions	West from Ely on A142. Left in Sutton onto B1381 for Earith. On south fringes of Sutton, right signed Sutton Gault. 1 mile north on left at bridge.

Adam Pickup & Carlene Bunten
Bury Lane, Sutton Gault, Ely,
Cambridgeshire CB6 2DB

Tel	01353 778537
Fax	01353 776180
Email	anchorinn@popmail.bta.com
Web	www.anchorsuttongault.co.uk

Travel Club Offer: see page 367 for details.

Hotel Felix

Propel your punt along the Cam and glide serenely past King's College Chapel, a wonder of old England. If this sounds too energetic, take advantage of special rates at a super-cool health club and loll about in its jacuzzi, where a huge window frames the river. Two miles north you find Hotel Felix, a metaphor for this resurgent city – a grand old villa now revamped in contemporary style. Two new wings run off at right angles creating a courtyard with statue and parterre garden. Bedrooms have a smart simplicity and mix corporate necessities (this is Silicon Fen, after all) with comfort and style: dark wood furniture, red leather chairs, Frette linen, silky curtains. Some rooms are bigger than others, but all come in similar style, with excellent bathrooms, fluffy robes and White Company lotions. There's a decked terrace for afternoon tea, a cool bar for pre-dinner drinks and an airy restaurant for super food with a Mediterranean touch, perhaps baby squid with lemon and thyme, cassoulet with confit of duck, vanilla panna cotta with Suffolk honey. Good weekend rates are often available.

Price	£180–£290. Singles from £145.
Rooms	52 twins/doubles.
Meals	Continental breakfast included; full English £7.50. Bar meals from £4.95. Lunch £12.95–£16.95. Dinner, 3 courses, £30–£35.
Closed	Rarely.
Directions	M11, junc. 13, then A1303 into Cambridge. Left at T-junction and immediately left into Huntingdon Road. Signed right after a mile.

 Travel Club Offer: see page 367 for details.

	Shara Ross
	Whitehouse Lane, Huntingdon Road, Cambridge, Cambridgeshire CB3 0LX
Tel	01223 277977
Fax	01223 277973
Email	help@hotelfelix.co.uk
Web	www.hotelfelix.co.uk

Hotel

Cornwall

Hell Bay

Magical Bryher. In winter, giant rollers crash against high cliffs; in summer, sapphire waters sparkle in the sun. There are sandy beaches, passing sail boats, waders and wild swans, absolute peace. The hotel lazes on the west coast with sublime watery views – there's nothing between you and America – so grab a drink from the bar and wander onto the terrace to watch a vast sky blush at sunset. Inside, you get stripped floors, coastal colours, excellent art and airy interiors that look out to sea. Step outside and find a heated pool in the garden and a courtyard stocked with rosemary and lavender; castaways would refuse rescue. Bedrooms offer beach-house heaven, most with terraces or balconies, most with views of sand and sea. You get tongue and groove panelling, walls of windows, crisp fabrics, super bathrooms. In summer dig into crab and lobster straight from the ocean, fresh asparagus from Tresco, succulent strawberries from the island There's a sauna, a PlayStation for kids, golf for the hopeful. Low-season deals are exceptional. *Surcharge for dogs £12 a night.*

Price	Half-board £150–£300 p.p. Child in parent's room £50 (incl. high tea). Under 2s free.
Rooms	25 suites.
Meals	Half-board only. Lunch £5–£15.
Closed	November-February.
Directions	Ship/helicopter from Penzance, or fly to St Mary's from Bristol, Southampton, Exeter, Newquay or Land's End; boat to Bryher. Hotel can arrange.

Philip Callan
Bryher, Isles of Scilly,
Cornwall TR23 0PR

Tel	01720 422947
Fax	01720 423004
Email	contactus@hellbay.co.uk
Web	www.hellbay.co.uk

Caradoc of Tregardock

Crashing breakers, wheeling gulls, carpets of wild flowers in spring – this place is a dream for artists and a tonic for everyone. Just two fields away from the coastal path, the old farm buildings are set around a grassy courtyard with west-facing patios that catch the setting sun or gathering storm. Some bedrooms look out to sea, all are airy with huge beds, white walls and pretty linen. You can B&B, self-cater, take the whole place. The first-floor drawing room has a magnificent Atlantic view, beams and a wood-burner; the farmhouse kitchen, also with a sea view, has a Rayburn and a large table that seats 12. Janet cooks a fabulous breakfast, but she'll stock the fridge with the best of Cornish and let you cook your own whenever you want. There are good restaurants, too, some within walking distance along the cliff path; alternatively hire a chef for special occasions. Caradoc and the cottage are perfect for extended families – and special-interest groups: there's a 60-foot studio. Books, music and videos, too, if staying in seems like a good idea. *Painting & yoga holidays available.*

Price	£90–£130. Singles £45–£65. Cottage £475–£2,000 per week.
Rooms	4 + 1: 4 twins/doubles. 1 self-catering cottage for 4.
Meals	Dinner with wine, £35, by arrangement. Private chef available.
Closed	Never.
Directions	Take turn to Treligga off B3314; 2nd farm road, signed.

 Travel Club Offer: see page 367 for details.

Janet Cant
Treligga, Port Isaac,
Cornwall PL33 9ED

Tel	01840 213300
Email	info@tregardock.com
Web	www.tregardock.com

Woodlands Country House

A big house in the country, half a mile west of Padstow, with long views across the fields down to the sea. Pippa and Hugo came west to renovate and have done a fine job. You get an honesty bar in the sitting room, a croquet lawn by the fountain and stripped floors in the airy breakfast room, where a legendary feast is served each morning. Spotless bedrooms are smart and homely, some big, some smaller, all with a price to match, but it's worth splashing out on the bigger ones, which are away from the road and have watery views. Expect lots of colour, pretty beds, floral curtains, Frette linen. One room has a four-poster, another comes with a claw-foot bath, there are robes in adequate bathrooms. All have flat-screen TVs and DVD players, with a library of films downstairs. WiFi runs throughout, there's a computer guests can use, taxis can be ordered – but make sure you book restaurants in advance, especially Rick Stein's or Jamie Oliver's Fifteen. Hire bikes in town and follow the Camel trail, take the ferry over to Rock, head down to the beach, walk on the cliffs. Dogs are very welcome.

Price	£92–£128. Singles from £58.
Rooms	8: 4 doubles, 3 twins/doubles, 1 four-poster.
Meals	Picnic £12. Restaurants in Padstow, 0.5 miles.
Closed	Mid-December to January.
Directions	On A389, just before Padstow, left for Newquay, then west on B3276. House signed on right in 1st village.

Hugo & Pippa Woolley
Treator, Padstow,
Cornwall PL28 8RU

Tel	01841 532426
Fax	01841 533353
Email	info@woodlands-padstow.co.uk
Web	www.woodlands-padstow.co.uk

Travel Club Offer: see page 367 for details.

Boskerris Hotel

A quietly swanky hotel with glass everywhere framing huge views of ocean and headland. Step inside and drift into the sitting room, then float onto the decked terrace and gaze at Godrevy lighthouse twinkling to the right, St Ives slipping into the sea to the left and the wide sands of Cabris Bay, Lelant and Gwithian lying in between. Back inside you find creamy walls to soak up the light. There are bleached boards and smart sofas in the sitting room, fresh flowers and blond wood in the dining room. Airy bedrooms are uncluttered, with silky throws, padded headboards, crisp white linen, flat-screen TVs and DVD players. Eleven rooms have the view, all have fancy bathrooms, some have deep baths and deluge showers. You get White Company lotions, Designers Guild fabrics, and in one room you can soak in the bath whilst gazing out to sea. Take the coastal path to St Ives and follow the mazy streets to the Tate; spin back for delicious locally sourced food in the restaurant or stop at Porthminster Café for the fanciest nosh in town.

Price	£95–£205. Singles from £70.
Rooms	15: 10 doubles, 3 twins, 1 family, 1 triple.
Meals	Dinner, 3 courses, about £25.
Closed	Christmas & New Year.
Directions	A30 past Hayle, then A3074 for St Ives. After 3 miles pass brown sign for Carbis Bay, then third right. Down hill, on left.

Travel Club Offer: see page 367 for details.

Jonathan & Marianne Bassett
Boskerris Road, Carbis Bay,
St Ives, Cornwall TR26 2NQ
Tel   01736 795295
Email   reservations@boskerrishotel.co.uk
Web   www.boskerrishotel.co.uk

Blue Hayes

The view from the terrace is hard to beat, a clean sweep across the bay to St Ives. You breakfast here in good weather in the shade of a Monterey pine, as if transported back to the fifties' French Riviera. As for the rest of the hotel, it's an unadulterated treat, mostly due to Malcolm, whose infectious generosity is stamped over every square inch. Few hoteliers close for four months to redecorate over winter, but that's the way things are done here and the house shines as a result. It comes in ivory white, with the occasional dash of colour from carpet and curtain. The bar has a vaulted ceiling and a wall of glass that runs along the front to weatherproof the view. Big bedrooms are gorgeous, two with balconies, one with a terrace, all with sparkling bathrooms. If you want to eat, light suppers are on hand, but Porthminster beach is a short stroll, so book a table at its eponymous café and treat yourself to the best food in town; torches are provided for the journey back up. Penzance, Zennor and the New Tate all wait – but no one will blame you if you hole up in luxurious isolation for a day or two.

Price	£160-£180. Singles from £130. Suite £190-£210.
Rooms	6: 4 doubles, 1 suite, 1 triple.
Meals	Packed lunches by arrangement. Light suppers from £8.
Closed	November-February.
Directions	A30, then A3074 to St Ives. Through Lelant & Carbis Bay, over mini-r'bout (Tesco on left) and down hill. On right immed. after garage on right.

	Malcolm Herring
	Trelyon Avenue, St Ives,
	Cornwall TR26 2AD
Tel	01736 797129
Fax	01736 799098
Email	bluehayes@btconnect.com
Web	www.bluehayes.co.uk

Travel Club Offer: see page 367 for details.

Primrose Valley Hotel

Roll out of bed, drop down for breakfast, slip off to the beach, stroll into town. If you want St Ives bang on your doorstep, you'll be hard pressed to find a better hotel; the sands are a 30-second stroll. Half the rooms have views across the bay, two have balconies for lazy afternoons. Inside, beautiful open-plan interiors revel in an earthy contemporary chic, with leather sofas, varnished floors, fresh flowers and glossy magazines. Bedrooms tend not to be huge, but you can't fault the price or style, so come for Hypnos beds, pastel colours, bespoke furniture and good bathrooms; the suite, with red leather sofa, hi-tech gadgetry and mind-blowing bathroom, is seriously fancy. Andrew and Sue are environmentally aware, committed to sustainable tourism and marine conservation. Their hugely popular breakfast is mostly sourced within the county; food providence is listed on the menu. There's a groovy bar with movie posters and leather sofas that's stocked with potions from far and wide. The New Tate and Barbara Hepworth's garden both wait. Great staff, too. *Minimum stay two nights at weekends.*

Price	£100–£155. Suite £175–£225.
Rooms	9: 6 doubles, 2 twins, 1 suite.
Meals	Platters £8.
Closed	25–26 December & January.
Directions	From A3074 Trelyon Avenue; before hospital sign slow down, indicate right & turn down Primrose Valley; under bridge, left, then back under bridge; signs for hotel parking.

Travel Club Offer: see page 367 for details.

Ethical Collection: Environment; Food.
See page 373 for details

Andrew & Sue Biss
Primrose Valley, Porthminster Beach,
St Ives, Cornwall TR26 2ED

Tel	01736 794939
Fax	01736 794939
Email	info@primroseonline.co.uk
Web	www.primroseonline.co.uk

The Gurnard's Head

The coastline here is utterly magical and the walk up to St Ives is hard to beat. Secret beaches appear at low tide, cliffs tumble down to the water and wild flowers streak the land pink in summer. As for the hotel, you couldn't hope for a better base. It's earthy, warm, stylish and friendly, with airy interiors, colourwashed walls, stripped wooden floors and fires at both ends of the bar. Logs are piled up in an alcove, maps and art hang on the walls, books fill every shelf; if you pick one up and don't finish it, take it home and post it back. Rooms are warm and cosy, simple and spotless, with Vi-Spring mattresses, crisp white linen, throws over armchairs, Roberts radios. Downstairs, super food, all homemade, can be eaten wherever you want: in the bar, in the restaurant or out in the garden in good weather. Snack on rustic delights – pork pies, crab claws, half a pint of Atlantic prawns – or tuck into more substantial treats, maybe fresh asparagus with a hollandaise sauce, fish stew with new potatoes, rhubarb crème brûlée. Picnics are easily arranged and there's bluegrass folk music in the bar most weeks.

Price	£80–£140. Singles from £70.
Rooms	7: 4 doubles, 3 twins/doubles.
Meals	Lunch from £4.50.
	Dinner, 3 courses, about £26.
Closed	Christmas & 4 days in mid-January.
Directions	On B3306 between St Ives & St Just, 2 miles west of Zennor, at head of village of Treen.

Charles & Edmund Inkin
Treen, Zennor, St Ives,
Cornwall TR26 3DE

Tel	01736 796928
Email	enquiries@gurnardshead.co.uk
Web	www.gurnardshead.co.uk

Travel Club Offer: see page 367 for details.

The Summer House

A glittering find, a small enclave of Mediterranean goodness a hundred yards up from the sea. It's stylish and informal, colourful and welcoming; what's more, it's super value for money. Linda and Ciro, English and Italian respectively, run the place with great affection – Ciro in the kitchen whisking up delights, Linda bubbling away out front. She's the designer, too, her breezy interiors warm and elegant with stripped floors, beautiful art, panelled windows and murals in the dining room (the breakfast chef is a sculptress). Ciro worked in some of London's best restaurants before heading west to go it alone and in good weather you can eat his ambrosial food in a small, lush courtyard garden, perhaps langoustine with mango and chives, rack of lamb with herbes de Provence, warm apple tart with crème Chantilly. Menus change weekly, fish comes from the market, and breakfast – served in the courtyard on good days – is a feast. Stylish rooms are the final delight: sunshine colours, well-dressed beds, freshly cut flowers, flat-screen TVs, super little bathrooms.

Price	£95-£125. Singles from £85.
Rooms	5: 4 doubles, 1 twin/double.
Meals	Dinner £25-£31.50. Not Monday-Wednesday.
Closed	November-March.
Directions	With sea on left, along harbourside, past open-air pool, then immediate right after Queens Hotel. House 30 yds up on left. Private car park.

Linda & Ciro Zaino
Cornwall Terrace, Penzance,
Cornwall TR18 4HL

Tel	01736 363744
Fax	01736 360959
Email	reception@summerhouse-cornwall.com
Web	www.summerhouse-cornwall.com

The Abbey Hotel

The Abbey is a rare gem, a hotel that refuses to enter the modern world, choosing instead to linger in its serenely elegant past. The feel is of a smart country house, and the drawing room – roaring fire, huge gilt mirror, walls of books, rugs on stripped floors – is hard to beat. Drinks are brought to you, there's a bust of Lafayette, exquisite art and huge arched windows that rise to the ceiling and open onto the loveliest walled garden; step out in summer for afternoon tea or a breakfast to remember. The house dates to 1660 and has views to the front of Penzance harbour and St Michael's Mount. Country-house bedrooms are grandly quirky (in one you pull open a cupboard to find an en suite shower). Sink into big comfy beds wrapped up in crisp white linen and woollen blankets. There are chandeliers, quilted bedspreads, French armoires, plump-cushioned armchairs. You breakfast indulgently in a panelled dining room with a fire crackling and assorted busts and statues for company. Kind staff don't act the part, they simply go the extra mile. The Abbey restaurant next door has a Michelin star. Exceptional.

Price	£105–£200. Suite £150–£210. Singles from £75. Flat £115–£170.
Rooms	7 + 1: 4 doubles, 1 twin, 1 family, 1 suite. Self-catering flat for 4.
Meals	Restaurants nearby.
Closed	Rarely.
Directions	Follow signs to town centre. Up hill (Market Jew St). Left at top, then fork left & 3rd on the left.

Thaddeus Cox
Abbey Street, Penzance,
Cornwall TR18 4AR

Tel	01736 366906
Email	hotel@theabbeyonline.co.uk
Web	www.theabbeyonline.co.uk

The Old Coastguard Hotel

Cornwall's hotels love a good view and the Old Coastguard is no exception. It stands 50 metres up from the sea, with a lush garden that tumbles down to the water. There are decks on two levels to make the most of it, while eight bedrooms have balconies with views across jostling boats to Mousehole's ancient harbour. Mousehole, sacked by the Spanish in 1595, hugs the coast, a warren of tiny lanes that cause havoc in summer, so take advantage of the handy car park and walk the coastal path into town. You'll find fishermen mending their nets before heading out to catch lobster, scallops and crab, much of which will land on your plate. Serious food in the ultra-airy restaurant is the raison d'être of the hotel, so come for a feast, perhaps foie gras with pear purée, wild sea bass with vanilla and shallots, raspberry soufflé with tea-infused chocolate sauce. Bedrooms (all but two have the view) come in uncluttered style: white walls to soak up the light, Egyptian cotton, flat-screen TVs and DVD players, robes in sparkling bathrooms. There's a small reading room with free internet access, too.

 Travel Club Offer: see page 367 for details.

Price	£120–£180. Single £90–£135. Suite £190–£210. Half-board from £85 p.p.
Rooms	14: 10 doubles, 2 twins/doubles, 1 single, 1 suite.
Meals	Lunch from £7.95. Dinner, 3 courses, £30–£40.
Closed	Christmas Day.
Directions	Follow A30 to Penzance & signs to Mousehole. Hotel on left as you enter the village. Limited parking on first come first served basis or public car park next door, £2 on departure.

Bill Treloar
The Parade, Mousehole,
Cornwall TR19 6PR

Tel	01736 731222
Fax	01736 731720
Email	bookings@oldcoastguardhotel.co.uk
Web	www.oldcoastguardhotel.co.uk

Mount Haven Hotel & Restaurant

A magical hotel with sublime views of St Michael's Mount, an ancient Cornish totem that's been pulling in the crowds for millennia. Most rooms look the right way, but there's a decked balcony in case yours doesn't and the causeway leads across at low tide, so stroll over to discover an ancient castle and church. Back at the hotel, sink in to comfy sofas in the bar where huge windows frame the view, making sunsets rather special. Elsewhere, Eastern deities jostle for space, local art hugs the walls, and there's a treatment room for soothing massage, the profits of which go to an orphanage in Sri Lanka. The restaurant comes in white with wood floors, big mirrors and doors that open onto a terrace, so try Newlyn crab cakes with mustard dressing, seared duck breast with a ginger glaze, then walnut tart with espresso syrup. Bedrooms are lovely: most aren't huge, all are airy, two have private patios and those on the top floor have unblemished views. They come with white walls, fresh flowers, crisp linen, flat-screen TVs. Bathrooms tend to be small but sweet, bigger rooms have sofas.

Price	£90–£150. Four-poster & suite £130–£190. Singles from £65.
Rooms	18: 10 doubles, 4 twins/doubles, 2 family, 1 four-poster, 1 suite.
Meals	Lunch from £9.95. Dinner, 3 courses, about £30.
Closed	One week before Christmas to 1st Friday in February.
Directions	From A30, A394 in Helston direction to r'bout. Tourist sign for Mount Haven, turn right; hotel 400 yds on left. Private parking.

Orange & Mike Trevillion
Turnpike Road, Marazion,
Cornwall TR17 0DQ

Tel	01736 710249
Fax	01736 711658
Email	reception@mounthaven.co.uk
Web	www.mounthaven.co.uk

Travel Club Offer: see page 367 for details.

The Rosevine

A super-smart family bolthole on the Roseland peninsular with views that tumble across trim lawns and splash down to the sea. Tim and Hazel welcome children with open arms and have created a small oasis where guests of all ages can have great fun. There's a playroom for kids (Xbox, plasma screen, DVDs, toys), an indoor pool, and a beach at the bottom of the hill. High teas are on hand, there are cots and highchairs, babysitters can be arranged. Parents don't fare badly either: an elegant sitting room with sofas in front of the wood-burner; sea views and Lloyd Loom furniture in an airy restaurant; sun loungers scattered about a semi-tropical garden. Suites and apartments come with small kitchens (fridge, sink, dishwasher, microwave/oven); you can self-cater, eat in the restaurant or mix and match (there's a deli menu for posh takeaways). Suites are open-plan with sofabeds, apartments have separate bedrooms. Expect airy, uncluttered interiors, flat-screen TVs and DVD players, Egyptian cotton and robes in good bathrooms. Eight rooms have a balcony or terrace. St Mawes is close.

Price	Suites £120-£285. Apartments £145-£305.
Rooms	12: 8 suites for 2-4, 4 apartments for 2-5. All with kitchenettes.
Meals	Breakfast £3-£8. Lunch from £5. Dinner, 3 courses, about £30.
Closed	January.
Directions	From A390 head south for St Mawes on A3078. Signed left after 8 miles. Right at bottom of road; on right.

 Travel Club Offer: see page 367 for details.

Hazel & Tim Brocklebank
Rosevine, Portscatho,
Cornwall TR2 5EW

Tel	01872 580206
Fax	01872 580230
Email	info@rosevine.co.uk
Web	www.rosevine.co.uk

Driftwood Hotel

A faultless position, one of the best, with six acres of garden that drop down to a private beach and coastal paths that lead to cliff-top walks. At the Driftwood, Cape Cod meets Cape Cornwall and airy interiors shine in white and blue. The sitting room is stuffed with beautiful things – fat armchairs, deep sofas, driftwood lamps, a smouldering fire – and there's a telescope in the bar with which to scan the high seas. Best of all are the walls of glass that pull in the spectacular watery views; in summer, doors open onto a decked terrace for breakfast, lunch and supper in the sun. Bedrooms are gorgeous (all but one has a sea view), some big, others smaller, one in a cabin halfway down the cliff with a private terrace. All have the same clipped elegance: big beds, white linen, wicker chairs and white walls to soak up the light. There are Roberts radios on bedside tables, cotton robes in excellent bathrooms. Drop down to the dining room for seriously good food that makes the most of the sea. High teas for children, hampers for beach picnics and rucksacks for walkers, too. *Minimum stay two nights at weekends.*

Price	£180–£240.
Rooms	15: 11 doubles, 3 twins, 1 cabin.
Meals	Dinner £40.
Closed	Mid-December to mid-February.
Directions	From St Austell, A390 west. Left on B3287 for St Mawes; left at Tregony on A3078 for approx. 7 miles. Signed left down lane.

Paul & Fiona Robinson
Rosevine, Portscatho,
Cornwall TR2 5EW

Tel	01872 580644
Fax	01872 580801
Email	info@driftwoodhotel.co.uk
Web	www.driftwoodhotel.co.uk

Trevalsa Court Hotel

An Arts and Crafts country house with sprawling lawns that run down to high cliffs. Steps drop to the beach and the coastal path takes you to Mevagissey, an old fishing village with a working quay. Don't dally too long: Trevalsa is a seaside treat, friendly, stylish and young at heart. You'll find American oak in the panelled dining room, a log fire in the airy sitting room and a couple of sofas in the candlelit bar. Best of all is the enormous mullioned window seat luxuriously padded with big white cushions, a great place to sit and watch the weather spin by. On fine days life spills onto the stone terrace amid beds of colour, or you can plonk a deckchair out on the lawn and fall asleep in the sun. Bedrooms are lovely, some big, others snug, all but two with fabulous sea views. Expect happy colours, crisp linen, wicker armchairs, padded bedheads. Head off to the Lost Gardens of Heligan and the Eden Project, both close, then return for a good meal, perhaps beetroot and orange soup, fish straight from the boats at Mevagissey, a rich chocolate mousse with toffee snaps. *Minimum stay two nights at weekends.*

Price	£100–£168. Singles from £70. Suites £178–£206.
Rooms	13: 7 doubles, 1 twin, 2 singles, 3 suites.
Meals	Dinner, 3 courses, £34.
Closed	Mid-November to mid-February.
Directions	From St Austell, B3273, signed Mevagissey, for 5.5 miles past beach caravan park, then left at top of hill. Over mini-r'bout. Hotel on left, signed.

Susan & John Gladwin
School Hill Road, Mevagissey,
Cornwall PL26 6TH

Tel	01726 842468
Fax	01726 844482
Email	stay@trevalsa-hotel.co.uk
Web	www.trevalsa-hotel.co.uk

The Old Quay House Hotel

The Old Quay House has everything going for it: an idyllic waterfront setting, an airy architect-designed interior, and a suite at the top of the house with huge views. Add to this owners passionate about good service and a loyal staff determined to deliver and you have a super little hotel. Stylish bedrooms spoil you all the way with goose-down duvets, Egyptian cotton, Javanese cabinets and seriously indulging bathrooms (bathrobes, the odd claw-foot bath, maybe a separate shower). Eight have balconies with glittering estuary views and flood with light, those further back look over Fowey's rooftops. Stop for a drink in the bar, then settle down to delicious modern European dishes in the 'Q' restaurant, smartly decorated in neutral tones, or spill out onto the terrace overlooking the estuary; you can breakfast here in the sun and watch the ferry chug past. Fowey is enchanting, bustles with life and fills with sailors for the August regatta. Come for the best of old Cornwall – narrow cobbled streets, quaint harbour, long-lost ways. A great place to unwind. *Minimum stay two nights at weekends in high season.*

Price	£160-£220. Singles £130-£220. Suite £300.
Rooms	11: 5 doubles, 5 twins/doubles, 1 suite.
Meals	Lunch about £15. Dinner £27-£35.
Closed	Rarely.
Directions	Entering Fowey, follow one-way system past church. Hotel on right where road at narrowest point, next to Lloyds Bank. Nearest car park 800 yds.

Jane & Roy Carson
28 Fore Street, Fowey,
Cornwall PL23 1AQ

Tel   01726 833302
Fax   01726 833668
Email   info@theoldquayhouse.com
Web   www.theoldquayhouse.com

The Cormorant Hotel

A supreme position on the side of a wooded hill with the magical Fowey river curling past below. Oyster catchers swoop low across the water, sheep bleat in the fields, sail boats tug on their moorings. The hotel is one room deep and every window looks the right way, but a recent renovation has added small balconies to most of the bedrooms, so doze in the sun and listen to the sounds of the river. As for the hotel, it couldn't have fallen into better hands. Mary rescued it from neglect, poured in love and money, and now it shines: new windows, new bathrooms, new swimming pool, new everything. A terrace sweeps along the front, a finger of lawn runs below, and inside, the river follows wherever you go. You get fresh flowers in the bar, an open fire in the sitting room, wooden floors in a smartly dressed dining room. Super bedrooms come without clutter: light colours, trim carpets, walls of glass, crisp white linen. One has a claw-foot bath from which you can gaze down on the water. Swim in the pool, tan on its terrace, dine on fabulous Cornish food. Boat trips can be arranged.

Price	£100–£170. Half-board £80–£125 p.p.
Rooms	14: 10 doubles, 4 twins.
Meals	Lunch from £10. À la carte dinner about £35.
Closed	Rarely.
Directions	A390 west towards St Austell, then B3269 to Fowey. After 4 miles, left to Golant. Into village, along quay, hotel signed right up very steep hill.

Mary Tozer
Golant, Fowey,
Cornwall PL23 1LL

Tel	01726 833426
Email	relax@cormoranthotel.co.uk
Web	www.cormoranthotel.co.uk

The Well House

Silence in a blissful valley, with sprawling lawns, a swimming pool, a tennis court and lilies on the pond. A stream runs though the garden. It's fed by a well that was blessed by St Keyne in 579; those who drink from it will rule their marriage. On a lane that goes nowhere, a Victorian country house that was built by a tea magnate, hence the tea menu at breakfast. Farrow & Ball colours run throughout, there's a snug bar with busts and prints, a marble fireplace in the airy sitting room and a mirrored restaurant for fabulous food – perhaps confit of Gressingham duck, seared black bream with prawn risotto, hot coconut soufflé with warm chocolate sauce. Bedrooms are scattered about and come in a fresh country-house style. Most have garden views (go for these) and flood with light. Expect quilted bedcovers, sheets and blankets, warm colours and spotless bathrooms. There's good art on the walls and garden suites open onto a stone terrace for glorious views of the Looe Valley. You can head down to the sea at Polperro, take the ferry across to Fowey or drop in at the Eden Project.

Price	£155–£180. Suites £215. Singles from £139. Half-board £110–£140 p.p.
Rooms	9: 4 doubles, 2 twins, 3 suites.
Meals	Lunch, 3 courses, £26.50, by arrangement. Dinner, 3 courses, £37.50. 6-course tasting menu £37.50
Closed	Rarely.
Directions	A38 to Liskeard, then B3254 south for Looe. Through St Keyne, then straight on down small lane at sharp right. House on left after half a mile.

Richard Farrow
St Keyne, Looe, Cornwall PL14 4RN

Tel	01579 342001
Email	enquiries@wellhouse.co.uk
Fax	01579 343891
Web	www.wellhouse.co.uk

 Travel Club Offer: see page 367 for details.

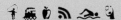

Aynsome Manor Hotel

A small country house with a big heart. It may not be the grandest place in the book but the welcome is genuine, the peace is intoxicating and the value is unmistakable. Stand at the front and a long sweep across open meadows leads south to Cartmel and its priory, a view that has changed little in 800 years. The house, a mere pup by comparison, dates to 1512. Step in to find red armchairs, a grandfather clock and a coal fire in the hall. There's a small bar at the front and a cantilever staircase with cupola dome that sweeps you up to a first-floor drawing room and panelled windows framing the view. Downstairs you eat under an ornate tongue-and-ball ceiling with Georgian colours and old portraits on the walls, so come for delicious cooking, perhaps cream of tomato and red pepper soup, roast leg of Cumbrian lamb, then rich chocolate mousse served with white chocolate sauce. Bedrooms are warm, cosy, simple, spotless, colourful. Some have views over the fields, one may be haunted, another has an avocado bathroom suite. Windermere and Coniston are both close. *Minimum stay two nights at weekends.*

Price	£90–£126. Singles from £80. Half-board £68–£89 p.p.
Rooms	12: 5 doubles, 4 twins, 1 four-poster, 2 family.
Meals	Dinner, 4 courses, £28.
Closed	25 & 26 December; January.
Directions	From M6 junc. 36 take A590 for Barrow. At top of Lindale Hill, follow signs left to Cartmel. Hotel on right 3 miles from A590.

 Travel Club Offer: see page 367 for details.

Christopher & Andrea Varley
Cartmel, Grange-over-Sands,
Cumbria LA11 6HH

Tel	015395 36653
Fax	015395 36016
Email	aynsomemanor@btconnect.com
Web	www.aynsomemanorhotel.co.uk

L'Enclume

Cartmel is idyllic, a tiny village that stands in the shadow of its magnificent 800-year-old priory. It is one of those spots that lifts the soul, nowhere more so than the garden at L'Enclume – paradise by the river with the priory's tower rising beyond. Not that you'll linger. This is one of Europe's most lauded restaurants, and a stream of pilgrims arrive each day for Simon's tantalizing Michelin-starred cooking. You eat amid a gleaming world of whitewashed walls, sandstone floors, beamed ceilings and contemporary art. Tasting menus bring course after course, each one listed by flavour and texture: foie gras served with foie gras ice cream, local venison with barley and banana, beef rib accompanied by watermelon and liquorice. Puddings are equally intriguing and exciting, perhaps coffee praline with green tea and apple, or parmesan cake with white chocolate and cardamom. Retire to the silence of princely rooms. One has bedside lights on plinths, another opens onto the garden; you get designer wallpapers, silky throws and robes in super bathrooms.

Price	£98–£158. Suites £178–£198.
Rooms	12: 10 doubles, 2 suites.
Meals	7-course tasting menu £50; 11-course tasting menu £70. (No lunch Monday-Friday; no dinner Monday.)
Closed	First week of January.
Directions	M6 junc. 36, then A590 west. Pass turning for Grange-Over-Sands, then left for Cartmel. In village.

Simon Rogan & Penny Tapsell
Cavendish Street, Cartmel,
Cumbria LA11 6PZ

Tel	015395 36362
Email	info@lenclume.co.uk
Web	www.lenclume.co.uk

The Mason's Arms

A perfect Lakeland inn tucked away two miles inland from Lake Windermere. You're on the side of a hill with huge views across lush fields to Scout Scar in the distance. In summer, all pub life decants onto a spectacular terrace – a sitting room in the sun – where window boxes and flowerbeds tumble with colour. The inn dates from the 16th century and is impossibly pretty. The bar is properly traditional with roaring fires, flagged floors, wavy beams, a cosy snug... and a menu of 70 bottled beers to quench your thirst. Rustic elegance upstairs comes courtesy of stripped floors, country rugs and red walls in the first-floor dining room – so grab a window seat for fabulous views and order delicious food, anything from a sandwich to Cumbrian duck. Self-catering cottages and apartments are a steal and come with fancy kitchens (breakfast hampers can be arranged). You get cool colours, fabulous beds, gleaming bathrooms and Bang & Olufsen TVs. Best of all, you have your own private terrace; order a meal in the restaurant and they'll bring it to you here. *Minimum stay two nights at weekends.*

Price	£65-£145. Cottages £130-£175.
Rooms	5 + 2: 5 suites. 2 self-catering cottages (1 for 4, 1 for 6).
Meals	Self-catering. Breakfast hampers £15-£25. Lunch & dinner £5-£30.
Closed	Never.
Directions	M6 junc. 36; A590 west, then A592 north. 1st right after Fell Foot Park. Straight ahead for 2.5 miles. On left after sharp right-hand turn.

Travel Club Offer: see page 367 for details.

John & Diane Taylor
Strawberry Bank, Cartmel Fell,
Cumbria LA11 6NW

Tel	015395 68486
Fax	015395 68780
Email	info@masonsarmsstrawberrybank.co.uk
Web	www.strawberrybank.com

The Punch Bowl Inn

You're away from Lake Windermere in a small village encircled by a tangle of lanes that defeat most tourists. A church stands next door; the odd bride ambles out in summer, bell ringers practise on Friday mornings. But while the Punch Bowl sits in a sleepy village lost to the world and doubles up as the local post office, it is actually a seriously fancy inn. It was rescued from neglect by Paul and Steph, who own the impeccable Drunken Duck, and after a top-to-toe renovation it now sparkles. Outside, honeysuckle climbs on old stone walls, inside four fires keep you warm in winter. A clipped elegance runs throughout: leather sofas in a beamed sitting room, Farrow & Ball colours on the walls, candles in vases on dining room tables. Bedrooms are delightful. Expect beautiful linen, super bathrooms, Roberts radios, flat-screen TVs. All are dressed in lovely fabrics, four have huge views down the Lyth valley and the fabulous suite, with double baths, is enormous. Don't miss the lakes and the hills. Wonderful.

Price	£110–£195. Suite £225–£280. Singles from £82.50.
Rooms	9: 1 twin/double, 5 doubles, 2 four-posters, 1 suite.
Meals	Lunch from £5. Dinner, 3 courses, about £30.
Closed	Never.
Directions	M6 junc. 36, then A590 for Newby Bridge. Right onto A5074, then right for Crosthwaite after 3 miles. Pub on southern flank of village.

Jenny Sisson
Crosthwaite, Kendal,
Cumbria LA8 8HR

Tel	015395 68237
Fax	015395 68875
Email	info@the-punchbowl.co.uk
Web	www.the-punchbowl.co.uk

Gilpin Lodge

One of the loveliest places to stay in the country, simple as that. Staff are delightful, the house is a treasure trove, and the food is heavenly. Run by two generations of the same family, Gilpin delivers at every turn. Clipped country-house elegance flows throughout: smouldering coals, Zoffany wallpaper, gilded mirrors, flowers everywhere. Afternoon tea, served wherever you want it, comes on silver trays. You're in 20 acres of silence, so throw open doors and sit on the terrace surrounded by pots of colour or stroll through the garden for magnolias, rhododendrons, cherry blossom or climbing roses and a fine copper beech. Bedrooms are predictably divine with crisp white linen, exquisite fabrics, delicious art; nothing is left to chance. Some have French windows that open onto the garden, others have hot tubs on private terraces, all have sofas or armchairs. As for Chris Meredith's sublime food, try lobster ravioli, fillet of beef, prune and Armagnac soufflé; a three-page breakfast menu offers nine different teas and strawberry sorbet served with pink champagne. *Minimum stay two nights at weekends.*

Price	Half-board £135–£195 p.p. Singles from £175.
Rooms	20: 4 doubles, 4 twins/doubles, 12 suites.
Meals	Half-board only. Lunch £10–£27. Dinner for non-residents, £47.
Closed	Never.
Directions	M6 junc 36, A591 north, then B5284 west for Bowness. On right after 4 miles.

 Travel Club Offer: see page 367 for details.

John, Christine, Barnaby & Zoe Cunliffe
Crook Road, Windermere,
Cumbria LA23 3NE

Tel	015394 88818
Fax	015394 88058
Email	hotel@gilpinlodge.co.uk
Web	www.gilpinlodge.co.uk

Linthwaite House Hotel & Restaurant

The view here is simply magnificent with Windermere sparkling half a mile below and a chain of peaks rising beyond; no great surprise to discover the terrace acts as a *de facto* sitting room in summer. Linthwaite is a grand Lakeland country house run in informal style. Everything is a treat: wonderful bedrooms, gorgeous interiors, glorious food and attentive staff. The house dates from 1900 and is sound-proofed by 15 acres of trim lawns, formal gardens and wild rhododendrons. Totter up through a bluebell wood to find a small lake surrounded by fields where you can fish, swim or retreat to the summer house and fall asleep in the sun. The house is no less alluring with logs piled high by the front door, fires smouldering, sofas everywhere and a clipped colonial elegance in the conservatory sitting room. Sublime food is served in elegant dining rooms (one is decorated with nothing but mirrors) and Keith Floyd occasionally comes to perform an act or two of culinary theatre. Gorgeous bedrooms are uncluttered and airy; those at the front have lake views. *Minimum stay two nights at weekends.*

Price	Half-board £95–£185 p.p. Singles from £128.
Rooms	27: 21 doubles, 4 twins/doubles, 1 single, 1 suite.
Meals	Half-board only. Lunch from £5.50. Dinner for non-residents, £50.
Closed	Rarely.
Directions	M6 junc. 36. Take A590 north, then A591 for Windermere. At roundabout, left onto B5284. Past golf course and hotel signed left after 1 mile.

Mike Bevans
Crook Road, Windermere,
Cumbria LA23 3JA

Tel	015394 88600
Fax	015394 88601
Email	stay@linthwaite.com
Web	www.linthwaite.com

 Travel Club Offer: see page 367 for details.

Holbeck Ghyll

Holbeck's majestic setting is unrivalled in the Lakes, a sublime position on the side of the hill with huge views of Lake Windermere shimmering below. Sixteen acres of gardens tumble downhill, there are sweeping lawns, a tennis court and colour in abundance. The house dates to 1888 and was built in Arts & Crafts-style by Charles Rennie Mackintosh for Lord Lonsdale. Inside, super-smart country-house interiors elate: grand sitting rooms, golden panelling, roaring fires, rugs on wood floors. Wellington boots stand at the front door, there are mullioned windows, fresh flowers everywhere and a sun terrace for alfresco meals in summer. Best of all is the Michelin-starred restaurant for ambrosial food, perhaps terrine of duck with pear and foie gras, roasted brill with a cider foam, cherry clafoutis with almond ice cream. Bedrooms have an overdose of elegance and style. Most in the main house have lake views, the Potter Suite has a hot tub on its terrace, Maddison House and The Sheilding are perfect for families, there's a huge gatehouse, too. Wonderful staff know every guest by name. Sunsets are amazing.

Price	Half-board £140–£195 p.p. Suites & cottages £175–£295 p.p.
Rooms	21 + 4: 15 twins/doubles, 6 suites. 4 self-catering cottages for 2–8.
Meals	Lunch from £22.50. Dinner £52.50. Tasting menu £67.50.
Closed	First 2 weeks in January.
Directions	M6 junc. 36, A591 to Windermere. On for Ambleside, pass Brockhole Visitor Centre, then right for Troutbeck (Holbeck Lane). 0.5 miles on left.

David & Patricia Nicholson
Holbeck Lane, Windermere,
Cumbria LA23 1LU

Tel	015394 32375
Fax	015394 34743
Email	stay@holbeckghyll.com
Web	www.holbeckghyll.com

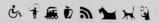

Drunken Duck Inn

Afternoon tea can be taken in the garden, where lawns run down to Black Tarn and Greek gods gaze upon jumping fish. You're up on the hill, away from the crowds, cradled by woods and highland fell. Huge views from the terrace shoot off for miles to towering Lakeland peaks. Roses ramble on the veranda, stone walls double as flower beds and burst with colour. As for the Duck, she may be old, but she sure is pretty, so step into a world of airy interiors – stripped floors in a beamed bar, timber-framed walls in the inspired restaurant. Wander at will and find open fires, grandfather clocks, rugs on the floor, exquisite art. They brew their own beer and have nine bitters on tap. Bedrooms are dreamy, smartly dressed in crisp white linen, with colours courtesy of Farrow & Ball and peaty water straight off the fell. Rooms in the main house are snug in the eaves; those across the courtyard are crisply uncluttered and indulgent. Some have private terraces, one comes with a balcony, several have walls of glass to frame the mighty mountains. Don't miss Duck Tarn for blue heron and brown trout.

Price	£120–£250. Singles from £90.
Rooms	17: 15 doubles, 2 twins.
Meals	Lunch from £5. À la carte dinner about £40.
Closed	Never.
Directions	West from Ambleside on A593, then left for Hawkshead on B5285. After 1 mile, left, signed. Up hill to inn.

Stephanie Barton
Barngates, Ambleside,
Cumbria LA22 0NG

Tel	015394 36347
Fax	015394 36781
Email	info@drunkenduckinn.co.uk
Web	www.drunkenduckinn.co.uk

New House Farm

A sublime position in the Vale of Lorton; Swinside rises on one side, Low Fell on the other, huge views shoot down the valley to Melbreak looming afar. Lie in a claw-foot bath and gaze on it all while planning your next ascent: you can from one room. This is a warm, chic, farmhouse B&B set in 17 lush acres. Horses graze in the fields, one the granddaughter of Nijinsky. There's a tearoom in summer for walkers, and grass paths in the garden lead up through an orchard to a small lake. Back at the house – 1650 at the front, 1820 at the back – are a stone-flagged entrance hall, a wood-burner in the dining room, warm reds and greens in snug sitting rooms. Bedrooms are fabulous – the feel of home, the style of a hotel – with bowls of fruit, smart red carpets, old beams, exposed stones. Both rooms in the converted stables have four-posters, all have exquisite bathrooms – claw-foots, an enormous shower, perhaps a bath for two. Hazel's delicious cooking – chicken liver pâté, roast Lakeland lamb, crème brûlée – is rounded off with a plate of local cheeses. Loweswater, Crummock Water and Buttermere are all close.

Price	£150-£160. Singles £75-£105.
Rooms	5: 2 doubles, 1 twin/double. Stables: 2 four-posters.
Meals	Lunch from £6 (April-November). Dinner, 3 courses, £26.
Closed	Never.
Directions	A66 to Cockermouth, then B5289 for Buttermere. Signed left 2.5 miles south of Lorton.

 Travel Club Offer: see page 367 for details.

Hazel Thompson
Lorton, Cockermouth,
Cumbria CA13 9UU

Tel	01900 85404
Fax	01900 85478
Email	enquiries@newhouse-farm.co.uk
Web	www.newhouse-farm.com

Hotel

Cumbria

The Pheasant

A 15th-century coaching inn with Sale Fell and Whythop Woods rising behind. A wonderfully English country-cottage garden (apple blossom, climbing roses, the trimmest lawn) looks the right way and is for guests only, so grab a deck chair on the lawn and settle in for an early evening drink. Interiors are no less spoiling; this is an extremely comfortable country-house inn, with open fires in elegant sitting rooms and a low beamed ceiling in the bright and breezy dining room. The snug bar, a treasured relic of times past, has a ceiling coloured by 300 years of tobacco smoke and polish, 40 malts, and a couple of Thompson sketches hanging on the wall (he exchanged them for drink). Cosseting bedrooms, warm in yellow, come with pretty pine beds, thick fabrics, Roberts radios, flat-screen TVs, and robes in spotless bathrooms. Most are in the main house, two are in a nearby garden lodge. Wander the corridors and meet Housekeeping armed with feather dusters. There's a kennel for visiting dogs, Skiddaw to be scaled, and Bassenthwaite – the only lake in the Lake District – is close. *Minimum stay two nights at weekends.*

Price	£150-£160. Singles from £85. Suites £176-£186. Half-board from £102 p.p. (min. 2 nights).
Rooms	15: 11 twins/doubles, 1 single, 3 suites.
Meals	Light lunch from £7. Dinner, 3 courses, £31.95.
Closed	Christmas Day.
Directions	From Keswick, A66 north-west for 7 miles. Hotel on left, signed.

Matthew Wylie
Bassenthwaite Lake, Cockermouth,
Cumbria CA13 9YE

Tel	01768 776234
Fax	01768 776002
Email	info@the-pheasant.co.uk
Web	www.the-pheasant.co.uk

Entry 48   Map 5

Swinside Lodge

Swinside is a Lakeland dream – a small, intimate country house that sits in silence at the foot of Cat Bells. Fells rise, spirits soar, and Derwent Water, Queen of the Lakes, is a stroll through the woods. Despite such impeccable credentials, it is Eric and Irene who shine most brightly. They excel in the art of proper hospitality; those who seek a gentle hand will find it here. Inside are warm colours, an open fire, a morning room with books and sofas, a drawing room with views of the hills. Spotless bedrooms suit the mood perfectly: double-pressed linen, super-comfy beds, country-style eiderdowns, wonderful bathrooms (some are small). Sash windows frame the view, so watch the weather change, while outside a host of characters visit the garden: a song thrush, red squirrels, wild pheasants, roe deer. You eat in style in the burnt-red dining room, the sort of food you'd hope for after a day on the hills, perhaps homemade soup, Cumbrian beef, liquorice panna cotta. As for breakfast, climb Cat Bells before 9am and find an extra sausage on your plate. Wonderful. *Children over 12 welcome. Minimum stay two nights at weekends in high season.*

Price	Half-board £96–£118 p.p.
Rooms	7: 5 doubles, 2 twins.
Meals	Half-board only. Dinner for non-residents, £40. Packed lunches £7.
Closed	Christmas.
Directions	M6 junc. 40. A66 west past Keswick, over r'bout, then 2nd left, for Portinscale & Grange. Follow signs to Grange for 2 miles. Signed on right.

Eric & Irene Fell
Grange Road, Newlands, Keswick,
Cumbria CA12 5UE

Tel	01768 772948
Fax	01768 773312
Email	info@swinsidelodge-hotel.co.uk
Web	www.swinsidelodge-hotel.co.uk

Crosby Lodge

A country house hotel with old-fashioned values: a pudding trolley is wielded each evening with great aplomb and housekeeping roam the corridors each morning armed with dusters and polish. Patricia is everywhere, always immaculately dressed, never seeming to stop, but never in a hurry. This castellated mansion stands in four acres of lawn and woodland, with lush views to the front; Michael and Patricia fell in love with it long before buying it 37 years ago. Inside, warm Victorian interiors are full of colour. Expect roaring fires, leather fenders, red chaise longues, vintage wallpaper and shiny wood floors. Reception rooms have high ceilings and oak-framed windows, there's a sparkling copper bar, a beautiful oval drawing room and an ornate ceiling in the restaurant... come for delicious food, perhaps onion and cider soup, pan-fried sea bass with asparagus, rich chocolate mousse. Country-house bedrooms have florals aplenty. You'll find the odd four-poster and those at the front have marvellous views. Gretna is close, so come to elope. Hadrian's Wall is just up the road.

Price	£160-£195. Singles £90-£95.	
Rooms	11: 2 doubles, 5 twins/doubles, 1 single, 3 family.	
Meals	Lunch from £5. Dinner, 3 courses, £38-£40.	
Closed	24 December-13 January.	
Directions	M6 junc. 44, A689 east for 3.5 miles, then right to Low Crosby. Through village. House on right.	

Michael & Patricia Sedgwick
High Crosby, Carlisle, Cumbria CA6 4QZ

Tel	01228 573618
Fax	01228 573428
Email	enquiries@crosbylodge.co.uk
Web	www.crosbylodge.co.uk

Augill Castle

A folly castle built in 1841 for John Bagot, the eldest of two feuding brothers, who wanted the grandest house. Outside, five acres of lush gardens patrolled by a family of free-range hens, whose eggs are served at breakfast each morning. Inside, grand interiors come properly furnished: chesterfield sofas in a vast hall, a grand piano in the music room, an honesty bar in the drawing room, ribbed ceilings, open fires, fine arched windows. The house is run informally: no uniforms, no rules, just Wendy, Simon and their staff to ply you with delicious food, scented hot-water bottles, big pillows, massive tubs. A stained-glass window on the staircase shines under a vaulted ceiling, then come wonderful country-house bedrooms. One is enormous, another has a wardrobe in the turret. You'll find beautiful beds, cavernous bathrooms, lattice windows and vintage luggage. Rooms in the house have the view, there are sofas if there's room, interesting art, antique wood, one huge dining table. Perfect for house parties and small weddings. The aptly named Eden Valley waits outside; the Dales are close.

Price	£160. Singles £80.
Rooms	12: 6 doubles, 3 twins/doubles, 3 four-posters.
Meals	Dinner, 4 courses, £40 (Fridays & Saturdays). Supper, 2 courses, £20 (not Wednesday or Sunday in winter).
Closed	Never.
Directions	M6 junc. 38; A685 through Kirkby Stephen. Just before Brough, right for South Stainmore; signed on left after 1 mile.

Ethical Collection: Environment;
Community; Food. See page 373 for details

Simon & Wendy Bennett
Brough, Kirkby Stephen,
Cumbria CA17 4DE
Tel   01768 341937
Email   enquiries@stayinacastle.com
Web   www.stayinacastle.com

Biggin Hall

Biggin isn't fancy for a moment, but you can't fault the price or its glorious position in the national park. Footpaths bisect the property and lead straight out into glorious country – the stepping stones at Dovedale, the lush beauty of Edale, the cycle tracks of the Tissington Trail. The house goes back to 1672 and stands in eight acres of the White Peaks with Dove River a mile from the front door. Interiors are comfortable without being plush: flagged floors, stone walls, beamed ceilings, a fire in the hall. Doors open onto a terrace for afternoon tea, where you are serenaded by birdsong. Bedrooms in the main house have better views, those in the converted outbuildings are good for people with pets. A simple country style offers the odd brass bed, perhaps a floral crown and adequate bathrooms. One is panelled, others come in neutral colours with white linen. There's a cooked breakfast buffet to set you up for the day and unpretentious home-cooking in the evenings, perhaps grilled pear and stilton salad, braised beef in red wine, fresh lemon meringue. A great base for walkers. *Minimum stay two nights at weekends.*

Price	£74–£130. Singles from £40. Half-board £55–£78 p.p.
Rooms	20: 6 doubles, 1 four-poster, 1 family. Outbuildings: 8 doubles, 4 twins/doubles.
Meals	Lunch from £5. Dinner £18.50. Sunday lunch from £11.95. Packed lunch available.
Closed	Never.
Directions	0.5 miles west of A515 midway between Ashbourne & Buxton.

James Moffett
Biggin-by-Hartington, Buxton,
Derbyshire SK17 0DH

Tel	01298 84451
Email	enquiries@bigginhall.co.uk
Web	www.bigginhall.co.uk

The Peacock at Rowsley

The Peacock began in 1652. It was once the dower house to Haddon Hall and stands by the bridge in the middle of the village. It opened as a coaching inn 200 years ago and its lawns sweep down to the river Derwent. Fishermen come to try their hand, but those who want to walk can follow the river up to Chatsworth, then sweep back over gentle hills and return for a night at this warmly contemporary hotel. Inside, the old and the new mix harmoniously. Expect mullioned windows, hessian rugs, open fires, fresh flowers everywhere and good art on the walls. The feel is light and airy. French windows in the restaurant open in summer onto a pot-festooned terrace; the fire in the bar smoulders all year. Rooms come in different shapes and sizes, all with a surfeit of style: crisp linen, good beds, Farrow & Ball paints, the odd fine antique. Drop down for dinner and nip into the restaurant for imaginative seasonal dishes, perhaps Dorset crab, breast of duck, green apple brûlée. Six circular walks start from the front door, so you can walk off any excess in the hills that surround you. *Minumum stay two nights at weekends.*

Price	£165–£210. Singles £85–£105. Half-board from £118 p.p.
Rooms	16: 6 doubles, 7 twins, 1 four-poster, 2 singles.
Meals	Breakfast buffet included; cooked dishes £3.50–£6.25. Lunch £21.50. Dinner, à la carte, about £45. Sunday lunch £18.50–£23.
Closed	Rarely.
Directions	A6 north through Matlock, then to Rowsley. On right in village.

Travel Club Offer: see page 367 for details.

Jenni MacKenzie
Bakewell Road, Rowsley, Matlock,
Derbyshire DE4 2EB
Tel   01629 733518
Fax   01629 732671
Email   reception@thepeacockatrowsley.com
Web   www.thepeacockatrowsley.com

The Devonshire Arms at Beeley

An old stone pub on the Chatsworth estate that carries the family name. The Duke and Duchess of Devonshire have renovated in fine style. Character comes courtesy of stone walls, roaring fires, flagged floors and timber frames, but the feel is fresh and elegant, with Designer's Guild fabrics and Farrow & Ball paints. A sympathetic extension houses the restaurant, where contemporary art adds much colour and a wall of glass looks onto the village. Scoff your bacon and eggs here, pop in for lunch, walk all day, then return for a good supper, perhaps Brixham scallops, Beeley lamb, Mrs Hill's lemon tart. In summer, sit out on the terrace with a pint of Chatsworth Gold and watch walkers pour off the hill. Bedrooms are split between the inn and next-door Brookside House. Expect extravagant headboards, period colours, beautifully dressed beds and super bathrooms (one has a claw-foot tub in the room). Also, all the expected gadgets: Bose sound systems, flat-screen TVs, DVD players, iPod docks. The Derbyshire Dales are all around and you can walk over the hill to Chatsworth. *Minimum stay two nights at weekends in high season.*

Price	£145–£165. Suite £165–£185.
Rooms	8: 4 doubles, 3 twins/doubles, 1 suite.
Meals	Lunch from £9.95.
	Dinner, 3 courses, about £25.
Closed	Never.
Directions	North from Matlock on A6, then right onto B6012 for Chatsworth & Beeley. Right in village and on right.

Alan Hill
Beeley, Matlock,
Derbyshire DE4 2NR

Tel   01629 733259
Email   res@devonshirehotels.co.uk
Web   www.devonshirebeeley.co.uk

Fischer's at Baslow Hall

Ambrosial food and country-house elegance combine in spades to make Fischer's a must for those in search of a welcoming bolthole in the Peak District. The house was built in 1907, but you'll think it belongs to the 17th century. It stands at the top of its own hill in lightly wooded grounds on the northern flank of town, with Baslow Edge running above – walk up for magnificent views. Inside you find grandeur on a small scale: plaster-moulded ceilings, old oak doors, mullioned windows through which the sun pours, a fire roaring in the half-panelled sitting room. Bedrooms in the main house come in country-house style (warm florals, smart fabrics, crisp white linen), while large garden rooms are more contemporary and have Italian marble bathrooms. Best of all is the Michelin-starred food. Rupert Rowley heads the kitchen alongside Max, a partnership that coaxes incredible flavours from their ingredients, so try terrine of foie gras with Yorkshire forced rhubarb, naturally-reared Derbyshire pork, raspberry soufflé with a sorbet to match. Chatsworth is close. Fabulous.

Price	£140-£195. Singles £100-£140.
Rooms	11: 5 doubles, 5 garden rooms, 1 suite.
Meals	Continental breakfast included; cooked extras £3-£9.50. Lunch, 2 courses, £23-£27. Dinner, à la carte, around £68. Menu de Jour (not Sat) £33-£38. Tasting menu £63.
Closed	25 & 26 December.
Directions	From Baslow north on A623. Signed on right on edge of town.

Max & Susan Fischer
Calver Road, Baslow,
Derbyshire DE45 1RR

Tel	01246 583259
Fax	01246 583818
Email	reservations@fischers-baslowhall.co.uk
Web	www.fischers-baslowhall.co.uk

Masons Arms

Lose yourself in tiny lanes, follow them down towards the sea, pass the Norman church, roll up at the Masons Arms. It stands in a village half a mile back from the pebble beach surrounded by glorious country, with a stone terrace at the front from which to gaze upon lush hills. It dates back to 1350 – a cider house turned country pub – and the men who cut the stone for Exeter Cathedral drank here, hence the name. Inside, simple, authentic interiors are just the thing: timber frames, low beamed ceilings, pine cladding, whitewashed walls and a roaring fire over which the spit roast is cooked on Sundays. Some bedrooms are above the shop, others are behind on the hill. Those in the pub are small but cute (warm yellows, check fabrics, leather bedheads, super bathrooms); those behind are bigger, quieter and more traditional; they overlook a garden and each has a private terrace for valley views that tumble down to the sea. Footpaths lead out – over hills, along the coast – so follow your nose, then return for super food: seared scallops, lamb cutlets, saffron and honey crème brûlée.

Price	£80–£130. Suites £170.
Rooms	21: 18 twins/doubles, 1 family, 2 suites.
Meals	Bar meals from £7.95. Dinner, 3 courses, about £29.95.
Closed	Never.
Directions	Barnscombe signed off A3052 between Seaton & Sidmouth. In village.

Colin & Carol Slaney
Main Street, Branscombe, Seaton,
Devon EX12 3DJ

Tel	01297 680300
Fax	01297 680500
Email	reception@masonsarms.co.uk
Web	www.masonsarms.co.uk

Combe House

Combe is immaculate, an ancient house on a huge estate, the full aristocratic works. You spin up a long drive, pass Arabian horses running wild in the distance, then skip through the front door and enter a place of architectural splendour. A fire roars in the magnificent hall, the muralled dining room gives huge views, the sitting room/bar in racing green opens onto the croquet lawn. Best of all is the way things are done: the feel is more home than hotel and you may mistake yourself for lord of the manor – a battalion of household staff to attend to your every whim. Wander around and see 600-year old flagstones, original William Morris wallpaper, Victorian greenhouses that provide much for the table, beehives for breakfast honey. Rooms are fabulous, expect the best: stately fabrics, wonderful beds, gorgeous bathrooms, outstanding views. The vast suite, once the laundry press, is now the stuff of fashion shoots and comes with an enormous copper bath. There are 3,500 acres to explore and fabulous food to keep you going, but it's Ruth and Ken who win the prize; they just know how to do it. *Minimum stay two nights at weekends.*

Price	£170–£280. Singles from £150. Suites £320–£375. Half-board from £120 p.p. Cottage £355 (B&B).
Rooms	15 + 1: 10 twins/doubles, 1 four-poster, 4 suites. 1 self-catering cottage for 2.
Meals	Lunch £22–£32. Dinner £42; tasting menu £59.
Closed	Rarely.
Directions	M5 junc. 28 or 29; across to Honiton. There, south for Sidmouth on A375. Right after a mile, brown signs through woods.

 Travel Club Offer: see page 367 for details.

Ruth & Ken Hunt
Gittisham, Honiton, Exeter,
Devon EX14 3AD
Tel   01404 540400
Fax   01404 46004
Email   stay@thishotel.com
Web   www.thishotel.com

Bark House Hotel

A country hotel on the southern flank of Exmoor where old-fashioned values win out. Martin whisks your bag into the house, Melanie greets you with the offer of cakes and tea. This may not be the fanciest hotel in the book but the way things are done is second to none – and much appreciated. You have at your disposal a cosy sitting room with books and open fire, a small garden popular with local birds and a candlelit dining room for delicious home cooking, perhaps spiced parsnip and apple soup, best end of lamb with rowan jelly, a creamy chocolate torte. Spotless bedrooms above are warmly comfortable, most in yellow, with trim carpets, comfortable beds and views across the road (never busy) to meadows running down to the river. Most have excellent little shower rooms; the lovely suite up in the eaves has a fancy bath, too. All come with padded bedheads, fresh flowers, small TVs and pretty linen. One is panelled, another has a beautiful bay window, a third is huge and comes with stone walls. Cream teas are served in the garden in good weather or by the fire in the sitting room in winter.

Price	£80–£120. Singles from £50.
Rooms	6: 3 doubles, 1 twin/double, 1 suite; 1 double with separate bath.
Meals	Dinner, 3 courses, £32.
Closed	Rarely.
Directions	From Tiverton, A396 north towards Minehead. Hotel on right, 1 mile north of junction with B3227.

Melanie McKnight & Martin French
Oakfordbridge, Bampton,
Devon EX16 9HZ

Tel   01398 351236
Email   barkhousehotel@btconnect.com
Web   www.thebarkhouse.co.uk

Heasley House

The sort of place you chance upon, only to return again and again. Everything here is lovely. It's a beautiful house in a sleepy village lost in a wild Exmoor valley, with stylish interiors, delicious food and very attractive prices. Inside, Paul and Jan have overseen a total refurbishment, recovering the grandness of a Georgian dower house, then dressing it up in contemporary clothes. You find stripped boards, stone walls, timber frames, a frieze on the fireplace. Harmonious colours run throughout, fires burn in the sitting rooms, there are gilt mirrors, a fancy bar and fresh flowers everywhere. Airy bedrooms are more than comfy with big beds, good linen and lovely bathrooms. Those at the front have country views, those in the eaves have beams. All have flat-screen TVs, DVD players, bathrobes and armchairs. Spin down to the restaurant for Aga-cooked food, perhaps mushroom risotto with white truffle oil, fillet of sea bass with spring onion mash, chocolate mousse with Gran Marnier. Paths lead out, so follow the river into the woods or head north for cliffs at the coast. Brilliant – and so hospitable.

Price	£120. Suite £140. Singles from £75.
Rooms	8: 7 twins/doubles, 1 suite.
Meals	Dinner £19.50-£24.
Closed	Christmas Day, Boxing Day & February.
Directions	M5 junc. 27, A361 to Barnstaple. Turn right at sign for North Molton, then left for Heasley Mill.

Paul & Jan Gambrill
Heasley Mill, North Molton,
Devon EX36 3LE

Tel	01598 740213
Fax	01598 740677
Email	enquiries@heasley-house.co.uk
Web	www.heasley-house.co.uk

St Vincent House & Restaurant

A hidden gem on the north Devon coast. Everything here is wonderful: owners, décor, food and price. Jean-Paul and Lin do their own thing brilliantly; boundless kindness and fabulous food are the hallmarks. Daisies grow on the lawn, a 100-year-old wisteria spreads its wings at the front, Jean-Paul's herbs lie hidden in pots and beds. Inside this charming house, built by Captain Green with monies from the battle of Cape St Vincent, you find stripped floors, warm rugs, gilt mirrors and polished brass in front of an open fire. Turn left for the sitting room, right for the restaurant. Spotless bedrooms upstairs are a delight. Expect good beds, warm colours and super little bathrooms. Aperitifs are served in the front garden in summer; you're in the middle of town, but lush plants screen you from it. Hop back into the restaurant for fabulous food: scallops cooked in butter and lemon; filet mignon with roasted garlic; lavender and vodka ice cream. John-Paul is Belgian, so are his beers, chocolate and waffles; the latter are served at breakfast with free-range eggs and local sausages. Moor and coast wait for walkers.

Price	£75–£80.
Rooms	5 twins/doubles.
Meals	Dinner £24–£27 (not Monday or Tuesday).
Closed	November–Easter.
Directions	In Lynton, ignore 1st sign to left; follow signs for car parks. Up hill, see car park on left, thatched house on right; on left after car park, next to Exmoor Museum.

Jean-Paul Salpetier & Lin Cameron
Market Street, Castle Hill, Lynton,
Devon EX35 6JA

Tel	01598 752244
Fax	01598 752244
Email	welcome@st-vincent-hotel.co.uk
Web	www.st-vincent-hotel.co.uk

The Old Rectory

The coastal road from Lynton is a great way in, a rollercoaster lane that snakes though woods clinging to the hill with the sea below. Wash up at the Old Rectory and find a warmly stylish hotel that must qualify as one of the quietest in England. Three acres of mature gardens wrap around you, only birdsong from a wide cast of characters disturbs you – though Exmoor deer occasionally come to drink from the small lake. Inside, Huw and Sam, corporate escapees who have taken to the hills, have already put their elegant mark on the place: uncluttered interiors, Farrow & Ball colours, and a revamp of the marvellous conservatory, where a 200-year old vine provides grapes for the cheese board. There are books and a computer for guests to use, an open fire in the snug sitting room and lovely bedrooms scattered about with big beds, crisp linen, cool colours and flat-screen TVs; one has a balcony, most have fancy bathrooms. Spin into the restaurant for an excellent meal, perhaps local asparagus, sea bass with a herb sauce, rhubarb crème brûlée. There's afternoon tea on the house, too. *Minimum stay two nights at weekends in high season.*

 Travel Club Offer: see page 367 for details.

Price	£140. Half-board (breakfast, dinner, afternoon tea) £100-£115 p.p. Cottage £325-£725 per week.
Rooms	8 + 1: 4 doubles, 4 twins/doubles. 1 self-catering cottage for 4.
Meals	Dinner, 4 courses, £33.
Closed	November-February.
Directions	M5 junc. 27, A361 to South Molton; A399 north. Right at Blackmore Gate onto A39 for Lynton. Left after 3 miles, signed Martinhoe, just past Woody Bay Station. In village, next to church.

Huw Rees & Sam Prosser
Martinhoe, Exmoor National Park,
Devon EX31 4QT

Tel	01598 763368
Fax	01598 763567
Email	info@oldrectoryhotel.co.uk
Web	www.oldrectoryhotel.co.uk

Northcote Manor

A divine retreat at the top of a hill built on the site of a 15th-century monastery. Those who want peace in glorious country will be in heaven. You wind up a one-mile drive, through a wood that bursts with colour in spring, then emerge onto a plateau of lush rolling hills. The house is as lovely as the land that surrounds it, built of local stone with wisteria wandering along the walls. There are sweeping lawns, a walled garden and a tennis court with country views. Inside, fires roar: in the airy hall, which doubles as the bar; in the country-house drawing room that floods with light; in the sitting room where you gather for pre-dinner drinks. Super food waits in a lovely dining room, steps lead down to a pretty conservatory, and doors open onto a gravelled terrace for summer breakfasts and exquisite views. Bedrooms are no less appealing, all recently refurbished in contemporary country-house style. Expect padded bedheads, mahogany dressers, flat-screen TVs, silky throws. Lovely walks start from the front door; Exmoor and the North Devon coast are fabulously close.

Price	£155–£215. Suites £255. Singles from £100. Half-board (min. 2 nights) from £105 p.p.
Rooms	11: 4 doubles, 2 twins/doubles, 1 four-poster, 4 suites.
Meals	Lunch from £15. Dinner £38.
Closed	Rarely.
Directions	M5 junc. 27, A361 to South Molton. Fork left onto B3227; left on A377 for Exeter. Entrance 4.1 miles on right, signed.

Cheryl King
Burrington, Umberleigh,
Devon EX37 9LZ

Tel	01769 560501
Fax	01769 560770
Email	rest@northcotemanor.co.uk
Web	www.northcotemanor.co.uk

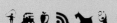 Travel Club Offer: see page 367 for details.

The Lamb Inn

This 16th-century inn is nothing short of perfect, a proper local in the old tradition with the odd touch of scruffiness to add authenticity to earthy bones. It stands on a cobbled walkway in a village lost down Devon's tiny lanes, and those lucky enough to chance upon it will leave reluctantly. Outside, all manner of greenery covers its stone walls; inside there are beams, but they are not sandblasted, red carpets with a little swirl, sofas in front of an open fire and rough-hewn oak panels painted black. Boarded menus trumpet wonderfully priced food – carrot and orange soup, whole baked trout with almond butter, an irresistible tarte tatin. There's a cobbled terrace, a small garden, an occasional cinema, a lovely open mic night... and a back bar, where two ales come straight from the barrel. Upstairs, three marvellous bedrooms elate. One is large with a bath and a wood-burner in the room, but all are lovely with super-smart power showers, sash windows that give village views, hi-fis, flat-screen TVs, good linen and comfy beds. Dartmoor waits but you may well linger. There's Tiny, the guard dog, too.

Price	£75–£95.
Rooms	3 doubles.
Meals	Lunch from £5.
	Dinner, 3 courses, £15–£20.
Closed	Rarely.
Directions	A377 north from Exeter. 1st right in Credion, signed Sandford. 1 mile up & in village.

Mark Hildyard & Katharine Lightfoot
Village Square, Sandford,
Crediton, Devon EX17 4LW

Tel	01363 773676
Email	thelambinn@gmail.com
Web	www.lambinnsandford.co.uk

Blagdon Manor

You'll have the warmest of welcomes from Steve and Liz in their supremely comfortable country house in the middle of nowhere – actually, in 20 acres of woodland and moor – with huge views stretching to Yes Tor. There are doors that open onto the garden in the stone-flagged library, an open fire in the sitting room, a panelled bar in what was the 16th-century kitchen, and a conservatory for breakfast where you can watch the birds flit by. Bedrooms are equipped to spoil. Come for decanters of sherry and fresh flowers, warm country florals and bathrobes. Colours are bold: blues, yellows, lilacs and greens; one room has a fine purple carpet. You get small sofas if there's room, the odd beam, a bit of chintz and comfortably snug bathrooms. All rooms are the same price; the first to book gets the biggest, but none are small. Steve's cooking is not to be missed, perhaps smoked duck breast, local lamb in a rosemary jus, a trio of citrus puddings. Blagdon is dog-friendly (a couple of labradors sleep in front of the fire) and there are towels, blankets, bowls, treats and toys.

Price	£135–£180. Singles from £85.
Rooms	8: 6 doubles, 2 twins/doubles.
Meals	Lunch from £17 (Wed-Sun). Dinner from £31.
Closed	2 weeks in January; 2 weeks in October; New Year.
Directions	A30, then north from Launceston on A388. Ignore signs to Ashwater. Right at Blagdon Cross, signed. Right; right again; house signed right.

	Steve & Liz Morey
	Ashwater, Devon EX21 5DF
Tel	01409 211224
Email	stay@blagdon.com
Web	www.blagdon.com

Percy's Country Hotel

There are days in summer when all the food you eat at dinner has come from the land that surrounds you. Tony and Tina came west not merely to cook but to grow their own; now even the meat is home-reared. Percy's – a restaurant with rooms on an organic farm – teems with life: pigs roam freely through 60 acres of woodland, Jacob sheep graze open pasture, geese, ducks and chickens supply the tastiest eggs. A kitchen garden is planted seasonally but much is harvested wild from the woods, a natural larder of mushrooms, juniper, crab apples and elderflower. Tina conjures up soups and salads, terrines and sausages, curing her own bacon and delicious hams: a meal at Percy's is no ordinary event. Bedrooms in the converted granary are lovely (super-comfortable beds, chic leather sofas, spotless bathrooms, flat-screen TVs), but Percy's is about more than just a bed. Grab a pair of wellies and lose yourself in the estate, or hitch a lift and lend a hand with the morning feed. Woodpeckers and kingfishers, deer and badger, old hedgerows, wild flowers and a huge sky wait.

Price	£150–£210. Singles £110–£185. Half-board £115–£145 p.p. (suite £195 p.p.)
Rooms	7: 6 twins/doubles, 1 suite.
Meals	Dinner, 3 courses, £40 for non-residents.
Closed	Never.
Directions	From Okehampton, A3079 for Metherell Cross. After 8.3 miles, left. Hotel on left after 6.5 miles.

Travel Club Offer: see page 367 for details.

Tina & Tony Bricknell-Webb
Coombeshead Estate, Virginstow,
Okehampton, Devon EX21 5EA

Tel	01409 211236
Fax	01409 211460
Email	info@percys.co.uk
Web	www.percys.co.uk

The Arundell Arms

A tiny interest in fishing would not go amiss, though the people here are so kind they welcome everyone. Anne has been at the helm for 45 years; her MBE for services to tourism is richly deserved. This is a *very* settled hotel, with Mrs VB, as staff call her fondly, quietly presiding over all; during a superb lunch – St Enodoc asparagus, scallops, homemade chocs – she asked after an 80th birthday party, ensuring their day was memorable. Over the years the hotel has resuscitated buildings at the heart of the village: the old police station and magistrates court is a pub, the old school a conference centre. Pride of place is the funnel-roofed cock-fighting pit, one of only two left in England; now it's the rod room, where local knowledge is shared generously every morning. Anne's late husband wrote about fly-fishing for *The Times* and it's no surprise to discover that this is one of the best fishing hotels in England – or that they own 20 miles of the Tamar. Come to try your luck or merely to search for otter and kingfisher on its banks. As for the hotel: it's newly refurbished, divine from top to toe.

Price	£160-£190. Singles from £99.
Rooms	21: 9 doubles, 7 twins, 3 singles, 2 suites.
Meals	Bar meals £7-£15. Dinner from £38.
Closed	Christmas.
Directions	A30 south-west from Exeter, past Okehampton. Lifton 0.5 miles off A30, 3 miles east of Launceston & signed. Hotel in centre of village.

Anne Voss-Bark
Lifton, Devon PL16 0AA

Tel	01566 784666
Fax	01566 784494
Email	reservations@arundellarms.com
Web	www.arundellarms.com

Travel Club Offer: see page 367 for details.

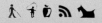

Tor Cottage

At the end of the track, a blissful valley lost to the world. This is an indulging hideaway, wrapped up in 28 acres of majestic country, and those who like to be pampered in peace will find heaven. Hills rise, cows sleep, streams run, birds sing. Bridle paths lead onto the hill, wild flowers carpet a hay meadow. Big rooms in converted outbuildings are the lap of rustic luxury, each with a wood-burner and private terrace. All are impeccable, one filled with Art Deco, one straight out of *House and Garden*, one whitewashed with ceilings open to the rafters. Best of all is the cabin in its own valley – a wonderland in the woods – with hammocks hanging in the trees and a stream passing below. You can self-cater here and eat on the deck while deer wander in the trees. Breakfasts served in the conservatory promise homemade muesli, local sausages and farm-fresh eggs, but if you get peckish later in the day, wash down smoked salmon sandwiches with a glass of sangria while sunbathing by the pool. Staff couldn't be nicer, guests return. *Minimum stay two nights. Special deals available.*

 Travel Club Offer: see page 367 for details.

Price	£140-£150. Singles £94. Self-catering from £100 (min. 3 nights).
Rooms	4 + 1: 2 doubles, 1 twin/double, 1 suite. 1 woodland cabin for 2 (B&B or self-catering).
Meals	Supper, 3 courses, £24. On request.
Closed	B&B: Christmas & New Year. Self-catering: Never.
Directions	In Chillaton keep pub & PO on left, up hill towards Tavistock. After 300 yds, right down bridleway (ignore No Access signs).

Maureen Rowlatt
Chillaton, Tavistock, Devon PL16 0JE

Tel	01822 860248
Fax	01822 860126
Email	info@torcottage.co.uk
Web	www.torcottage.co.uk

Browns Hotel

This is a popular spot. The Romans came first and left a well: you can stand on a sheet of glass in the conservatory and peer into it. Then came the Benedictines, who built an abbey: old carved stones are on show in the bar. If tradition holds they'll find Roberts radios and leather sofas when they rebuild in 200 years. Helena swept in armed with ideas and has already made her mark: Lloyd Loom wicker sits in the courtyard, a hidden terrace is being brought back to life. The house dates to 1700 and was Tavistock's first coaching inn. It's still the best place to stay in town, with armchairs in front of the fire, wood floors in the restaurant, and a stone-flagged conservatory for delicious breakfasts. Clutter-free bedrooms have a clipped elegance: Farrow & Ball colours, Egyptian cotton, latticed windows and comforting bathrobes. Some in the coach house are huge, with cathedral ceilings. Dine under beams on Cornish scallops, roast lamb, rhubarb and custard crumble. Tavistock is an old market town, its famous goose fair takes place in October. Don't miss Dartmoor for uplifting walks.

Price	£99–£239.
Rooms	21: 15 doubles, 3 twins, 3 singles.
Meals	Continental breakfast included. Cooked dishes £6.00–£12.50. Lunch from £9. Dinner £32–£37. 5-course tasting menu £45.
Closed	Never.
Directions	Leave A386 for Tavistock. Right, at statue, for town centre. Left at T-junction, them immediately left into West Street. Hotel on right. Ask about parking.

Helena King & Phil Biggin
80 West Street, Tavistock,
Devon PL19 8AQ

Tel	01822 618686
Fax	01822 618646
Email	enquiries@brownsdevon.co.uk
Web	www.brownsdevon.co.uk

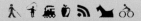

The Horn of Plenty

This country-house hotel has been thrilling guests for 40 years. It's won just about every award going and the food is glorious, so if you're looking for somewhere very special, you'll find it here. You get fabulous rooms, jaw-dropping views, exceptional service. Staff come to meet you on arrival – with an umbrella if it's wet – then escort you into this impeccable house. Airy interiors are the essence of graceful simplicity with stripped floors, gilt mirrors, exquisite art and flowers everywhere. Bedrooms elate wherever you go, some with terraces that look down on the Tamar, others with painted wooden floors, shimmering throws or crushed velvet headboards. All come fully armed with an excess of hi-tech gadgetry, bathrooms are predictably divine. As for the food, well, just don't miss it. Try foie gras crème brûlée, loin of venison with spiced pear, then chocolate truffle mousse with raspberry sauce. In summer you can eat on the terrace with views of the Tamar cutting through the valley below. You're in five acres of silence. Tavistock is close, as is Dartmoor.

Price	£160–£250. Singles £150–£240.
Rooms	10 twins/doubles.
Meals	Lunch, 3 courses, £26.50. Dinner, 3 courses, £45.
Closed	25 & 26 December.
Directions	A386 north to Tavistock. Left onto A390, following signs to Callington. After 3 miles, right at Gulworthy Cross. Signed.

 Travel Club Offer: see page 367 for details.

Paul Roston & Peter Gorton
Gulworthy, Tavistock, Devon PL19 8JD

Tel	01822 832528
Fax	01822 834390
Email	enquiries@thehornofplenty.co.uk
Web	www.thehornofplenty.co.uk

The Dartmoor Inn

There aren't many inns where you can sink into Zoffany-clad winged armchairs in the dining room, snooze on a pink silk bed under a French chandelier, or shop for rhinestone brooches and Provençal quilts while you wait for the wild sea bass to crisp in the pan. Different rules apply at the Dartmoor. This is the template of deep-country chic, a fairytale inn dressed up as a country local. True, there is a snug bar at the front where you can perch on a stool and knock back a glass of ale, but then again the walls are coated in textured wallpaper, gilded mirrors sit above smouldering fireplaces and upstairs a shimmering velvet throw is spread out across a sublimely upholstered sleigh bed. Come for stripped wood floors, timber-framed walls, sand-blasted settles and country-house rugs. Add to this wonderful staff and Philip's ambrosial food (corned beef hash for breakfast, ham hock terrine for lunch, free-range duck for dinner) and you have a very special place. Triple-glazed bedroom windows defeat road noise and ensure a good night's rest. The moors are on your doorstep, so walk in the wind, then eat, drink and sleep.

Price	£100–£120.
Rooms	3 doubles.
Meals	Lunch from £5. Dinner from £15.
Closed	Occasionally.
Directions	North from Tavistock on A386. Inn on right at Lydford turnoff.

	Karen & Philip Burgess
	Lydford, Okehampton, Devon EX20 4AY
Tel	01822 820221
Fax	01822 820494
Email	info@dartmoorinn.co.uk
Web	www.dartmoorinn.com

Oxenham Arms

In a pretty village on the edge of Dartmoor, a grand inn that that dates from the 12th century. It may have started life as a monastery and has held a licence since 1477 – a mere 630 years of continuous service to locals and travellers alike (Dickens and Nelson both stayed). Inside, you find timber frames, flagged floors, oak beams and mullioned windows, but Mark has come to breathe new life into old bones and the paint brush has been wielded with aplomb. One restaurant comes in lilac with a huge stone inglenook, the other has whitewashed walls and Lloyd Loom furniture. The front bar is trapped in aspic: roaring fire, oak settles, varnished wood bar, even a canon ball. Locals gather here, as do shooting parties and tale-telling fishermen. There's a back bar with a stone reputed to be 5,000 years old, a terrace for dining, a garden for beer and a paddock beyond, for Shakespeare in summer. Bedrooms are a work in progress; most have had their florals evicted in favour of oak four-posters, cool colours and excellent bathrooms. Magical Dartmoor beckons – bring your boots.

Price	£105–£165.
Rooms	7: 2 doubles, 1 twin, 4 four-posters.
Meals	Lunch from £6. Dinner, 3 courses, £20–£25.
Closed	Never.
Directions	M5 junc. 31, then A30 west to Whiddon Down. South thro' village on A382, then left for South Zeal. In village.

 Travel Club Offer: see page 367 for details.

Mark Payne
South Zeal, Okehampton,
Devon EX20 2JT

Tel	01837 840244
Fax	01837 840791
Email	theoxenhamarms@aol.com
Web	www.theoxenhamarms.co.uk

Sandy Park Inn

A thatched pub in a tiny Dartmoor village. The river Teign runs through the valley; fishing can be arranged or you can follow it along for views that lift the soul. Those of a more sedentary disposition can sit in the beer garden and take in the view while sampling local delicacies. This is a cracking country boozer, loved by locals, with food that punches above its weight. Barry the butcher brings in slow-grown pork off the moor, the cod comes battered in beer, cheeses are all local. It's snug, with low ceilings, flagged floors, country rugs and huge logs crackling in an old stone fire. Standing room only at the bar at weekends; local musicians occasionally play on Sunday nights. Bedrooms sparkle with unexpected treats – flat-screen TVs, CD players, padded headboards, colourful throws – but the bar is lively, and a night here will only suit those who want to have some fun. Most rooms have pretty views over the village; some are en suite, others not, so come to practise the dying art of smiling at strangers on the landing. Also: kippers at breakfast, maps for walkers and dog biscuits behind the bar.

Price	£92. Singles £59.
Rooms	5: 1 twin, 1 double, each en suite; 3 doubles each with separate bath/shower.
Meals	Lunch from £5. Dinner from £8.
Closed	Never.
Directions	A30 west from Exeter to Whiddon Cross. South 2 miles to Sandy Park. Pub on right at x-roads.

Nick Rout
Sandy Park, Chagford,
Devon TQ13 8JW
Tel   01647 433267
Email   sandyparkinn@aol.com
Web   www.sandyparkinn.co.uk

 Travel Club Offer: see page 367 for details.

Gidleigh Park

Gidleigh is a perfect place, ten out of ten on all counts. It stands in 54 acres of lush silence with the North Teign river pottering through and huge views shooting off to Meldon Hill. Inside, you find a faultless country house. A fire smoulders in the oak-panelled hall, ferns tumble from silver champagne bowls, sofas come crisply dressed in dazzling fabrics. Bedrooms are divine, impeccably presented with hand-stitched linen, woollen blankets, upholstered headboards and polished wooden furniture; the panelled suite comes with an enormous bathroom that opens onto a private balcony. Back downstairs, beautiful art adorns the walls, while summer life spills onto a view-filled terrace. As for the food, Michael Caines brings two Michelin stars to the table, so expect the best, perhaps terrine of foie gras with rhubarb and lemon grass jelly, Cornish duckling with roast garlic and honey, poached peach with vanilla mousse and nectarine sorbet. Breakfast offers porridge with whisky among other delicacies. Best of all is sublime service from the loveliest staff. Matchless. *Minimum stay two nights at weekends.*

Price	Half-board £240–£310 p.p. Suites £350–£662.50 p.p.
Rooms	24: 15 twins/doubles, 6 doubles, 3 suites.
Meals	Half-board only. Lunch £33–£41. Dinner for non-residents, £85.
Closed	Never.
Directions	A30 west from Exeter to Whiddon Down. A382 south, then B3206 into Chagford. Right in square, right at fork. Signed straight across at x-roads.

Susan Kendall
Chagford, Devon TQ13 8HH

Tel	01647 432367
Fax	01647 432574
Email	gidleighpark@gidleigh.co.uk
Web	www.gidleigh.com

Mill End

Another Dartmoor gem. Mill End is flanked by the Two Moors Way, one of the loveliest walks in England. It leads along the river Teign, then up to Castle Drogo – not a bad way to follow your bacon and eggs. So step inside to find an extremely comfortable country retreat. Labradors snooze in front of the fire, there are timber frames, nooks and crannies, bowls of fruit, pretty art. Warm, uncluttered, traditional interiors are just the ticket, with vases of flowers on plinths in the sofa'd sitting room and smartly upholstered dining chairs in the airy restaurant. Bedrooms come in clipped country-house style: white linen, big beds, moor views, the odd antique. You might find a chandelier, a large balcony or padded window seats. All come with flat-screen TVs, some have big baths stocked with Radox. Drop down for a delicious dinner, perhaps pea and truffle soup, local venison with roasted pears, hot chocolate fondant with white chocolate foam. In the morning there's porridge with cream and brown sugar, as well as the usual extravagance. Dogs are very welcome; bowls, leads and blankets all wait.

Price	£90-£160. Suites £160-£220.
Rooms	14: 10 doubles, 2 twins, 2 suites.
Meals	Lunch by arrangement.
	Dinner £28-£38.
Closed	3 weeks in January.
Directions	M5, then A30 to Whiddon Down.
	South on A382, through Sandy Park,
	over small bridge and on right.

Keith Green
Sandy Park, Chagford, Devon TQ13 8JN

Tel	01647 432282
Fax	01647 433106
Email	info@millendhotel.com
Web	www.millendhotel.com

 Travel Club Offer: see page 367 for details.

Prince Hall Hotel

An avenue of beech trees sweeps you down to this very peaceful hotel, in six acres of woodland and lawns, with views at the back across majestic Dartmoor. Inside is a warm and welcoming country house. It's not the grandest place in the book but colour and comfort go hand in hand and those who want to escape the city can do so here. Follow your nose and find leather sofas in front of the fire in the sitting room, old pine windows framing the view in the bar and a newly refurbished restaurant that comes in airy whites for super food – perhaps seared squid with lemon oil, saddle of venison with toasted wild mushrooms, then white chocolate custard tart. Bedrooms above come in different shapes and sizes. Expect wallpaper, white linen, dressing mirrors and warm florals. The more expensive rooms have the view and a couple have fancy bathrooms too, but Fi and Chris have arrived armed with plans, so expect things to change. Outside, lawns run down to paddocks, the river passes beyond, then nothing but moor and sky. Foxgloves and primroses bring colour in spring. Dogs are very welcome. *Minimum stay two nights at weekends.*

Price	£120–£140. Singles from £60.
Rooms	9: 4 doubles, 4 twins/doubles, 1 single.
Meals	Lunch from £5.50. Dinner, 3 courses, £35.
Closed	1st two weeks in January.
Directions	A38 to Ashburton, then follow signs through Poundsgate & Dartmeet. Hotel signed on left 1 mile before Two Bridges.

 Travel Club Offer: see page 367 for details.

Fi & Chris Daly
Two Bridges, Dartmoor,
Devon PL20 6SA

Tel   01822 890403
Fax   01822 890676
Email info@princehall.co.uk
Web   www.princehall.co.uk

Lydgate House

You're in 36 acres of heaven, so come for the sheer wonder of Dartmoor: deer and badger, fox and pheasant, kingfisher and woodpecker. A 30-minute circular walk takes you over the East Dart, up to a wild hay meadow where rare orchids flourish, then back down to a 12th-century clapper bridge; sensational. Herons dive in the river by day; you may get a glimpse from the conservatory as you dig into your bacon and eggs. The house is a dream, a nourishing stream of homely comforts: a drying room for walkers, deep white sofas, walls of books and a wood-burner in the sitting room. Anna bakes delicious scones, Douglas keeps the garden trim; somehow they find time to double up as host and hostess extraordinaire: expect a good chat, delicious cooking and peace when you want it. Bedrooms – two huge – are warmly cossetting: crisply floral with comfy beds and Radox in the bathrooms. Rescued sheep live in the top field and are partial to a slice of toast, moonwort grows in the hay meadow. Legend says if gathered by moonlight it unleashes magical properties; clearly someone has.

Price	£100-£120. Singles £45-£50.
Rooms	7: 4 doubles, 1 twin/double, 2 singles.
Meals	Dinner, 3 courses, £27.50.
Closed	January.
Directions	From Exeter A30 west to Whiddon Down, A382 south to Moretonhampstead, B3212 west to Postbridge. In village, left at pub. House signed straight ahead.

Anna & Douglas Geikie
Postbridge, Newton Abbot,
Devon PL20 6TJ

Tel	01822 880209
Fax	01822 880360
Email	lydgatehouse@email.com
Web	www.lydgatehouse.co.uk

Entry 76   Map 2

Kingston House

It's hard to know where to begin with this stupendous house – the history in one bathroom alone would fill a small book. "It's like visiting a National Trust home where you can get into bed," says Elizabeth, your gentle, erudite host. Set in a flawless Devon valley, Kingston is one of the finest surviving examples of early 18th-century English architecture. Arrive down a long country lane and at the brow of the last hill the house comes into view... along with the Great Danes that bound out to greet you. Completed in 1735 for a wealthy wool merchant, original features remain including numerous open fires, murals peeling off the walls, a sitting room in the old chapel (look for the drunken cherubs) and 24 chimneys. The craftsman who carved the marble hallway later worked on the White House, the marquetry staircase is the best in Europe, and the magnificent bed in the Green Room has stood there since 1830. The cooking is historic, too – devilled kidneys, syllabub and proper trifle. Flowers by the thousand in various gardens and a small pool with a jet stream so you can swim 20 miles.

Price	£180–£200. Singles £110–£120.
Rooms	3: 2 doubles, both en suite; 1 double with separate bath.
Meals	Lunch from £25. Dinner, 3 courses, £38. On request.
Closed	Christmas & New Year.
Directions	From A38, A384 to Staverton. At Sea Trout Inn, left fork for Kingston; halfway up hill right fork; at top, ahead at x-roads. Road goes up, then down to house; right to front of house.

Michael & Elizabeth Corfield
Staverton, Totnes,
Devon TQ9 6AR

Tel	01803 762235
Fax	01803 762444
Email	info@kingston-estate.co.uk
Web	www.kingston-estate.co.uk

Bickley Mill

A small inn full of good things. David and Tricia recently orchestrated a total refurbishment and their stylishly cosy interiors are just the ticket. Come for wood floors, stone walls, hessian rugs, cushioned sofas. Three fires burn in winter, there are Swedish benches, colourful art and a panelled breakfast room in creamy yellow. Everywhere you look something lovely catches the eye, be it a huge sofa covered with mountainous cushions, old black and white photos hanging on the walls or a decked terrace at the side for a pint or two in the summer sun. Bedrooms have a simple beauty in warm colours, pretty pine, trim carpets, crisp white linen – and with reasonable prices they're an absolute steal. Downstairs you'll find helpful staff, local ales and loads to eat (light bites to a three-course feast) perhaps devilled kidneys, salmon fishcakes, banana and toffee pancakes; there's a menu for children and baby chairs, too. You're in the lush Stoneycombe valley with Dartmouth, Dartmoor and the south Devon coast all close. A very generous place, so don't delay.

Price	£80–£90. Singles £60–£65.
Rooms	8: 5 doubles, 2 twins, 1 family room.
Meals	Lunch from £5. Dinner from £11.
Closed	Rarely.
Directions	South from Newton Abbot on A381. Left at garage in Ipplepen. Left at T-junc. after 1 mile. Down hill, left again, pub on left.

David & Tricia Smith
Stoneycombe, Kingskerswell,
Devon TQ12 5LN

Tel	01803 873201
Fax	01803 875129
Email	info@bickleymill.co.uk
Web	www.bickleymill.co.uk

Travel Club Offer: see page 367 for details.

Browns Hotel

Browns is all things to all men, a trendy little eatery bang in the middle of town. You can pop in for breakfast, stop for coffee, stay for lunch, drop by for a beer or book in for a slap-up dinner. The building goes back to 1812 but the interiors are unmistakably contemporary, with sofas by the fire in the bar and Philippe Starck chairs in the airy restaurant. An open-plan feel runs throughout and fine Georgian windows look onto the high street, so sink into a comfy armchair and watch the world go by. Colours come courtesy of Farrow & Ball, big seaside oils hang on the walls, flames leap from a pebbled fire, stripped floors mix with sandstone tiles. Bedrooms upstairs may not be huge but they're clean, comfortable and pretty. Expect padded bedheads, flat-screen TVs, tub leather armchairs and warm colours. Rooms at the back are quieter, but all have radios, good bathrooms and a book that spills local secrets (the best walks and beaches, which ferries to use). Bistro-style food waits in the restaurant: super paella, local halibut, spicy lamb kofta. And the river is close. *Minimum stay two nights at weekends.*

Price	£85–£150. Four-poster £170. Singles from £60 (Sunday–Thursday).
Rooms	10: 8 doubles, 1 twin, 1 four-poster.
Meals	Lunch from £6.95. Dinner, 3 courses, about £25.
Closed	January.
Directions	Into Dartmouth on A3122. Left at 1st r'bout, straight over 2nd r'bout, then 3rd right (Townstal Road). Down into town. On right.

James & Clare Brown
27-29 Victoria Road, Dartmouth,
Devon TQ6 9RT

Tel	01803 832572
Email	enquiries@brownshoteldartmouth.co.uk
Web	www.brownshoteldartmouth.co.uk

Fingals

People love the defiant individualism of Fingals. It is so different, so satisfyingly unusual, that the less easy-going among us should give it a miss. Richard runs things in a rare laissez-faire style; informality and a sense of fun are the hallmarks. Sheila, behind every scene, is impossibly kind. Guests, many old fans, wander around as if at home, children and dogs mill about, tennis is played on the lawn. The clock in the bar has one hand only and dinner comes whenever it's ready, but this laid-back atmosphere has its benefits: breakfast is served until 11am. You'll make friends, stay up too late, get to know Richard, Sheila and their friends. The setting is a handsome house next to a stream with small indoor pool, panelled dining room, log fires and lots of books. It is not for the over fastidious – the odd spider web may be overlooked. Rooms are eclectically cluttered or plainly traditional; bathrooms tend not to be fancy. For every visitor who is uncomfortable with the Fingals style, there are legions of fans. It is a generous place and one that cocks a welcome snook at more conventional hotels. *Minimum stay two nights at weekends.*

Price	£80–£160. Barn £500–£800 per week.
Rooms	10 + 1: 8 doubles, 1 twin, 1 family. Self-catering barn for 4.
Meals	Dinner £30.
Closed	2 January–April.
Directions	From Totnes, A381 south; left for Cornworthy. Right at x-roads for Cornworthy; right at ruined gatehouse for Dittisham. Down steep hill, over bridge. Signed on right.

Richard & Sheila Johnston
Dittisham, Dartmouth, Devon TQ6 0JA

Tel	01803 722398
Fax	01803 722401
Email	richard@fingals.co.uk
Web	www.fingals.co.uk

Hazelwood House

Crest the hill, drop down the drive and dive into a hidden valley. If you are looking to escape the outside world, you can here. Sixty-seven wild acres wrap around you with a river galloping through. You'll find native woodlands, ancient rhododendrons, fields of wild flowers, a shepherdess grazing her flock. Hazelwood isn't your standard hotel or B&B, it's a country venue with accommodation for all who wish to rest, retreat and recoup – you may occasionally find yourself among guests on a residential course. It's a comfy, no frills house with open fires, sublime peace and a large drawing and dining room. Bedrooms are homely with an assortment of furniture, some have huge views over the valley, some face the back, others have brass beds and quilted bedcovers or big mirrors and a Victorian fireplace. Cream teas on the wisteria-shaded veranda are wonderful and you get lectures, exhibitions, courses, even recitals. Wellington boots wait at the front door. Pull on a pair, pick up a map, lope past a Frederick Frank sculpture in the garden and a boathouse on the river.

Price	£80–£160. Singles £48–£115.
Rooms	14: 4 doubles, 2 twins, 1 family room, all en suite; 2 doubles, 2 twins, 2 family rooms, 1 single, sharing 4 baths.
Meals	Lunch £10–£18. Dinner £25–£35.
Closed	Never.
Directions	From Exeter, A38 south; A3121 south. Left onto B3196 south. At California Cross, 1st left after petrol station. After 0.75 miles, left.

Janie Bowman, Gillian Kean &
Anabel Watson
Loddiswell, Kingsbridge, Devon TQ7 4EB

Tel	01548 821232
Fax	01548 821318
Email	info@hazelwoodhouse.com
Web	www.hazelwoodhouse.com

Buckland Tout-Saints

Tiny lanes lead up to this William and Mary manor house. It stands in four acres of parkland gardens with views at the front sweeping across an ancient quilt of field and copse. The land was listed in the Domesday book, the current house dates to the 17th century, its dovecote is one of England's oldest. Inside you find grandly panelled reception rooms dressed in shimmering Russian pine. Old oils adorn the walls, flames leap in the marble fireplace, there are scattered sofas, bowls of fruit, vast displays of flowers. There's a bar in red leather that resembles a gentleman's club, a ceiling rose in the stately dining room, a terrace with big views for afternoon tea. First-floor bedrooms come in country-house style: high ceilings, warm colours, thick fabrics, fine views. Those above in the eaves are smaller but funkier, with padded headboards, neutral colours, flat-screen TVs, comfy beds. Excellent food is often organic, perhaps fish terrine with horseradish cream, rack of lamb with a black olive sauce, ginger crème brûlée with plum chilli sorbet. Salcombe and Dartmouth are both close.

Price	£120–£280. Singles from £90.
Rooms	15: 11 doubles, 2 twins, 2 suites.
Meals	Lunch from £15. Dinner, 3 courses, about £39.
Closed	Never.
Directions	A381 south from Totnes for Kingsbridge. Hotel signed right three miles south of Halwell. Follow signs up narrow lanes to hotel.

	Matthew Gibbs Goveton, Kingsbridge, Devon TQ7 2DS
Tel	01548 853055
Fax	01548 856261
Email	buckland@tout-saints.co.uk
Web	www.tout-saints.co.uk

Seabreeze

A Mediterranean-style beach café at the end of Slapton Sands: the sea laps ten paces from the front door, the rolling hills of Devon soar behind. Seabreeze is a treat, small, cute and nicely relaxed, a little piece of homespun magic. It's not grand, but what you get is priceless. Andrew organises kite surfing, Charlotte runs the café. There are kayaks and bikes for intrepid adventures, cliff walks for fabulous views. Those who want to stay put can soak up the sun on the terrace at the front and tuck into homemade smoothies and grilled paninis while seaside life ambles by. Inside, airy interiors are just as they should be: colourful and comfy. You get stripped floors, halogen lighting, sky-blue tongue and groove panelling. You can buy sun cream and kites, there are sofas, candles and a fire in the café. Airy bedrooms are perfect for the price: crisp linen, seaside colours, flat-screen TVs, super bathrooms. Two have huge sea views; padded window seats oblige. Fabulous seafood at the Start Bay Inn is yards away. There's a surf school at Bigbury and sailing at Salcombe. *Minimum stay two nights at weekends.*

Price	£60–£100. Singles from £40.
Rooms	3: 1 double, 1 twin/double, 1 family.
Meals	Lunch (March–October) from £5. Restaurants in village.
Closed	Rarely.
Directions	A379 south from Dartmouth to Torcross. House on seafront in village.

Andrew & Charlotte Barker
Torcross, Kingsbridge, Devon TQ7 2TQ

Tel	01548 580697
Email	info@seabreezebreaks.com
Web	www.seabreezebreaks.com

White House

A super cool boutique hotel with dazzling interiors and a fabulous garden. Sun loungers dot the lawn, there's a gorgeous terrace for lunch in summer and views that stretch off to forest and hill. A footpath across the lane winds off to the beach at Torcross for two miles of nothing but sand with cliff-top walks and fabulous views, though some won't make it: White House encourages a certain laziness. Bedrooms are fabulous: stripped floors, Florence Broadhurst wallpapers, handmade beds and Frette linen. One has a hammock, another has a huge chrome lamp. You'll find flat-screen TV/DVDs, iPod docks, coffee machines and chests full of liquid refreshments. All have spectacular bathrooms: deluge showers or claw-foot baths, robes and fancy oils. Downstairs, airy uncluttered interiors come as standard, with leather sofas in the sitting room, a small bar that opens onto the terrace, even a screening room for the local film club. As for the restaurant, it's mostly made of glass and overlooks the garden, with fabulous food to boot: don't miss the plates of cheese and charcuterie. Seriously spoiling. *Minimum stay two nights at weekends.*

Price	£155–£175. Singles from £140.
Rooms	5 doubles.
Meals	Breakfast £8.50–£12.50. Lunch from £7. Dinner, 3 courses, about £30.
Closed	Never.
Directions	East from Kingsbridge on A379 for Dartmouth. In village, last house on right.

	Tamara Costin
	Chillington, Kingsbridge, Devon TQ7 2JX
Tel	01548 580505
Fax	01548 581196
Email	frontofhouse@whitehousdevon.com
Web	www.whitehousedevon.com

Burgh Island

Burgh is unique – grand English Art Deco trapped in aspic. Noel Coward loved it, Agatha Christie wrote here. It's much more than a hotel – you come to join a cast of players – so bring your pearls and come for cocktails under a stained-glass dome. By day you lie on steamers in the garden, watch gulls wheeling above, dip your toes into Mermaid's pool or try your hand at a game of croquet. At night you dress for dinner, sip vermouth in a palm-fringed bar, then shuffle off to the ballroom and dine on delicious organic food while the sounds of swing and jazz fill the air. Follow your nose and find flowers in vases four-feet high, bronze ladies thrusting globes into the sky, walls clad in vitrolite, a 14th-century smugglers inn. Art Deco bedrooms are the real thing: Bakerlite telephones, ancient radios, bowls of fruit, panelled walls. Some have claw-foot baths, others have balconies, the Beach House suite juts out over rocks. There's snooker, tennis, massage, a sauna. You're on an island; either sweep across the sands at low tide or hitch a ride on the sea tractor. *Minimum stay two nights at weekends.*

Price	Half-board £355-£380 per room. Suites £355-£550.
Rooms	24: 10 doubles, 3 twins, 12 suites.
Meals	Half-board only. Lunch £38. Dinner for non-residents, 3 courses, £55.
Closed	Rarely.
Directions	Drive to Bigbury-on-Sea. At high tide you are transported by sea tractor, at low tide by Landrover. Walking takes three minutes.

Deborah Clark & Tony Orchard
Bigbury-on-Sea,
Devon TQ7 4BG

Tel	01548 810514
Fax	01548 810243
Email	reception@burghisland.com
Web	www.burghisland.com

The Henley

A small house above the sea with fabulous views, super bedrooms and some of the loveliest food in Devon. Despite such credentials, it's Martyn and Petra who shine most brightly, and their kind, generous approach makes this a memorable place to stay. Warm Edwardian interiors come with stripped wood floors, seagrass matting, Lloyd Loom wicker chairs, the odd potted palm. Beyond, the Avon estuary slips out to sea: at high tide surfers ride the waves; at low tide you can walk on the sands. There's a pretty garden with a path down to the sea, binoculars in each room, a wood-burner in the snug and good books everywhere. Bedrooms are a steal, not large but in warm yellows with crisp linen, tongue-and-groove panelling and robes in super little bathrooms. As for Martyn's table d'hôte dinners, expect something special. Fish comes daily from Kingsbridge market, you might have cream of parsnip, apple and potato soup, roasted monkfish with king prawns and a garlic and butter sauce, then hot chocolate soufflé with fresh raspberries. Gorgeous Devon is all around. Don't miss it. *Minimum stay two nights at weekends.*

Price	£101–£128. Singles from £60.
Rooms	5: 2 doubles, 3 twins/doubles.
Meals	Dinner £30.
Closed	November–March.
Directions	From A38, A3121 to Modbury, then B3392 to Bigbury-on-Sea. Hotel on left as road slopes down to sea.

Martyn Scarterfield & Petra Lampe
Folly Hill, Bigbury-on-Sea,
Devon TQ7 4AR

Tel	01548 810240
Fax	01548 810240
Email	thehenleyhotel@btconnect.com
Web	www.thehenleyhotel.co.uk

Entry 86   Map 2

The Bull Hotel

With Dorset's star firmly on the rise, it was only a matter of time before a funky hotel appeared on the radar. Step forward The Bull, a sparkling bolthole that comes in cool hues and which stands on the high street in the middle of town. It's smart enough for a masked ball on New Year's Eve, and informal enough for ladies who lunch to pop in unannounced. It's a big hit with the locals and lively most days; at weekends the bar rocks. All of which makes it a lot of fun for guests passing through. Gorgeous rooms wait upstairs; French and English country elegance entwine with a touch of contemporary flair. Expect beautiful beds, pashmina throws, old radiators, perhaps an armoire. Most come in airy whites, some have striking wallpaper, maybe a claw-foot bath at the end of the bed. There are digital radios, flat-screen TVs, super little bathrooms. Back downstairs — stripped floorboards, Farrow & Ball walls, sofas in the bar, candles everywhere — dig into brasserie style food; moules frites is on the menu every Wednesday night. Lyme Regis and Chesil Beach are close. *Minimum stay two nights at weekends.*

Price	£70-£180. Suite from £190.
Rooms	14: 6 doubles, 3 four-posters, 2 family, 1 twin, 1 single, 1 suite.
Meals	Lunch, 2 courses, from £10. Dinner, 3 courses, around £25.
Closed	Never.
Directions	On main street in town. Car park at rear.

 Travel Club Offer: see page 367 for details.

Nikki & Richard Cooper
34 East Street, Bridport,
Dorset DT6 3LF

Tel	01308 422878
Fax	01306 426872
Email	info@thebullhotel.co.uk
Web	www.thebullhotel.co.uk

BridgeHouse Hotel

Beaminster – Emminster in Thomas Hardy's *Tess* – sits in a lush Dorset valley. From the hills above, rural England goes on show: quilted fields lead to a country town, the church tower soars towards heaven. At BridgeHouse stone flags, mullioned windows, old beams and huge inglenooks sweep you back to a graceful past. This is a comfortable hotel in a country town – intimate, friendly, quietly smart. There are rugs on parquet floors, a beamed bar in a turreted alcove, a sparkling dining room with Georgian panelling. Breakfast is served in the brasserie, where huge windows look onto the lawns, so watch the gardener potter about as you scoff your bacon and eggs. Delicious food – local and organic – is a big draw, perhaps seared scallops, Gressingham duck, champagne sorbet. And so to bed. Rooms in the main house are bigger and smarter, those in the coach house are simpler and less expensive; all are pretty with chic fabrics, crisp linen, flat-screen TVs and stylish bathrooms. There are river walks, antique shops and Dorset's Jurassic coast. *Minimum stay two nights at weekends.*

Price	£116-£200. Four-poster £200. Singles from £76. Half-board (min. 2 nights) from £83 p.p.
Rooms	13: 6 twins/doubles, 2 four-posters, 1 single. Coach House: 3 doubles, 1 family room.
Meals	Brasserie lunch & dinner from £10.50. À la carte dinner £30-£35.
Closed	Never.
Directions	From Yeovil, A30 west; A3066 for Bridport to Beaminster. Hotel at far end of town, as road bends to right.

Mark & Jo Donovan
3 Prout Bridge, Beaminster,
Dorset DT8 3AY

Tel	01308 862200
Fax	01308 863700
Email	enquiries@bridge-house.co.uk
Web	www.bridge-house.co.uk

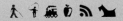

Entry 88   Map 2

Plumber Manor

A grand stone house lost in Dorset's sleepy lanes. It stands in 60 acres of lawns, field and woodland with the river Develish running through. It dates from 1650 and comes with mullioned windows, huge stone flags and a fine terrace for afternoon tea. An avenue of horse chestnuts leads up to the front door, inside which a pair of labradors rule the roost. Interiors pay no heed to designer trends – Plumber is not the place to come to glimpse the latest fashions – but the first-floor landing has the biggest velvet sofa you are ever likely to see, plus a gallery of family oils covering the walls and a grand piano for good measure. Bedrooms are split between the main house and converted barns. The latter tend to be bigger and are good for people with dogs. Décor is dated – 1980s florals – as are the bathrooms, but the family triumvirate of Brian (in the kitchen), Richard (behind the bar) and Alison (simply everywhere) excel in the art of old-fashioned hospitality. Delicious country food waits in the restaurant. Bulbarrow Hill is close. *Pets by arrangement.*

Price	£120–£180. Singles from £100.
Rooms	16: 2 doubles, 13 twins/doubles, all en suite; 1 twin/double with separate bath.
Meals	Sunday lunch £23. Dinner £26–£30.
Closed	February.
Directions	West from Sturminster Newton on A357. Across traffic lights, up hill & left for Hazelbury Bryan. Hotel signed left after 2 miles.

Richard, Alison & Brian Prideaux-Brune
Sturminster Newton, Dorset DT10 2AF

Tel	01258 472507
Fax	01258 473370
Email	book@plumbermanor.com
Web	www.plumbermanor.com

Stapleton Arms

An inn with a big heart. There are no pretensions here, just kind, knowledgeable staff committed to running the place with informal panache. A recent face lift has brought a streak of glamour back to this old coaching inn, infusing it with a warm colourful style. Downstairs there are sofas in front of the fire, a piano for live music in the bar and a restaurant in Georgian blue with shuttered windows and candles in the fireplace. You can eat wherever you want. Pork pies, Serrano ham and Tête de Moine cheese all wait at the bar, but if you want a bowl of soup or a three-course feast you can have it; try salmon and crab fishcakes, home-baked Dorset ham, banana tarte tatin. There's a beer menu (ale matters here), on Sundays groups can order their own joint of meat, and there's always a menu for kids. Rooms above are soundproofed to ensure a good night's sleep. They're comfy-chic with Egyptian linen, fresh flowers, happy colours, perhaps a claw-foot bath. Also: maps and picnics, wellies if you want to walk, games for children, DVDs for all ages. Wincanton is close for the races.

Price	£72–£120. Singles £72–£96
Rooms	4: 3 doubles, 1 twin/double.
Meals	Lunch from £5.50. Dinner, 3 courses, about £23.
Closed	Rarely.
Directions	A303 to Wincanton. Into town, right after fire station, signed Buckhorn Weston. Left at T-junc. after 3 miles. In village, left at T-junc. Pub on right.

Kaveh Javvi
Church Hill, Buckhorn Weston,
Gillingham, Dorset SP8 5HS

Tel	01963 370396
Email	relax@thestapletonarms.com
Web	www.thestapletonarms.com

Travel Club Offer: see page 367 for details.

The Museum Inn

Dorset is fabulous: rolling hills, tiny villages, a Jurassic coast… old England at its best. The Museum is just as good, a smart country inn in the middle of a pretty village that is lost in a web of meandering lanes. Inside, style and comfort abound: a country-house sitting room with open fire and books galore; a gorgeous bar with flagged floors and cushioned window seats; a conservatory dining room which opens onto a sun-trapping terrace. Wander at will and find painted shutters, country oils and an elegant breakfast room with ferns and high ceiling. Outside, roses wander along red-brick walls and you can glimpse the listed remains of 18th-century stocks. Bedrooms – big in the main house, smaller in the old stables – are extremely comfortable as they stand, but David is hell bent on refurbishing nonetheless and cool colours, fancy bathrooms and hi-tech gadgetry are on the way in. One room has a Georgian four-poster and French windows that open to a balcony. The food is fantastic: Gloucester Old Spot sausages for breakfast, south-coast fish for lunch, Dorset duck for dinner. Superb.

Price	£95–£120. Four-poster £150.
Rooms	8: 5 doubles, 2 twins/doubles, 1 four-poster.
Meals	Lunch & dinner £5–£30.
Closed	Never.
Directions	From Blandford, A354 for Salisbury for 6.5 miles, then left, signed Farnham. Inn on left in village.

David Sax
Farnham, Blandford Forum,
Dorset DT11 8DE

Tel	01725 516261
Fax	01725 516988
Email	enquiries@museuminn.co.uk
Web	www.museuminn.co.uk

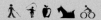

The Priory Hotel

Come for a slice of old England. The lawns of this 16th-century priory run down to the river Frome. Behind, a church rises, beyond, a neat Georgian square; in short, a little bit of time travel. A stone-flagged courtyard leads up to the hotel, where comfortable country-house interiors include a first-floor drawing room with views of the garden and a stone-vaulted dining room in the old cellar. Best of all is the terrace; 200 yards of dreamy English gardens front the river, so sit in the sun and watch yacht masts flutter. Bedrooms in the main house come in different sizes, some cosy under beams, others grandly adorned in reds and golds. Also: mahogany dressers, padded window seats, bowls of fruit, the odd sofa. Bathrooms — some new, some old — come with white robes. Eight have river views, others look onto the garden or church. Rooms in the boathouse, a 16th-century clay barn, are opulent, with oak panelling, stone walls, the odd chest and sublime views. Four acres of idyllic gardens have climbing roses, a duck pond and banks of daffs. Wonderful. *Minimum stay two nights at weekends in summer.*

Price	£225-£270. Suites £315-£345. Half-board (obligatory at weekends) from £137.50 p.p.
Rooms	18: 13 twins/doubles, 5 suites.
Meals	Lunch from £27. Dinner from £39.95.
Closed	Never.
Directions	West from Poole on A35, then A351 for Wareham and B3075 into town. Through lights, 1st left, right out of square, then keep left and entrance on left beyond church.

Jeremy Merchant
Church Green, Wareham,
Dorset BH20 4ND

Tel	01929 551666
Fax	01929 554519
Email	reservations@theprioryhotel.co.uk
Web	theprioryhotel.co.uk

urban beach hotel

Urban beach operates to different rules: Janusz is in charge of making girls laugh, Alex is responsible for being nice. The spirit here is infectious: very friendly with buckets of style – surfer chic in Bournemouth with seven miles of sandy beach waiting at the end of the road. Inside, gaze upon a total renovation. Walls have disappeared downstairs to create one large airy room and the bar/restaurant now comes with a ceiling rose and plaster moulding to complement chrome stools and the odd decorative surf board. There are big circular leather booths, driftwood lamps, a house guitar and surf movies projected onto a wall in the bar. In summer, doors open onto a decked terrace for cocktails, fresh fruit smoothies and barbecues in the sun. Excellent bedrooms, some big, some smaller, are all fitted to the same spec: Egyptian linen, flat-screen TVs, crushed velvet curtains, wonderful bathrooms. Drop down for a good breakfast: freshly squeezed orange juice, hot croissants, the full cooked works. A brasserie-style menu runs all day. It's a 20-minute seaside walk into town. *Minimum stay two nights at weekends.*

Price	£95–£170. Singles from £70.
Rooms	12: 9 doubles, 1 twin/double, 2 singles.
Meals	Lunch & dinner £5–£25.
Closed	Never.
Directions	South from Ringwood on A338; left for Boscombe (east of centre). Over railway, right onto Centenary Way, keep with the flow (left, then right) to join Christchurch Rd; 2nd left (St John's Rd); 2nd left.

 Travel Club Offer: see page 367 for details.

Mark & Fiona Cribb
23 Argyll Road, Bournemouth,
Dorset BH5 1EB

Tel	01202 301509
Email	info@urbanbeachhotel.co.uk
Web	www.urbanbeachhotel.co.uk

Lord Bute Hotel

For a small hotel the Lord Bute sure packs a big punch. Its heart and soul is a wonderfully glamorous restaurant that comes in black and gold, with fairy lights hung around mirrors, Lloyd Loom wicker in its conservatory, and a grand piano that gets played at weekends. Part grand ocean liner, part colonial outpost, it is never short of an interesting view, be it flowers erupting from a vase on a plinth or a cut-glass chandelier glistening with grace. Spotless bedrooms are equally pleasing, the quietest away from the road, and if there's a fault, it is this: the larger doubles are so good, you really don't need to go for the suites. They come with super beds, padded heads, thick fabrics and lots of colour. You get flat-screen TVs, sofas if there's room, bathrooms with potions galore. Dinner is unmissable, with live jazz on Wednesdays. Try Poole Bay crab, roast partridge with garlic and thyme, delicious banana crème brûlée. The gate house, built by Robert Adam, belonged to Highcliffe Castle, home to the Earl of Bute, prime minister in 1762. Make sure you drop in, then head to the beach for fine views of the Needles.

Price	£98–£108. Suites £160–£225.
Rooms	13: 8 doubles, 1 twin, 3 suites. Coach House: 1 family suite.
Meals	Lunch from £8.50. Sunday lunch £21.95. Dinner, 3 courses, £32.50. Not Mondays.
Closed	Never.
Directions	From Christchurch, A337 towards Lymington to Highcliffe. Hotel 200 yds past castle.

Gary Payne & Simon Box
Lymington Road, Highcliffe,
Christchurch, Dorset BH23 4JS

Tel	01425 278884
Fax	01425 279258
Email	mail@lordbute.co.uk
Web	www.lordbute.co.uk

Rose and Crown

An idyllic village of mellow stone where little has changed in 200 years. The Rose and Crown dates from 1733 and stands on the green, next to the village's Saxon church. Roses ramble above the door in summer, so pick up a pint and search out the sun on the gravelled forecourt. Inside is just as good. You can sit at settles in the tiny locals' bar and roast away in front of the fire while reading the *Teesdale Mercury*, or seek out sofas in the peaceful sitting room and tuck into afternoon tea. Bedrooms are lovely. Those in the converted barn have padded headboards and tumble with colour; those in the main house come with antique pine, padded window seats and warm country colours. All have crisp white linen, Bose sound systems and quietly fancy bathrooms. Fabulous food can be eaten informally in the brasserie (smoked salmon soufflé, confit of duck, sticky toffee pudding) or grandly in the panelled dining room (farmhouse ham with fresh figs, grilled sea bass, honey and whisky ice cream). High Force waterfall and Hadrian's Wall are close and there's a drying room for walkers. *Minimum stay two nights at weekends.*

Price	£135–£165. Singles from £85. Suites £175–£190.
Rooms	12: 6 doubles, 4 twins, 2 suites.
Meals	Bar meals from £8. Dinner, 4 courses, £30.
Closed	Christmas.
Directions	From Barnard Castle, B6277 north for 6 miles. Right in village towards green. Inn on left.

 Travel Club Offer: see page 367 for details.

Christopher & Alison Davy
Romaldkirk, Barnard Castle,
Durham DL12 9EB

Tel	01833 650213
Fax	01833 650828
Email	hotel@rose-and-crown.co.uk
Web	www.rose-and-crown.co.uk

The Pier at Harwich

You're bang on the water, overlooking the historic Ha'penny pier, with vast skies and watery views that shoot across to Felixstowe. The hotel was built in 1862 in the style of a Venetian palazzo and has remained in continuous service ever since. Inside are boarded floors, big arched windows, a granite bar and travel posters framed on the walls. Eat informally in the bistro downstairs (fish pie, grilled bream, beef stew and dumplings) or grab a window seat in the first-floor dining room and tuck into lobster bisque while huge ferries glide past outside. The owners took over the adjoining pub several years ago and have carved out a pretty lounge with port-hole windows, leather sofas, coir matting, timber frames, even a piano. Bedrooms are scattered about, some above the sitting room, others in the main house. All are pretty, with padded bedheads, seaside colours, crisp white linen, super bathrooms; if you want the best view in town, splash out on the Mayflower suite. Don't miss Dovercourt beach for exhilarating walks, or the Electric Palace, the second oldest cinema in Britain.

Price	£105–£125. Suite £185. Singles from £80.
Rooms	14: 13 doubles, 1 suite.
Meals	Lunch from £8.95. Sunday lunch £26. Dinner, à la carte, £25–£35.
Closed	Never.
Directions	M25 junc. 28, A12 to Colchester bypass, then A120 to Harwich. Head for quay. Hotel opposite pier.

Chris & Vreni Oakley
The Quay, Harwich,
Essex CO12 3HH

Tel	01255 241212
Fax	01255 551922
Email	pier@milsomhotels.com
Web	www.milsomhotels.com

 Travel Club Offer: see page 367 for details.

The Mistley Thorn

This Georgian pub stands on the high street and dates back to 1746, but inside you find a fresh contemporary feel that will tickle your pleasure receptors. The mood is laid-back with a great little bar, an excellent restaurant and bedrooms that pack an understated punch. Downstairs, an open-plan feel sweeps you through high-ceilinged rooms that flood with light. Expect tongue-and-groove panelling, Farrow & Ball colours, blond wood furniture and smart wicker chairs. Climb up to excellent rooms for smartly dressed beds, flat-screen TVs, DVD players and iPod docks. You get power showers above double-ended baths, those at the front have fine views of the Stour estuary, all are exceptional value for money. Back down in the restaurant dig into delicious food; Sherri runs a cookery school next door and has a pizzeria in town. Try smoked haddock chowder, Debden duck with clementine sauce, chocolate mocha tart (if you stay on a Sunday or Monday, dinner is free). Constable country is all around. There's history, too; the Witch-finder General once lived on this spot.

Price	£80–£105. Singles from £65.
Rooms	5: 3 doubles, 2 twins/doubles.
Meals	Lunch from £7.95. Dinner, 3 courses, about £25.
Closed	Rarely.
Directions	From A12, Hadleigh/East Bergholt exit north of Colchester. Thro' East Bergholt to A137; follow signs to Manningtree; drive thro' to Mistley High Street.

David McKay & Sherri Singleton
High Street, Mistley,
Colchester, Essex CO11 1HE

Tel	01206 392821
Fax	01206 390122
Email	info@mistleythorn.co.uk
Web	www.mistleythorn.co.uk

The Sun Inn

An idyllic village made rich by mills in the 16th century. These days you can hire boats on the river, so order a picnic at the inn, float down the glorious Stour, then tie up on the bank for lunch al fresco. You're in the epicentre of Constable country; the artist attended school in the village and often returned to paint St Mary's church with its soaring tower; it stands directly opposite. As for the Sun, you couldn't hope to wash up in a better place. Step in to find open fires, stripped floors and an easy elegance. A panelled lounge comes with sofas and armchairs, the bar is made from a slab of local elm and the dining room is beamed and airy, so settle in for fresh seafood, wild boar, slow-cooked lamb and English cheeses. Rooms are gorgeous: creaking floorboards, a panelled four-poster, timber-framed walls, decanters of sherry. You get Farrow & Ball colours on the walls, crisp Egyptian linen on the beds, super little power-showered bathrooms. There's afternoon tea on arrival, a garden for summer barbecues and the inn owns a traditional grocer's next door.

Price	£80-£150. Singles from £67.50.
Rooms	5: 4 doubles, 1 four-poster.
Meals	Lunch & dinner £5-£25.
Closed	25-27 December.
Directions	A12 north past Colchester. 2nd exit, marked Dedham.

Piers Baker
High Street, Dedham,
Colchester, Essex CO7 6DF

Tel	01206 323351
Email	office@thesuninndedham.com
Web	www.thesuninndedham.com

The Bell Inn & Hill House

A 600-year-old timber-framed coaching inn, as busy today with happy locals as it was when pilgrims stopped on their way to Canterbury. Everything here is a treat: hanging lanterns in the courtyard, stripped boards in the bar, smartly dressed staff in the restaurant, copious window boxes bursting with colour. This is a proper inn, warmly welcoming, with thick beams, country rugs, panelled walls and open fires. Stop for a pint of cask ale in the lively bar, then potter into the restaurant for sensational food, perhaps Stilton ravioli, grilled Dover sole, orange and passion fruit tart. Christine grew up here, John joined her 35 years ago; both are much respected in the trade, as is Joanne, their loyal manager of many years and Master Sommelier. An infectious warmth runs throughout this ever-popular inn. As for the bedrooms, go for the suites above the shop: cosy, traditional, individual, rather wonderful. In the morning stroll up the tiny high street to breakfast with the papers at elegant Hill House, then head north into Constable country or east to the pier at Southend. London is close.

Price	£50–£60. Suites £85.
Rooms	15: 7 doubles, 3 twins, 5 suites.
Meals	Breakfast £4.50–£9.50. Bar meals from £8.50. Dinner, à la carte, around £27. No food bank holidays.
Closed	Christmas Day & Boxing Day.
Directions	M25 junc. 30/31. A13 for Southend for 3 miles; B1007 to Horndon on the Hill. On left in village.

Christine & John Vereker
High Road, Horndon-on-the-Hill,
Essex SS17 8LD

Tel	01375 642463
Fax	01375 361611
Email	info@bell-inn.co.uk
Web	www.bell-inn.co.uk

The Kings Chipping Campden

A gorgeous small hotel bang on the market place in this idyllic Cotswold town. Flower baskets dripping with colour hang from golden stone walls while interiors sparkle in cool rustic style. Follow your nose and find sofas in reception, stripped floors in the granite bar and sandblasted beams in a super restaurant, where a huge curved settle dominates the room. Elsewhere, there's a wood-burner for winter nights, grand oils hanging from the walls and doors that open onto a terrace and lawn – perfect for lazy summer afternoons. Bedrooms are all upstairs. Those at the front overlook the square, those at the back have the peace of the garden. All come in smart country style, with pretty beds, crisp white linen, airy colours and lovely bathrooms. You get flat-screen TVs, good books and White Company lotions. Back downstairs, eat wherever you want, informally in the brasserie/bar or a three-course feast in the restaurant – perhaps homemade ravioli, fish stew with saffron and garlic, then white chocolate cheesecake. There's a tea room, too, for champagne cream teas. Fabulous. *Minimum stay two nights at weekends.*

Price	£95–£175. Singles from £85. Half-board from £82 p.p.
Rooms	14: 11 doubles, 3 twins.
Meals	Lunch from £6.95. Dinner, 3 courses, £25–£30.
Closed	Never.
Directions	From Oxford, A44 north for Evesham. 5 miles after Moreton-in-Marsh, right on B4081 to Chipping Campden. Hotel in square by town hall.

	Charlotte Rides
	The Square, Chipping Campden, Gloucestershire GL55 6AW
Tel	01386 840256
Fax	01386 841598
Email	info@kingscampden.co.uk
Web	www.kingscampden.co.uk

The Malt House

A wonderfully pretty Cotswold village of sculpted golden stone. The Malt House sits in the middle of it all, delightful inside and out. An impeccable country garden runs down to a stream, beyond which fruit trees blossom in spring. There's a summer house, a croquet lawn and Lloyd Loom furniture: pull up a seat and snooze in the sun. Equally impressive is Judi's kitchen garden which provides freshly cut flowers for beautiful bedrooms and summer fruits for the breakfast table. Inside, clipped country-house interiors are just the thing: parquet flooring, sparkling wallpaper, mullioned windows and a mantelpiece that almost touches the ceiling. There are original beams, books and papers, an honesty bar and sofas by the fire. Spotless bedrooms are warmly elegant and hugely comfortable: big mirrors, Jane Churchill silks, Italian fabrics, crisp white linen. You'll find maps for walkers, a list of local restaurants, hot-water bottles and umbrellas to keep you dry. Breakfast is a feast: fresh fruit salad, homemade granola, hot bread straight from the oven, the full cooked works. *Minimum two nights weekends April-October.*

Price	£120–£140. Singles from £85. Suite from £150.
Rooms	7: 1 double, 4 twins/doubles, 1 four-poster, 1 suite.
Meals	Pub 1 mile. Dinner by arrangement (min. 12 people).
Closed	One week over Christmas.
Directions	From Oxford, A44 through Moreton-in-Marsh; right on B4081 north to Chipping Campden. Entering village, 1st right for Broad Campden. Hotel 1 mile on left.

Travel Club Offer: see page 367 for details.

	Judi Wilkes
	Broad Campden, Chipping Campden, Gloucestershire GL55 6UU
Tel	01386 840295
Fax	01386 841334
Email	info@malt-house.co.uk
Web	www.malt-house.co.uk

Entry 101   Map 3

Lower Brook House

The village is a Cotswold jewel, saved from the tourist hordes by roads too narrow for coaches. Lower Brook is no less alluring. It was built in 1624 to house workers from one of the 12 silk mills that made Blockley rich. Step inside to find country rugs on flagged floors, Farrow & Ball paints on timber framed walls, mullioned windows, vases of flowers and piles of vintage luggage. Winter logs smoulder in a huge inglenook in the sitting room – slide onto the leather sofa and roast away. Bedrooms are crisply stylish with beautiful fabrics, pristine linen, bowls of fresh fruit and handmade soaps in super little bathrooms. All but one overlooks the garden; views fly up the hill. Outside, colour bursts from the beds in summer and a small lawn runs down to a shaded terrace for afternoon tea in good weather. Walks start from the door: you can be deep in the country within half a mile. Come back to Anna's delicious cooking, perhaps mustard and cress soup, roast loin of lamb, rhubarb crumble; breakfast treats include smoothies, croissants and freshly squeezed juice. *Minimum stay two nights at weekends.*

Price	£95–£175.
Rooms	6: 3 doubles, 2 twins, 1 four-poster.
Meals	Dinner, 3 courses, £28.
Closed	Christmas.
Directions	A44 west from Moreton-in-Marsh. At top of hill in Bourton-on-the-Hill, right signed Blockley. Down hill to village, on right.

Julian & Anna Ebbutt
Lower Street, Blockley,
Gloucestershire GL56 9DS

Tel	01386 700286
Fax	01386 701400
Email	info@lowerbrookhouse.com
Web	www.lowerbrookhouse.com

Travel Club Offer: see page 367 for details.

Horse and Groom

You're at the top of the hill, so grab the window seats for views that pour over the Cotswolds. This is a hive of youthful endeavour, with brothers at the helm; Will cooks, Tom pours the ales, and a cheery conviviality flows throughout. Recently refurbished interiors mix the old (open fires, stone walls, beamed ceilings) with the new (halogen lighting, crisp coir matting, a cool marble bar), making this a fine place in which to hole up for a night or two. There are settles and boarded menus in the bar, stripped wooden floors and old rugs in the dining room. Tuck into homemade soups, Cornish sardines, Cotswold lamb, then sinful chocolate puddings. In summer you can eat in the back garden under the shade of damson trees and watch the chefs raid the kitchen garden for raspberries and strawberries, onions, fennel, broad beans and herbs. Bedrooms are wonderfully plush, smart but uncluttered, and those at the front are sound-proofed to minimise noise from the road. One room is huge, while the garden room has doors that open onto the terrace. *Minimum stay two nights at weekends April-September.*

Price	£100-£140. Singles from £70.
Rooms	5 doubles.
Meals	Bar meals all day from £9.50. Dinner, à la carte, from £25. Pub closed Sunday night & Monday lunchtime.
Closed	Christmas Day & New Year's Eve.
Directions	West from Moreton-in-Marsh on A44. Climb hill in Bourton-on-the-Hill; pub at top on left.

Tom & Will Greenstock
Bourton-on-the-Hill,
Moreton-in-Marsh GL56 9AQ

Tel	01386 700413
Fax	01386 700413
Email	greenstocks@horseandgroom.info
Web	www.horseandgroom.info

Wesley House

A 15th-century timber-framed house on Winchcombe's ancient high street; John Wesley stayed in 1755, hence the name. Not satisfied with one excellent restaurant, Matthew has opened another bang next door. The elder statesman comes in traditional style with sofas in front of a roaring fire, candles flickering on smartly dressed tables and a fine conservatory for delicious breakfasts with beautiful views of town and country. Next door, the young upstart is unashamedly contemporary with a smoked-glass bar, faux-zebra-skinned stools and alcoves to hide away in. Both buildings shine with original architecture: timber frames, beamed ceilings, stone flags and stripped boards. Quirky bedrooms up in the eaves tend to be cosy, but one has a balcony with views over rooftops to field and hill. All come in a warm country style with good beds, pretty fabrics, small showers, smart carpets and wonky floors. Back downstairs, dig into food as simple or rich as you want, anything from fish cakes or a good burger to a three-course feast. The Cotswolds Way skirts the town, so bring your walking boots.

Price	£80–£95. Singles from £65. Half-board (for 1-night stays on Saturdays) £90–£100 p.p.
Rooms	5: 1 twin, 1 twin/double, 3 doubles.
Meals	Restaurant: lunch from £19.50; dinner £32.50–£42. Bar & grill: main courses from £7.95.
Closed	Never.
Directions	From Cheltenham, B4632 to Winchcombe. Restaurant on right. Drop off luggage, parking nearby.

Matthew Brown
High Street, Winchcombe,
Gloucestershire GL54 5LJ

Tel	01242 602366
Fax	01242 609046
Email	enquiries@wesleyhouse.co.uk
Web	www.wesleyhouse.co.uk

Corse Lawn House Hotel

Old-fashioned values win out at Corse Lawn. It may not be the fanciest place in the book, but excellent service, delicious food and generous prices make it a must for those in search of an alternative to contemporary minimalism. This impeccable Queen Anne manor house was built on the ruins of a Tudor inn where Cromwell is thought to have slept before the battle of Worcester (1651); it is now the hub of a small community. The Rotary Club dine once a week, shooting parties lunch here in winter, locals bring the family for birthdays. At the front, a willow dips its branches into the country's last surviving coach-wash; in summer you can sit out under parasols and dig into a cream tea while ducks glide by. Inside, slightly eccentric furnishings prevail. There are palms in the swimming pool, a sofa'd bistro for light meals, an open fire in the sitting room and a paddock at the back for visiting horses. Big bedrooms may be chintzy, but they're eminently comfortable, with crisp white linen, bowls of fruit, fresh milk and leaf tea. As for the food, it's all homemade, utterly delicious, and breakfast is a treat.

Price	£150–£170. Suites £185. Singles £95. Half-board from £100 p.p.
Rooms	19: 14 twins/doubles, 2 four-posters, 2 suites, 1 single.
Meals	Lunch & dinner £10–£35.
Closed	Christmas Day & Boxing Day.
Directions	West from Tewkesbury on A438 for Ledbury. After 3 miles left onto B4211. Hotel on right after 2 miles.

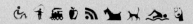 Travel Club Offer: see page 367 for details.

Baba Hine
Corse Lawn, Gloucestershire GL19 4LZ

Tel	01452 780771
Fax	01452 780840
Email	enquiries@corselawn.com
Web	www.corselawn.com

Three Choirs Vineyards

England's answer to the Napa Valley. After 15 years tilling the soil (very sandy, good drainage), Thomas's 75 acres of Gloucestershire hillside now produce 300,000 bottles a year. This is no mean feat and locals love it; the restaurant was packed for lunch the day we visited. There's a shop where you can buy a bottle and paths that weave through the vines – a perfect stroll after a good meal. What's more, three fabulous lodges have recently been built down by the lake, all with decks and walls of glass, so you can camp out in savannah style and listen to the woodpeckers. Rooms up at the restaurant are extremely spacious with terraces that overlook the vineyard. Delightful interiors reveal padded bedheads, walls of colour, leather armchairs, flat-screen TVs, super little bathrooms. Up at the restaurant (squashy sofas, claret walls and big views) a good meal is assured, perhaps ravioli of fresh salmon, Gressingham duck with buttered cabbage, warm treacle tart. World wines are on the list, but you can drink from the vines that surround you; there's a microbrewery, too. Fabulous. *Minimum stay two nights at weekends.*

Price	£95-£135. Lodges £135-£165. Singles from £75. Half-board from £80 p.p. (min. 2 nights).
Rooms	11: 8 twins/doubles, 3 vineyard lodges.
Meals	Lunch from £21. Dinner, à la carte, about £35.
Closed	Christmas & New Year.
Directions	From Newent, north on B4215 for about 1.5 miles, follow brown signs to vineyard.

Thomas Shaw
Newent, Gloucestershire GL18 1LS

Tel	01531 890223
Fax	01531 890877
Email	info@threechoirs.com
Web	www.threechoirs.com

Thirty Two

A magnificent regency townhouse on Cheltenham's loveliest square. Strictly speaking this is simply a B&B, but nothing here is simple and those who come find divine interiors on a grand scale, a match for any design hotel. The building doubles up as a showroom for Jonathan Parkin's predictably successful interior design company, and anything that can move is for sale. Climb up stairs clad in smart red carpet and find a first-floor sitting room to beat most others. French windows soar to the ceiling and open onto a small balcony; when the jazz festival comes to town, cool tunes float in. You get varnished wooden floors, candles everywhere, the odd Thai deity carved in stone, beautifully upholstered armchairs. Bedrooms are just as you'd expect: sublime to behold and kitted out with all the best names: Cole & Son wallpaper, Whites of London linen, natural travertine marble bathrooms and the same showers as Buckingham Palace. Delicious breakfasts are eaten communally or brought up to your room, and Cheltenham's restaurants lie outside the door. Exceptional. *Minimum stay two nights at weekends July-September.*

Price	£164–£198. Singles from £149.
Rooms	4: 2 twins/doubles, 2 doubles.
Meals	Restaurants nearby.
Closed	Rarely.
Directions	A40 west into Cheltenham. Left onto one-way system. Swing right, heading east; 3rd left; hotel on the left.

Jonathan Parkin & Jonathan Sellwood
32 Imperial Square, Cheltenham,
Gloucestershire GL50 1QZ

Tel	01242 771110
Fax	01242 771119
Email	stay@thirtytwoltd.com
Web	www.thirtytwoltd.com

Cowley Manor

Cowley is imperious – a 17th-century mansion set in 55 acres of sculpted parkland that could double as the estate of a Jane Austen hero. It was mentioned in the Domesday Book and stands next door to a Norman church, but inside, graceful interiors come beautifully adorned in crisp, contemporary style – a contrast that is never out of place. In fact, much of the house still basks in its original grandeur, so expect the best of both worlds: a panelled dining room that opens onto a sublime terrace, a glass bar that bursts with colour, and some very funky bedrooms. Best of all is the über-cool spa – sleek lines, treatment rooms, a wall of glass that separates the inside pool from its outside neighbour… and there are Wellington boots at the front door for those who want to explore the grounds. Beautiful bedrooms come with contemporary furniture, blond wood, Egyptian cotton and matchless bathrooms. All have DVD players and fancy TVs, while a couple have balconies. As for the food, you can eat informally in the bar or spin into the restaurant for a three-course feast. Seriously spoiling. *Minimum stay two nights at weekends.*

Price	£245–£470.
Rooms	30: 25 doubles, 5 twins/doubles.
Meals	All-day bar meals from £8.50. Dinner, 3 courses, about £40.
Closed	Never.
Directions	South from Cheltenham on A435 for three miles, then village signed right. On left.

Stuart McPherson
Cowley, Cheltenham,
Gloucestershire GL53 9NL

Tel	01242 870900
Fax	01242 870901
Email	stay@cowleymanor.com
Web	www.cowleymanor.com

Westcote Inn

The village is tiny, the view is fantastic, the bar is lively, the rooms are a treat. This 300-year-old malt house recently had a face lift and now looks rather good for its age. Interiors mix all the old originals — stone walls, timber frames, beamed ceilings, open fires — with a cool contemporary style. There's a zinc-topped champagne bar, modern art in the airy restaurant, local ales on tap in the bar, the odd winged armchair. Bedrooms upstairs are lovely. One is enormous, two have great views, beds are dressed in crisp linen, all come with an explosion of extras: coffee machines, flat-screen TVs, DVD players and iPod docks. Most have power showers, one has a claw-foot bath, all have robes. Back downstairs, a varied crowd gathers: shooting parties, city slickers, local farmers, Morris men. This is racing country and the bar is popular with local jockeys (TV tipsters gather here before Cheltenham and Aintree to dole out valuable advice). Country cooking waits in the restaurant (pies, casseroles, local game). In summer life spills into the garden with picnic hampers and country rugs.

Price	£85–£110.
Rooms	4: 3 doubles, 1 family.
Meals	Lunch from 6.95.
	Dinner, 3 courses, about £25.
Closed	Never.
Directions	From A40 at Burford, A361 then A424 dir. Stow-on-the-Wold. After 6 miles, right for Nether Westcote; signs to inn.

Julia Reed
Nether Westcote, Chipping Norton,
Gloucestershire OX7 6SD

Tel	01993 830888
Fax	01933 831657
Email	info@westcoteinn.co.uk
Web	www.westcoteinn.co.uk

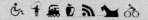

Lords of the Manor

A 1650 mansion fit for a king that was originally built for a rector. The setting is spectacular, eight acres of lush lawns and formal gardens flanked by the river Eye; there's a 19th-century skating pond, too. Inside, interiors glisten after a recent facelift, so step in to find parquet flooring, mullioned windows, roaring fires and porters' chairs in a sitting-room bar. Fabrics come courtesy of Osborne & Little, views from the drawing room spin down to the river, old oils adorn the walls. A serious restaurant overlooks a courtyard garden. There's a complimentary wine tasting for guests on Saturday evenings, not a bad way to choose your tipple before sitting down to a brilliant dinner… perhaps crab tian with smoked salmon and lemon, roast loin of lamb with a rosemary jus, pistachio and chocolate soufflé with bitter chocolate sorbet. Super-smart bedrooms come in contemporary country-house style with Egyptian cotton, excellent art, padded bedheads, bowls of fruit. Expect flat-screen TVs and iPods, fancy bathrooms with robes and power showers. Church bells chime on Sunday.

Price	£195–£310. Suites £370–£380. Half-board from £132.50 p.p.
Rooms	26: 21 twins/doubles, 5 suites.
Meals	Lunch from £19.50. Dinner, 3 courses, £49. Tasting menu £65.
Closed	Never.
Directions	North from Cirencester on A429 for 17 miles, then left for The Slaughters. In Lower Slaughter, left over bridge, into Upper Slaughter. Hotel on right in village, signed.

Ingo Wiangke
Upper Slaughter,
Bourton-on-the-Water GL54 2JD

Tel	01451 820243
Fax	01451 820696
Email	reservations@lordsofthemanor.com
Web	www.lordsofthemanor.com

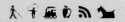

The Dial House

Bourton – Venice of the Cotswolds – is bisected by the river Windrush; willow branches bathe in its waters, ducks preen for tourists. Dial House is equally alluring, a sublime retreat set back from the high street. It dates from 1698, but skip past the trim lawns and hanging baskets and find the old world made new. Mullioned windows and stone fireplaces shine warmly, the fire crackles, armchairs are dressed in Zoffany, Cole & Son wallpaper sparkles on some walls. You're in the heart of the village with a peaceful garden at the back in which to escape the summer hordes. You can eat here in good weather or just pull up a deckchair and read in the sun. Stripped floors in the restaurant, cool colours in the bar, old oils on the walls, and bedrooms in different shapes and sizes: grand four-posters and cool colours in the main house; airy pastels and silky quilts in the coach house; small but sweet garden rooms with fancy little bathrooms. There's fabulous food, too, perhaps hand-dived scallops with lemon purée, Scottish beef with Madeira jus, and a magnificent caramel soufflé. Heaven. *Minimum stay two nights at weekends.*

Price	£120–£220. Half-board (midweek only, min. 2 nights) from £92.50 p.p.
Rooms	13: 10 doubles, 2 four-posters, 1 suite.
Meals	Lunch from £4.95. Dinner, 3 courses, about £40.
Closed	Never.
Directions	From Oxford, A40 to Northleach, right on A429 to Bourton. Hotel set back from High St opp. main bridge.

Martyn & Elaine Booth
The Chestnuts, Bourton-on-the-Water,
Gloucestershire GL54 2AN

Tel	01451 822244
Fax	01451 810126
Email	info@dialhousehotel.com
Web	www.dialhousehotel.com

The New Inn at Coln

The New Inn is old – 1632 to be exact – but well-named nonetheless; a top-to-toe renovation has recently swept away past indiscretions. These days, it's all rather smart. The pub stands in a handsome Cotswold village with ivy roaming on original stone walls and a sun-trapping terrace where roses bloom in summer. Inside, airy interiors come with low ceilings, painted beams, flagged floors and fires that roar. There are padded window seats, eastern busts, gilt mirrors and armchairs in the bar. Bedrooms are a treat, all warmly elegant with perfect white linen, flat-screen TVs and cotton robes in good little bathrooms (a couple have claw-foot baths). There are wonky floors and the odd beam in the main house, while those in the old dovecote come in bold colours and have views across water meadows to the river; walks start from the front door. Bibury, Burford and Stow are all close, so spread your wings, then return for a good meal, perhaps grilled goat's cheese with poached pear, roasted lemon sole with pink grapefruit, vanilla panna cotta with plum crumble.

Price	£120–£150. Singles from £85.
Rooms	13 doubles.
Meals	Lunch & dinner £5–£35. Sunday lunch £19–£24.
Closed	First week in January.
Directions	From Oxford, A40 past Burford, B4425 for Bibury. Left after Aldsworth to Coln St Aldwyns.

Jeremy du Plessis
Coln St Aldwyns, Cirencester,
Gloucestershire GL7 5AN

Tel   01285 750651
Fax   01285 750657
Email   info@thenewinnatcoln.co.uk
Web   www.new-inn.co.uk

 Travel Club Offer: see page 367 for details.

Bibury Court Hotel

A Jacobean mansion that stands next to the church in one of Gloucestershire's loveliest villages. The six-acre garden is reason enough to come; it's utterly English, with croquet on the lawn, clipped yew hedges, a rose arbour flanked by lavender and the river Coln ambling past on one side. You can fish from its banks or follow the footpath into glorious country; just wonderful. This is a very friendly place, grand, but not stuffy. There's a panelled drawing room for afternoon teas, a conservatory for indulgent breakfasts and a smart dining room for serious dinners; in summer, life spills out onto the stone terrace for sundowners in a scented garden. Antiques are scattered about: oak chests, mahogany dressers, writing desks and oil paintings by the score. A refurbishment is underway to remove all trace of the 1980s, but it wouldn't matter if it wasn't; what wins here is the relaxed atmosphere and the kind staff. Bedrooms tend to be large, with mullioned windows, old radiators, parkland views, crisp linen, the odd four-poster and a grand piano in the suite. *Minimum stay two nights at weekends April-September.*

Price	£160-£200. Suite £240. Singles from £135.
Rooms	18: 12 twins/doubles, 5 four-posters, 1 suite.
Meals	Lunch from £12.50. Dinner, 3 courses, about £35.
Closed	Never.
Directions	West from Burford on B4425. Cross bridge in village & house signed right along high street.

Travel Club Offer: see page 367 for details.

Philip Mason-Gordon
Bibury, Gloucestershire GL7 5NT

Tel	01285 740337
Fax	01285 740660
Email	info@biburycourt.com
Web	www.biburycourt.com

The King's Arms Inn

A 17th-century country inn three miles south of Westonbirt. It stands on the main road and was once a doctor's surgery. After a sympathetic refurbishment, it is now back doing what it was built to do: cook great food, serve good beer, deliver a comfortable bed. Inside, you find Farrow & Ball colours on the walls and logs piled high in the alcove. You get crackling fires, terracotta tiles, padded window seats and painted settles. There's a back bar for a game of darts, a front bar for a glass of champagne and a restaurant in Eating-Room Red for excellent food, anything from Wiltshire ham and free-range eggs to pan-roasted duck breast cooked with ginger and lime. Bedrooms are here and there. Those in the house come in simple contemporary style: crisply laundered sheets, padded bedheads, pretty lime throws, flat-screen TVs. Three cottages across the drive come in country style and are perfect for families, with lots of space and fully equipped kitchens. There's a pretty garden for summer suppers, but don't miss Westonbirt Arboretum, one of England's Seven Wonders.

Price	£95. Single from £65. Cottages from £100.
Rooms	4 + 3: 1 double, 2 twins/doubles, 1 single. 3 self-catering cottages (2 for 4, 1 for 6).
Meals	Lunch from £5.95. Dinner, 3 courses, £20–£25.
Closed	Never.
Directions	M4 junc. 18, A46 north, then A433 for Tetbury. In village on right.

Alastair & Sarah Sadler
The Street, Didmarton, Badminton,
Gloucestershire GL9 1DT

Tel	01454 238245
Fax	01454 238249
Email	bookings@kingsarmsdidmarton.co.uk
Web	www.kingsarmsdidmarton.co.uk

The Peat Spade

Hampshire is as lovely as any county in England, deeply rural with lanes that snake through glorious countryside. As if to prove the point, the Peat Spade serves up a menu of boundless simplicity and elegance. First there's this dreamy thatched village in the Test valley, then there's the inn itself, packed to the gunnels with lip-licking locals for Sunday lunch in early February (and there's a 4pm sitting to satisfy demand). A Roberts radio on the bar brings news of English cricket, gilt mirrors sparkle above smouldering fires, fishing rods hang from the ceiling (fish the Test while you're here) and a pith helmet sits in an alcove. There's a horseshoe bar, flowers everywhere, varnished wood floors and claret walls. Upstairs, a snug residents' sitting room, a roof terrace for summer breakfasts and a couple of bedrooms above the bar. Others are in next-door Peat House, all are as lovely as you'd expect. Fired Earth colours, sisal matting, big wooden beds, Roberts radios, crisp white linen – the works. There's no space left to describe how utterly wonderful the food is, but be assured it is.

Price	£120.
Rooms	6 doubles.
Meals	Lunch & dinner £5–£25.
Closed	Christmas Day & New Year's Day.
Directions	A3057 north from Stockbridge; left after a mile for Longstock. In village.

Lucy Townsend & Andy Clarke
Longstock, Stockbridge
Hampshire SO20 6DR

Tel	01264 810612
Fax	01264 811078
Email	info@peatspadeinn.co.uk
Web	www.peatspadeinn.co.uk

The Anchor Inn

A super-smart country dining pub, renovated recently in imperious style. The house is Edwardian with 14th-century roots, and its treasure-trove interiors are full of beautiful things: timber frames, wavy beams, oils by the score, trumpets and pith helmets, a piano in the bar. Old photographs of Charterhouse School cover the walls, there are sofas by the fire in the panelled bar and busts on plinths in the airy restaurant, where you dine on proper English food: devilled kidneys, lemon sole, treacle tart with clotted cream. Doors open onto a lawned garden with country views, so come in summer for lunch in the sun. Bedrooms upstairs are seriously indulging. Expect beautifully upholstered armchairs, seagrass matting, fine linen on comfy beds, flat-screen TVs. There are power showers, huge towels and bathrobes, too. One suite is open to the rafters and comes with Nelson and friends framed on the wall; another has an enormous window that opens onto a private balcony. Don't come looking for a gastropub; do come looking for good ales, sublime food and old-world interiors. A treat! *Minimum stay two nights at weekends.*

Price	£130-£150. Suite £170.
Rooms	6: 5 doubles, 1 suite.
Meals	Continental breakfast included, full English £10.50. Lunch & dinner £5-£30 (not Sunday evenings).
Closed	Christmas Day.
Directions	Leave A31 for Bentley, 4 miles west of Farnham. West through village, north for Lower Froyle. Inn on left in village.

Lucy Townsend & Andy Clarke
Lower Froyle, Alton,
Hampshire GU34 4NA

Tel	01420 23261
Email	info@anchorinnlowerfroyle.co.uk
Web	www.anchorinnatlowerfroyle.co.uk

The Old House Hotel & Restaurant

A 1707 creeper-clad townhouse that stands on the village square. After 35 years running Rowley's in Jermyn Street, John escaped the city and snapped up the Old House. With a swift refurbishment under his belt, things are looking rather good – airy interiors, painted panelling, leather sofas in front of the fire, a conservatory/breakfast room that opens onto the garden. Bedrooms are a treat. Those in the main house have the character – high ceilings, low ceilings, timber frames, uneven floors. There are sleigh beds, four-posters, rooms in the eaves, crisp white linen, and those at the front have views of the square. Four gorgeous garden rooms are a different bag. Two are big, two are huge, all come in contemporary style with padded heads, light oak frames, power showers, perhaps a claw-foot bath; two open onto a private terrace. Back in the house there's a cosy bar and a restaurant for tasty food, perhaps seared pigeon with chestnut purée, red mullet with scallop ravioli, spiced pear tarte tatin with roquefort ice cream. Chichester, Portsmouth and the New Forest are close.

Price	£90–£125. Suites £165. Cottage £350.
Rooms	12 + 1: 7 doubles, 1 twin, 4 suites. 1 self-catering cottage for 6.
Meals	Continental breakfast included. Cooked extras from £5.95. Lunch from £8.95. Dinner, 3 courses, about £30.
Closed	Never.
Directions	M27 junc. 10; A32 north. Left into village, right into square. On right.

John Guess
The Square, Wickham,
Hampshire PO17 5JG

Tel	01329 833049
Fax	01329 833672
Email	enquiries@oldhousehotel.co.uk
Web	www.oldhousehotel.co.uk

Hotel TerraVina

Nina and Gerard, co-founders of Hotel du Vin, have returned to the fray, unable to keep out of the wine cellar. The result is predictably divine, a small intimate hotel with a cool contemporary design that delivers at every turn: impeccable wine, fabulous food, excellent service and delightful rooms. Outside, you find a pool with a terrace and a shaded deck for meals in summer. Inside, a top-to-toe refurbishment in warm Mediterranean colours with beautiful oak floors, a fancy chrome staircase, and a granite-topped bar for a glass of champagne. Best of all is the brasserie, where you can watch the chefs at work. A huge leather banquette dominates the room; beyond, a wall of glass frames the wine cellar. Dig into linguini with truffles and parmesan, char-grilled rib-eye with Chateaubriand sauce, lemon tart with raspberry sorbet, all washed down by one of Gerard's magical wines (he's one of the world's great wine men). Rooms are heavenly, with super-comfy beds, flat-screen TVs, gorgeous bathrooms, speakers in the ceiling; some have terraces or claw-foot baths in the room. *Minimum stay two nights at weekends.*

Price	£130–£210.
Rooms	11: 9 doubles, 2 twins/doubles.
Meals	Lunch from £10. Dinner, 3 courses, about £35.
Closed	Rarely.
Directions	M27 junc. 2, A326 south, then A336 west for Netley Marsh. Left in village at White Horse pub. One mile down and signed on left.

Gerard & Nina Basset
Woodlands Road, Woodlands,
Southampton, Hampshire SO40 7GL

Tel	02380 293784
Fax	02380 293627
Email	info@hotelterravina.co.uk
Web	www.hotelterravina.co.uk

Entry 118   Map 3

Whitley Ridge Hotel

It's hard to fault Whitley Ridge, and, with its attractive prices, harder still to resist. The setting is glorious – 14 acres of garden and parkland soundproofed by the New Forest. Then there's the small matter of the house itself, a 1748 hunting lodge that glitters in grand country-house style. Amazingly, all this fades into relative insignificance when you step into the dining room for something to eat. Alex Aitken has held his Michelin star for 15 years and for good reason: his food is out of this world. Splash out on the tasting menu for course after course of perfection: seared foie gras with apple and vanilla purée, ravioli of quail's egg, roasted scallop with baby artichoke, sea bass gnocchi, veal with wild mushrooms, camembert calvados and hot passion fruit soufflé. Wash it down with excellent wines, saunter into the drawing room for a digestif by the fire. As you'd expect bedrooms are divine (with ludicrously comfy beds), the service is wonderful, and breakfast is an unremitting joy. Paths lead out into the forest, so work off your indulgence in style. *Minimum stay two nights at weekends in high season.*

Price	Half-board £100–£150 p.p. Singles from £125.
Rooms	19: 5 doubles, 6 twins/doubles, 1 four-poster, 5 suites, 2 family.
Meals	Lunch, 2 courses, £15. Dinner, 3 courses, £45. Tasting menu £60.
Closed	Never.
Directions	South from Lyndhurst on A337, then left for Beaulieu on B3055. Under railway bridge & signed left.

Travel Club Offer: see page 367 for details.

The Aitken Family
Beaulieu Road, Brockenhurst,
Hampshire SO42 7QL

Tel	01590 622354
Fax	01590 622856
Email	info@whitleyridge.co.uk
Web	www.whitleyridge.co.uk

Westover Hall

A small-scale country house by the sea with levels of service that surpass most others. Views from the back stretch across the Solent to the Isle of Wight, so sip champagne cocktails in the sunroom before supper, spill out into the garden for afternoon tea or follow the path down to the beach – and the private beach hut. Inside, oak panelling astounds, not least in the hall, which soars up to a minstrels' gallery. A fire burns in an opulent sitting room, tartan curtains mix with leather stools in the bar, and a huge bay window in the restaurant looks out to sea (though excellent food holds your attention and you may not notice). Bedrooms upstairs may be pricey but they're lavish too. Go for the bigger rooms (two are small); those at the front have long views across to the Needles. Enjoy gilt mirrors, antique beds, grand armoires and smart sofas – and crisp linen, marble bathrooms, waffle bathrobes and flat-screen TVs. Excellent art hangs on the walls. There's great walking, too; drop down to the sea and follow the fabulous coastal path. *Minimum stay two nights at weekends.*

Price	£206-£266. Half-board from £145 p.p.
Rooms	15: 9 doubles, 2 twins, 1 family, 3 suites.
Meals	Light lunch £15-£20. Dinner, 3 courses, £42. Tasting menu £60.
Closed	Rarely.
Directions	A337 west from Lymington, then B3058 to Milford-on-Sea. Through village; house on left.

Christine & David Smith
Park Lane, Lymington,
Hampshire SO41 0PT

Tel	01590 643044
Fax	01590 644490
Email	info@westoverhallhotel.com
Web	www.westoverhallhotel.com

Travel Club Offer: see page 367 for details.

The Mill at Gordleton

A 400-year-old listed mill; plans are afoot to reactivate the wheel in order to draw electricity from it. The house sits in two acres of English country garden with Avon Water tumbling over the weir; ducks, lampreys, Indian runners and leaping trout all call it home. It's an idyllic spot, the terrace perfect for summer suppers with the stream brushing past below. Inside, low ceilings, warm colours and wonky walls give the feel of cottage life. A fire roars in reception, a panelled bar serves pre-dinner drinks. Colourful bedrooms are full of character; one is directly above the wheel house and comes with mind-your-head beams. Expect check fabrics, furry throws, sheets and blankets, bowls of fruit. Three rooms have watery views (you can fall asleep to the sound of the river), two have small sitting rooms, most have fancy new bathrooms, and while a lane passes outside, you are more likely to be woken by birdsong. Downstairs, the restaurant offers delicious locally sourced food: confit of duck, loin of pork and an irresistible banana soufflé. The coast is close. *Minimum stay two nights at weekends April-October.*

Price	£130-£150. Suites £150-£210.
Rooms	7: 1 double, 4 twins/doubles, 2 suites.
Meals	Lunch from £8.95.
	Dinner, 3 courses, about £35.
Closed	Christmas Day.
Directions	South from Brockenhurst on A337. Under railway bridge, over roundabout, and 1st right, signed Hordle. On right after 2 miles.

Ethical Collection: Environment; Food.
See page 373 for details

	Liz Cottingham
	Silver Street, Hordle, Lymington, Hampshire SO41 6DJ
Tel	01590 682219
Email	info@themillatgordleton.co.uk
Web	www.themillatgordleton.co.uk

Chewton Glen

Chewton Glen is one of England's loveliest country-house hotels. It opened in 1964 with eight bedrooms; now it has 58. Despite this growth it still remains wonderfully intimate and hugely welcoming, and, with a ratio of two staff to every guest, there's sublime service too. As for the hotel, it has everything you could ever want: a pillared swimming pool, a hydrotherapy spa, plunge pools and treatment rooms, a small golf course, a tennis centre and vast parkland gardens. Beauty at every turn, be it in the fabric of a sofa in one of the sitting rooms or afternoon tea served on the croquet terrace. Bedrooms are exemplary, as their price demands. Some come in warm country-house style, others bask in contemporary flair. Expect the best: marble bathrooms, private balconies, designer fabrics, faultless housekeeping. Fires burn, Wellington boots wait at the front door, five gardeners work minor miracles. Exquisite food, too, and a pianist who plays at dinner each evening. The beach is a 20-minute walk, and you can ride in the New Forest. Hard to beat. *Minimum stay two nights at weekends.*

Price	£299–£517. Suites £517–£1,280.
Rooms	58: 35 twins/doubles, 23 suites.
Meals	Lunch £17.50–£24.50.
	Dinner, 3 courses, £65.
	Light meals available throughout day.
Closed	Never.
Directions	A337 west from Lymington. Through New Milton for Christchurch. Right at r'bout, signed Walkford. Right again; hotel on right.

Andrew Stembridge
Christchurch Road, New Milton,
Hampshire BH25 6QS

Tel	01425 275341
Fax	01425 272310
Email	reservations@chewtonglen.com
Web	www.chewtonglen.com

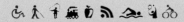

Moccas Court

Glorious Moccas. Sweep down the drive, plunge into ancient parkland, pass a 12th-century Norman church and discover this thrilling mansion. The river Wye flows past serenely behind; you can fish from its banks, or follow a path down to the red cliffs and spy on peregrine falcons. As for the interiors, enormous stately rooms come in classical design: stripped wood floors and a Broadwood piano forte in the music room; library steps and a moulded marble fireplace for open fires in the sitting room; original wallpaper in the circular dining room. Windows open onto balustraded terraces that lead down to the river. Bedrooms (two big, three huge) have Zoffany wallpapers, Jane Churchill fabrics, gigantic beds, mahogany dressers, padded window seats, the original 1785 shutters. Those at the front look towards the deer park where an enclosed fallow herd have run since Norman times (now they eat the garden) and the Moccas beetle is found nowhere else. Dinner – a set menu discussed in advance – is served communally; Ben's cooking hits the spot, perhaps goat's cheese salad, rack of lamb, lemon tart.

Price	£140-£224.
Rooms	5: 4 twins/doubles, 1 double.
Meals	Dinner, 3 courses, £40.
Closed	Christmas; occasionally in February & March.
Directions	South from Hereford on A465, then west on B4352 to Moccas. Right by stone cross in village, 200 yds to drive, signed.

Travel Club Offer: see page 367 for details.

Ben & Mimi Chester-Master
Moccas, Hereford,
Herefordshire HR29LH

Tel	01981 500019
Fax	01981 500095
Email	info@moccas-court.co.uk
Web	www.moccas-court.co.uk

Wilton Court

A Grade-II listed stone house with a Grade-I listed mulberry tree; in season, its berries are turned in sorbets and pies. The house dates to 1510 and looks out across the river to Wye; herons dive, otters swim, kingfishers nest. Roses ramble on the outside, happy guests potter within. This may not be the fanciest place in the book, but Roger and Helen go the extra mile, and, with good prices, a pretty position on the river and a restaurant for great food, Wilton Court has won itself a devoted following. Bedrooms upstairs come in different shapes and sizes. Splash out on the more expensive ones for watery views, William Morris wallpaper, lots of space, perhaps a four-poster. A couple of rooms are small, but so are their prices and you can lose yourself in the rest of the hotel. Drop down for a drink in the smart panelled bar, then nip across to the airy conservatory / dining room for super food, perhaps tiger prawns in garlic butter or rack of Welsh lamb with rosemary mash. A small garden across the lane drops down to the river for summer sundowners.
Minimum stay two nights at weekends.

Price	£95–£145. Suite £125–£165. Singles from £80. Half-board from £70 p.p. (minimum 2 nights).
Rooms	10: 3 doubles, 5 twins/doubles, 1 four-poster, 1 family suite.
Meals	Lunch from £9.75. Dinner, 3 courses, about £30. Sunday lunch £14–£17.50.
Closed	Never.
Directions	South into Ross at A40/A49 roundabout. 1st right into Wilton Lane. Hotel on right.

Roger & Helen Wynn
Ross-on-Wye,
Herefordshire HR9 6AQ

Tel	01989 562569
Fax	01989 768460
Email	info@wiltoncourthotel.com
Web	www.wiltoncourthotel.com

Travel Club Offer: see page 367 for details.

Glewstone Court Country House Hotel & Restaurant

Grand, yet relaxed enough to have no rule book. Bill does front of house, Christine cooks brilliantly, both are charming and fun. A rather appealing faded elegance is the hallmark. You'll find eastern rugs, stripped floors and delightful clutter, but best of all is the drawing room bar, where resident dogs snooze in front of a roaring fire. The centre of the house is early Georgian with a fine staircase that spirals up to a galleried landing. Rooms are warm, comfortable and traditional with pleasant furniture. The big ones are rather grand with long views across to the Forest of Dean. Those at the back are simpler and more homely and overlook a cherry orchard; bathrooms aren't excessively fancy, but all are more than adequate. There's croquet on the lawn in the shade of an ancient Cedar of Lebanon and a small terrace for lunch in the summer sun. Fabulous food is reason enough to come, with Herefordshire beef served pink with a claret gravy for Sunday lunch; Christine's award-winning textiles are on display in the restaurant.. Heaven for those in search of the small and friendly.

Price	£118-£135. Singles £58-£99.
Rooms	8: 5 doubles, 1 four-poster, 1 single, 1 suite.
Meals	Lunch from £12.95. Dinner, 3 courses, about £28. Sunday lunch £18.
Closed	25-27 December.
Directions	From Ross-on-Wye, A40 for Monmouth, right 1 mile south of Wilton r'bout, for Glewstone. Hotel on left after 0.5 miles.

Christine & Bill Reeve-Tucker
Glewstone, Ross-on-Wye,
Herefordshire HR9 6AW

Tel	01989 770367
Fax	01989 770282
Email	glewstone@aol.com
Web	www.glewstonecourt.com

The Hambrough

You look out on a carpet of sea rolling off towards France. Splash out on the best rooms and you get a balcony – the Hambrough's equivalent of the royal box. There are loungers and tables and they'll bring up your breakfast, freshly juiced oranges and a plate of peeled fruits, then bacon and eggs with coffee and toast. Rooms are exquisite with huge beds, high ceilings, espresso machines and LCD TVs. Mosaic bathrooms are faultless (underfloor heating, thick white bathrobes, the deepest baths); from those on the top floor you can gaze out to sea as you bathe. Despite all this the Hambrough's chief passion is its food. Come down for champagne cocktails at the bar, then dig into Isle of Skye scallops with a pea bavoise, fillet of beef with a ravioli of braised blade, chocolate fondant with coffee ice cream. Back upstairs you'll find your bed turned down and a bowl of popcorn in case you want to watch a movie. Ventnor, an old-fashioned English seaside town, is worth exploring. Don't miss the botanic gardens or Osborne House, Queen Victoria's favourite home. *Minimum stay two nights at weekends.*

Price	£95–£220.
Rooms	7 doubles.
Meals	Lunch from £7. Dinner from £30. 7-course tasting menu £50.
Closed	Rarely.
Directions	A3055 into Ventnor. On western edge of town, south into Hambrough Rd, following blue sign to police station. House on left overlooking sea.

	Daniel Edwards
	Hambrough Road, Ventnor,
	Isle of Wight PO38 1SQ
Tel	01983 856333
Fax	01983 857260
Email	info@thehambrough.com
Web	www.thehambrough.com

Travel Club Offer: see page 367 for details.

The George Hotel

The George is a kingly retreat; Charles II stayed in 1671 and you can sleep in his room with its panelling and high ceilings. The house, a grand mansion in the middle of tiny Yarmouth, has stupendous views of the Solent; Admiral Sir Robert Holmes took full advantage of them when in residence, nipping off to sack passing ships. These days country-house interiors mix with contemporary flourishes. Ancient panelling and stone flags come as standard in the old house, but push on past the crackling fire in the bar to find an airy brasserie with walls of glass that open onto the terrace. You can eat here in summer, next to the castle walls, with sailboats zipping past – a perfect spot for black truffles and scrambled eggs, New Forest venison with peppercorn butter, fig tart with honey and almond ice cream. Bedrooms come in country-house style, some with crowns above the bed, others with fabulous views. Two rooms have balconies that overlook the water, but smaller rooms at the back have the same homely style. Head off to Osborne House, Cowes for the regatta or the Needles for magical walks. *Minimum stay two nights at weekends.*

Price	£180–£255. Singles from £130.
Rooms	16 twins/doubles.
Meals	Lunch & dinner from £20.
Closed	Rarely.
Directions	Lymington ferry to Yarmouth, then follow signs to town centre.

Jeremy Wilcock
Quay Street, Yarmouth,
Isle of Wight PO41 0PE

Tel	01983 760331
Fax	01983 760425
Email	res@thegeorge.co.uk
Web	www.thegeorge.co.uk

Priory Bay Hotel

An imperious setting one field up from the sea, with paths that lead down through a ridge of trees to a long sandy beach. Stone-age axes have been discovered here, medieval monks made this their home, Tudor farmers and Georgian gentry followed. The house dates to the 14th century. Inside, sleeping dogs lie in front of roaring fires. The drawing room comes in grand style with high ceilings, a baby grand and huge windows that frame sea views. Wander freely and find country rugs on parquet flooring, red leather armchairs in the bar, vintage luggage, a children's playroom and golf clubs for the six-hole course. In summer, loungers flank the swimming pool and croquet hoops stand on the lawn. Bedrooms have an uncluttered country-house feel: seaside colours, tongue-and-groove bathrooms, padded bedheads, a sofa if there's room. Some are enormous with timber frames or an exposed stone wall. You can eat in a muralled dining room or out on the terrace in good weather, perhaps foie gras terrine, pan-fried sea bass, dark chocolate tart. And there's opera on the lawn in summer. *Minimum stay two nights at weekends.*

Price	£120–£270. Singles from £70.
Rooms	18: 16 twins/doubles, 2 family.
Meals	Lunch £22.50.
	Dinner, 3 courses, £32.50.
Closed	Rarely.
Directions	South from Ryde on B3330. Through Nettlestone and hotel signed left and left again.

Andrew Palmer
Priory Drive, Seaview,
Isle of Wight PO34 5BU

Tel	01983 613146
Fax	01983 616539
Email	enquiries@priorybay.co.uk
Web	www.priorybay.co.uk

Seaview Hotel

Everything here is a dream. You're 50 yards from the water in a small seaside village that sweeps you back to a nostalgic past. Locals pop in for a pint, famished yachtsmen step ashore for a meal, those in the know drop by for a luxurious night in indulging rooms. This small hotel manages to be all things to all men, making it one of the most inclusive places in this book. The pitch pine bar has a roaring fire and every conceivable nautical curio nailed to its walls, the terrace buzzes with island life in summer, the restaurants hum with the contented sighs of happy diners. The whole show is orchestrated by Andrew and a battalion of kind staff, who book taxis, carry bags, send you off in the right direction. Interior designer Graham Green oversaw the fabulous refurbishment; some rooms come in super-smart country-house style (upholstered four-posters, padded headboards), others are more contemporary (Farrow & Ball colours, very fancy bathrooms). Don't miss the food; the crab ramekin is an island institution, and the fish comes fresh from the sea. *Minimum stay two nights at weekends.*

Price	£120–£199.
Rooms	Main house: 14 twins/doubles, 3 four-posters. Seaview Modern: 4 doubles, 3 twins/doubles, 4 family suites.
Meals	Lunch & dinner £5–£30.
Closed	Never.
Directions	From Ryde, B3330 south for 1.5 miles. Hotel signed left.

Andrew Morgan
High Street, Seaview,
Isle of Wight PO34 5EX

Tel	01983 612711
Fax	01983 613729
Email	reception@seaviewhotel.co.uk
Web	www.seaviewhotel.co.uk

Cloth Hall Oast

Sweep up the rhododendron-lined drive to this immaculate Kentish oast house and barn. For 40 years Mrs Morgan lived in the 15th-century manor next door where she tended both guests and garden; now she has turned her perfectionist's eye upon these five acres. There are well-groomed lawns, a carp-filled pond, pergola, summer house, heated pool and flower beds – two of orange and yellow, four all-white. Light shimmers through swathes of glass in the dining room; there are off-white walls and pale beams that soar from floor to rafter. Mrs Morgan is a courteous hostess and an excellent cook; discuss in the morning what you'd like for dinner – duck with cherries, sole Véronique – later you dine at an antique table gleaming with crystal and candelabra. There are three bedrooms for guests: a four-poster on the ground floor, a triple and a queen-size double on the first. Colours are soft, fabrics are frilled but nothing is busy or overdone; you are spoiled with good bathrooms and fine mattresses, crisp linen and flowered chintz. And there's a sitting room for guests, made snug by a log fire on winter nights.

Price	£95–£125.
Rooms	3: 1 four-poster, 1 triple, 1 double.
Meals	Dinner, 4 courses, £26.
Closed	Christmas.
Directions	Leave village with windmill on left, taking Golford Road east for Tenterden. After a mile, right, before cemetery. Signed right.

Mrs Katherine Morgan
Cranbrook, Kent TN17 3NR

Tel	01580 712220
Fax	01580 712220
Email	clothhalloast@aol.com

Travel Club Offer: see page 367 for details.

The Place at the Beach

A boutique motel, a 'diner with rooms' – friendly, stylish, very well priced. Across the road, enormous dunes tumble down to Camber Sands for two miles of uninterrupted beach, so watch the kite-surfing or walk up to the river Rother and follow it into Rye (three miles). Back at The Place comfy bedrooms come in light colours, with crisp white linen, digital radios, big mirrors, a sofa if there's room; spotless bathrooms provide for a good soak after a hard day on the beach. Doors in the airy brasserie open onto a dining terrace in summer, where menus offer local food when possible, with Dover sole and mackerel fresh from the market. Try Rye Bay scallops, moules frites, char-grilled rib eye, then a famous ice cream sundae – or weekend barbeques in summer. There's a good DVD library at reception; great photography on the walls; big family rooms (busy in summer); and body boards and beach towels for those who want to ride the waves. Lympne Castle is close, as is Dungeness; Derek Jarman's Prospect Cottage is worth a look. *Minimum stay two nights at weekends.*

Price	£80–£120. Family £99–£140.
Rooms	18: 13 doubles, 1 twin, 3 family, 1 triple.
Meals	Lunch & dinner £5–£30.
Closed	Christmas Day.
Directions	A259 east from Rye, then B2075 for Camber & Lydd. On left after 2 miles.

Harry Cragoe
New Lydd Road, Camber Sands,
Camber, Rye, Kent TN31 7RB

Tel	01797 225057
Fax	01797 227003
Email	enquiries@theplacecambersands.co.uk
Web	www.theplacecambersands.co.uk

Romney Bay House

Hollywood tales linger at Romney Bay. The house, built by Clough William-Ellis – creator of Portmeirion – was owned by Hedda Hooper, and Cary Grant was a regular guest. The position here is sublime with huge views of the Straits of Dover; a telescope in the first-floor library reveals much, even France on a good day. Elsewhere, an honesty bar that looks like a small pub, a sitting room with florals and flowers, and a conservatory/dining room for delicious food. Clinton, once deputy head chef at the Ritz, whisks local ingredients into seasonal dishes, perhaps wild sea bass and saffron risotto, Romney Bay lamb with rosemary mash, baked apples stuffed with sweet mince; in case you're still hungry, there's cheese, too. Airy rooms come in warm country style – pretty fabrics, padded headboards, white linen, hot water bottles. Seven have sea views, two have claw-foot baths, all come with robes, fresh flowers, TVs and DVD players. A golf course passes behind, so watch members hole out on the 16th green while you scoff your bacon and eggs. Guests return again and again, the picture doesn't lie. *Minimum stay two nights at weekends.*

Price	£90–£160. Singles £65–£95.
Rooms	10: 8 doubles, 2 twins.
Meals	Dinner, 4 courses, £42.50.
	Cream teas from £5.95.
Closed	One week at Christmas.
Directions	M20 junc. 10, A2070 south, then A259 east through New Romney. Right to Littlestone; left at sea & on for 1 mile.

Clinton & Lisa Lovell
Coast Road, Littlestone,
New Romney, Kent TN28 8QY
Tel   01797 364747
Fax   01797 367156

Travel Club Offer: see page 367 for details.

Elvey Farm

This ancient Kentish farmhouse stands in six acres of blissful peace half a mile up a private drive. It's a deeply rural position, a nostalgic sweep back to old England. White roses run riot on red walls, a cooling vine shades the veranda, trim lawns are flanked by colourful borders. Inside you find timber frames at every turn, but the feel is airy and contemporary with smart furniture sitting amid stripped boards and old beams. Bedrooms come in similar vein. The two in the main house are big and very family-friendly, while those in the stable block are seriously indulging with chunky beds wrapped in crisp cotton, small sitting areas with flat-screen TV/DVDs, and fabulous wet rooms (two have slipper baths). The four-poster suite comes with a hot tub in a secret garden, but all open onto the veranda, beyond which tables and chairs are scattered across the lawn. As for the restaurant, seasonal menus of Kentish fare offer long-lost treats: potted ham, hop-pickers pie… and chocolate fondue with marshmallows. Leeds Castle is close; the *Darling Buds of May* was filmed in the village. *Minimum stay two nights at weekends.*

Price	£90–£145. Four-poster £140.
Rooms	7: 1 suite for 4, 1 suite for 5. Stable block: 1 four-poster, 4 suites.
Meals	Dinner £21–£25 (Wed-Sat). Sunday lunch from £11.95.
Closed	Never.
Directions	M20 junc. 8, then A20 to Lenham. At Charing r'bout, 3rd exit for A20 Ashford. Right at the lights to Pluckley. Bypass village, down hill, right at pub, then right & right again.

Jeff Moody & Simon Peek
Pluckley, Ashford, Kent TN27 0SU

Tel	01233 840442
Fax	01233 840726
Email	bookings@elveyfarm.co.uk
Web	www.elveyfarm.co.uk

Wife of Bath

With Canterbury on your doorstep, you'd guess this restaurant took its name from Chaucer's famous tale, but the wife in question belonged to the original owner, whom he met in Bath. Named in her honour, it opened in 1963 to great acclaim, one of the first restaurants with rooms to appear in the country. Over the years it has reinvented itself several times, always keeping its reputation for fabulous food; current chef, Robert Hymers, has been at the helm for 16 years. A recent refurbishment has brought Georgian interiors back to life. Expect airy whites, timber frames, the odd roll of fancy wallpaper. There's a bar for cocktails, after which you are whisked through to feast on super food, perhaps watercress and nettle soup with grated horseradish, pressed shoulder of lamb with pistachio pesto, warm pear tart with rosemary ice cream. Bedrooms give every reason to make the most of the wine list, so knock back a good claret, then retire to pretty rooms (crisp linen, Farrow & Ball colours, the odd beam and bathrobes). Great walks start from the village; Ashford is close for Eurostar.

Price	£85–£95. Singles from £65.
Rooms	5: 3 doubles, 1 twin, 1 four-poster.
Meals	Lunch £15–£18.
	Dinner, 3 courses, £30–£35.
Closed	Sunday & Monday nights.
Directions	M20 junc. 10; A2070 & immediately right for Wye. Follow signs for 3 miles into Wye. Left in village; on left.

Helen Fowler
4 Upper Bridge Street, Wye, Ashford,
Kent TN25 5AF

Tel	01233 812232
Email	relax@thewifeofbath.com
Web	www.thewifeofbath.com

The Relish

It's not just the super-comfy interiors that make The Relish such a tempting port of call. There's a sense of generosity here: a drink on the house each night in the sitting room; tea and cakes on tap all day; free internet throughout. This is a grand 1850s merchant's house on the posh side of town with warmly contemporary interiors; wind up the cast-iron staircase to find bedrooms that make you smile. Hypnos beds with padded headboards wear crisp white linen and pretty throws. You get a sense of space, a sofa if there's room, big mirrors and fabulous bathrooms. All are great value for money. Downstairs there are candles on the mantelpieces above an open fire, stripped wooden floors and padded benches in the dining room; in summer, you may decamp onto the terrace for breakfast, a four-acre communal garden stretching out beyond. You're one street back from Folkestone's cliff-top front for huge sea views; steps lead down to smart gardens and the promenade. There are takeaway breakfasts for early Eurostar departures and a local restaurant guide in every room. *Minimum stay two nights at weekends in summer.*

Price	£90–£120. Four-poster £140. Singles from £59.
Rooms	10: 2 twins/doubles, 6 doubles, 1 four-poster, 1 single.
Meals	Restaurants nearby.
Closed	22 December–2 January.
Directions	In centre of town, from Langholm Gardens, head west on Sandgate Road. 1st right into Augusta Gardens/Trinity Gardens. Hotel on right.

Chris & Sarah van Dyke
4 Augusta Gardens, Folkestone,
Kent CT20 2RR

Tel	01303 850952
Fax	01303 850958
Email	reservations@hotelrelish.co.uk
Web	www.hotelrelish.co.uk

Wallett's Court Country House Hotel & Spa

A fabulous position at the end of England, with sweeping fields heading south towards white cliffs; you can follow paths across to a lighthouse for rather good views. The hotel stands opposite a Norman church on land gifted by William the Conqueror to his brother Odo. The current building dates from 1627, but recent additions include an indoor swimming pool which opens onto the garden, and cabins for treatments hidden in the trees. Eight acres of grounds include lush lawns, a tennis court, a boules pitch and a climbing frame for kids. Timber-framed interiors come with contemporary art on ancient brick walls, a fire roars in a sitting-room bar and sublime food waits in the whitewashed restaurant – perhaps crab cakes with a chilli sauce, Gressingham duck with a spring onion rösti, a faultless banana tarte tatin. Bedrooms are scattered about, some grandly traditional with four-posters in the main house, others simpler and quieter in the outbuildings; the suites above the pool come in contemporary style. Canterbury cathedral, Sandwich golf course and Dover Castle are close. *Minimum two nights at weekends half-board.*

Price	£129-£199. Singles £109-£139.
Rooms	16: 12 twins/doubles, 4 suites.
Meals	Lunch from £5. Sunday lunch £25. Dinner, 3 courses, £40.
Closed	Christmas.
Directions	From Dover, A2/A20, then A258 towards Deal, then right, signed St Margaret's at Cliffe. House 1 mile on right, signed.

Chris, Lea & Gavin Oakley
Westcliffe, St Margaret's at Cliffe,
Dover, Kent CT15 6EW

Tel	01304 852424
Fax	01304 853430
Email	stay@wallettscourt.com
Web	www.wallettscourt.com

Travel Club Offer: see page 367 for details.

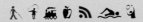

The White Cliffs Hotel & Trading Co.

You're lost in the last folds of England with the beach at the bottom of the hill and the White Cliffs of Dover soaring above, so climb up for views that stretch across to France. This pretty weatherboard hotel stands a mile back from the water with a fine Norman church across the road that's shielded by a curtain of lush trees. Inside, airy interiors come with stripped floors, sandblasted beams, contemporary art and an open fire in the sitting room/bar. Best of all is the walled garden with climbing roses, colourful borders and a trim lawn that plays host to Sunday lunch in summer. Bedrooms are all over the place. Those in the main house are bigger and more sophisticated, and come in bold colours with silky curtains, gilt mirrors and the odd four-poster. Garden rooms are altogether more simple, but good value for money. Expect summer colours, wooden beds, trim carpets and crisp linen. In the restaurant there's meat from Kent, fish from local waters and a children's menu, too. Dover Castle is close, as is Sandwich for golf, and you can use the pool and spa at Wallett's Court, the other half of Gavin's empire.

Price	£89–£99. Family suites £129. Singles from £49.
Rooms	15: 4 doubles, 1 triple, 1 four-poster. Mews cottages: 4 doubles, 1 twin, 2 singles, 2 family suites.
Meals	Lunch from £4. Dinner, 3 courses, £20–£30.
Closed	Rarely.
Directions	M20/A20 into Dover, then A2 north. At roundabout, right for Deal, then right again for St Margaret's. Right in village; hotel on left.

Chris, Lea & Gavin Oakley
High Street, St Margaret's-at-Cliffe,
Dover, Kent CT15 6AT

Tel	01304 852229
Fax	01304 851880
Email	mail@thewhitecliifs.com
Web	www.thewhitecliffs.com

Royal Harbour Hotel

A delightfully quirky townhouse hotel that stands on a Georgian crescent with magnificent views of harbour and sea. Simplicity, elegance and a quiet eccentricity go hand in hand. The sitting room is a dream with stripped floors, gorgeous armchairs, a crackling fire and an honesty bar. Beautiful things abound: a roll top desk, super art, potted palms, a miniature orange tree bearing fruit. There are binoculars with which to scan the high seas (Ramsgate was home to the Commander of the Channel Fleet), books by the hundred for a good read (Dickens's Bleak House is up the road in Broadstairs) and a library of DVDs for the telly in your room or the cinema in the basement (home to an inspiring film production company). Bedrooms at the front are tiny, but have the view, those at the back are bigger and quieter. The suite is enormous with a coal fire and French windows that open onto a balcony. All have good linen, excellent shower rooms and flat-screen TVs. Breakfast is a leisurely feast with cured hams from James's brother, a Rick Stein food hero. *Minimum stay two nights at weekends in high season.*

Price	£98–£138. Singles from £78. Suite £198.
Rooms	20: 15 doubles, 2 family, 2 singles, 1 suite.
Meals	Restaurants in town.
Closed	Never.
Directions	M2, A229, then A256 into Ramsgate. Follow signs for town centre, pick up coast on right. On left as road drops down hill.

James Thomas
Nelson Crescent, Ramsgate,
Kent CT11 9JF

Tel	01843 591514
Fax	01843 570443
Email	info@royalharbourhotel.co.uk
Web	www.royalharbourhotel.co.uk

 Travel Club Offer: see page 367 for details.

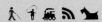

Hipping Hall

You get a bit of time travel at Hipping Hall: 15th-century bricks and mortar, 21st-century lipstick and pearls. It's all the result of a total refurbishment, and funked-up classical interiors elate. Zoffany wallpaper in a swanky sitting room, red leather armchairs in an airy bar, and varnished floorboards in the old hall — overlooked by a minstrels' gallery, its ceilings open to the rafters. The flagged conservatory is home to an ancient well and opens onto a courtyard where tables and chairs are scattered in summer. Upstairs, fabulous bedrooms in various shades of white contrast with the vibrant colours of the ground floor. Fine ivory carpets, white leather headboards, muslin canopies and padded window seats. Bathrooms are the best and come in slate or creamy limestone, some with power showers, others with deep baths too, all with fluffy white towels and bathrobes. As for the food, expect something special, perhaps English asparagus with a garlic purée, fillet of veal with glazed sweetbreads, then caramelised pears with a prune and armagnac ice cream. *Minimum stay two nights at weekends.*

Price	£160–£260. Singles from £105. Half-board from £105 p.p.
Rooms	9: 7 doubles, 2 twins/doubles.
Meals	Sunday lunch £29.50. Dinner, 3 courses, £49.50.
Closed	First 2 weeks in January.
Directions	M6 junc. 36, then A65 east. House on left, 2.5 miles after Kirkby Lonsdale.

Andrew Wildsmith
Cowan Bridge, Kirkby Lonsdale,
Lancashire LA6 2JJ

Tel	01524 271187
Fax	01524 272452
Email	info@hippinghall.com
Web	www.hippinghall.com

The Inn at Whitewell

It is almost impossible to imagine a day when a better inn will grace the English landscape. Everything here is perfect. The inn sits just above the river Hodder with five-mile views across blistering parkland to rising fells; doors in the bar lead onto a terrace where guests sit in a row and gaze upon it. Inside, fires roar, the papers wait, there are beams, sofas, maps and copies of Wisden. Bedrooms are exemplary and come with real luxury, perhaps a peat fire, a lavish four-poster, a fabulous Victorian power shower. All have beautiful fabrics, Egyptian linen and gadgets galore; many have the view – you can fall asleep at night to the sound of the river. There's a restaurant for splendid food (the Queen once popped in for lunch), so dig into seared scallops, Bowland lamb, a plate of cheese or something sweet; there are bar meals for those who want to watch their weight and the Whitewell fish pie is rightly famous. Elsewhere, a small vintners in reception, seven miles of private fishing and countryside as good as any in the land. Magnificent.

Price	£96–£170. Suite £172–£197. Singles from £70.
Rooms	23: 9 twins/doubles, 13 four-posters, 1 suite.
Meals	Bar meals from £8. Dinner, à la carte, £25–£35.
Closed	Never.
Directions	M6 junc. 31a, B6243 east through Longridge, then follow signs to Whitewell for 9 miles.

Charles Bowman
Whitewell, Clitheroe,
Lancashire BB7 3AT
Tel   01200 448222
Fax   01200 448298
Email   reception@innatwhitewell.com
Web   www.innatwhitewell.com

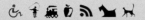

Temple Lodge

Temple Lodge, once home to the painter Sir Frank Brangwyn, is sandwiched between a courtyard and a lushly landscaped garden. The peace here is remarkable, making it a very restful place – simple yet human and warmly comfortable. Michael and a small devoted team run it with quiet energy. You breakfast overlooking the garden, there are newspapers to browse, no TVs, and bedrooms to make you smile. Expect crisp linen, garden views and prints of famous artists (each room is named after a painter). They are surprisingly stylish – clean, uncluttered with a hint of country chic – and represent exceptional value for money. None has its own bathroom; if you don't mind that, you'll be delighted. The Thames passes by at the end of the road (you can follow it down to Kew); the Riverside Studios – for theatre and film – are close. The Gate Vegetarian Restaurant is nearer still, ten paces across the courtyard; it is a well-known eatery and was Brangwyn's studio, hence the enormous artist's window. The house is a non-denominational Christian centre with two services a week, which you may take or leave as you choose.

Price	£50–£70. Singles £42.50.
Rooms	9: 1 double, 3 twins, 5 singles all sharing 3 baths & 1 shower.
Meals	Continental breakfast included. Restaurants nearby.
Closed	Never.
Directions	Tube: Hammersmith (3-minute walk). Bus: 9, 10, 27, 295.

Michael Beaumont
51 Queen Caroline Street,
Hammersmith, London W6 9QL

Tel	020 8748 8388
Fax	020 8748 8322
Email	templelodgeclub@btconnect.com
Web	www.templelodgeclub.com

The Troubadour

Bob Dylan played here in the 1960s, so did Jimi Hendrix, Joni Mitchell, Paul Simon and the Rolling Stones. The Troubadour is a slice of old London cool, a quirky coffee house/bar with a magical garden and a small club in the basement where bands play most nights. Outside, pavement tables make the best of the weather, inside the past lives on: rows of teapots elegantly displayed in the windows date from 1954, when the bar opened. The ceiling drips with musical instruments, you find stripped boards, tables and booths, the odd pew. The kitchen is open all day (if you wear a hat on Tuesday nights, pudding is free), so try Welsh rarebit, bangers and mash, Belgium waffles with chocolate ice cream; in summer, you can eat in the courtyard garden. Next door, three floors above the champagne bar, a vibrant suite up in the eaves gives views to the back of London rooftops. Expect lots of colour, a super-comfy bed, leather armchairs in front of the flat-screen TV, an alcoholic fridge. There's a kitchen, too: wake before 9am and make your own breakfast, or come down after for bacon and eggs served late into the afternoon.

Price	£165. Singles £150.
Rooms	1 suite for 2-4.
Meals	Breakfast from £4.25. Lunch & dinner £5-£25.
Closed	25 & 26 December; 1 January.
Directions	Tube: Earl's Court or West Brompton (both 5-minute walk). Bus: 74, 328, 430, C1, C3. Parking: £35 a day.

Simon & Susie Thornhill
263-267 Old Brompton Road,
London SW5 9JA
Tel 020 7370 1434
Email susie@troubadour.co.uk
Web www.troubadour.co.uk

Travel Club Offer: see page 367 for details.

base2stay Kensington

Stylish rooms and attractive prices make this is a brilliant base for those in town for a night or longer. Part hotel, part serviced apartments, the idea here is to keep things simple and pass on the savings to guests. You won't find a bar or a restaurant, you will find a tiny kitchen cleverly concealed behind cupboard doors in each room. You get fridges, kettles, sinks and microwaves, so chill drinks, make your own breakfast or zap up an evening meal. Super rooms come in a cool contemporary style and offer a lot for the money: halogen lighting, crisp white linen, air conditioning – and flat-screen TVs through which you can surf the internet at no cost (there are points for laptops too). Watch movies on demand, play games, raid the hotel's music library for 1,500 tracks. Bathrooms are equally good and come with limestone tiles, big white towels and power showers. There's a directory of local restaurants that deliver to the door, 24-hour reception, good security, a daily maid service. Some rooms interconnect, and a base breakfast box can be delivered to your door. Bars, clubs and restaurants are close.

Price	£107–£147. Triples £157–£181. Suites £197–£227. Singles £93–£107.
Rooms	67: 33 twins/doubles, 13 triples, 17 singles, 4 suites, all with kitchenettes.
Meals	Base breakfast £3.95.
Closed	Never.
Directions	Tube: Earl's Court (3-minute walk). Bus: 74, 328, C1, C3. Parking: £30 a day, off-street.

Nassar Khalil
25 Courtfield Gardens, Earl's Court,
London SW5 0PG

Tel	0845 262 8000
Fax	0845 262 8001
Email	info@base2stay.com
Web	www.base2stay.com

The Cranley Hotel

In a charming quiet London street of brightly painted Georgian houses, the Cranley has a neat front garden with wooden tables and chairs, clipped bay trees and wide steps up to the front door. The hall leads straight into a calm drawing room with deep Wedgewood blue walls, original fireplaces, good antiques, coir carpets and the odd lively rug. Bedrooms, some with private terraces, are extremely comfortable: pale carpets, lilac walls, embroidered headboards over huge beds, plain cream curtains with bedspreads to match, pretty windows and cream-tiled snazzy bathrooms. Robes and slippers, state-of-the-art technology, air conditioning, prettily laid tables for breakfast if you don't want it in bed... A cream tea with warm scones and clotted cream in the afternoon comes with the package, along with champagne and canapés at 7pm before you go off to an excellent local restaurant booked by the friendly staff. South Kensington and the Kings Road are both close.

Price	£175–£275. Suites £235–£365. Singles £140–£225.
Rooms	39: 19 doubles, 6 twins, 8 four-posters, 4 singles, 2 suites.
Meals	Continental breakfast £12.50; English £17.50. Restaurants nearby.
Closed	Never.
Directions	Tube: Gloucester Road (4-min walk). Bus: 49, 74, 430, C1. Parking: £30 a day, off-street.

	John Alexander
	10 Bina Gardens, South Kensington, London SW5 0LA
Tel	020 7373 0123
Fax	020 7373 9497
Email	info@thecranley.com
Web	www.steinhotels.com/thecranley

Parkes Hotel

A smart Knightsbridge townhouse tucked away in a peaceful square three minutes' walk from Harrod's. Those who like to stroll along smart London streets will have much to aim for: Hyde Park, the Albert Hall and the V&A are all close. Inside, you find a panelled reception hall, fresh blooms bursting from vases and a country-house sitting room for drinks before heading out to dinner. Bedrooms are seriously indulging, with a lift to whisk you up and down. Expect the very best: thick fabrics, stately colours, smart beds, Egyptian cotton. Suites are enormous and come with small kitchens hidden away behind cupboard doors; all rooms have sofas or armchairs, bowls of fruit and flat-screen TVs with movies on demand. Bathrooms are predictably luxurious; expect yellow and green marble, underfloor heating, power showers, bathrobes and piles of towels. A delicious breakfast is served downstairs but can be brought to your room; there's 24-hour room service, too. Endless restaurants wait on your doorstep with San Lorenzo around the corner in Beauchamp Place.

Price	£199–£297. Suites £325–£550. Singles from £135.
Rooms	33: 11 doubles, 18 suites, 4 singles.
Meals	Continental breakfast £12.50, full English £17.50.
Closed	Never.
Directions	Tube: Knightsbridge. Bus: 14, 74, C1. Parking: £30 a day off-street.

 Travel Club Offer: see page 367 for details.

Susan Burns
41 Beaufort Gardens, Knightsbridge,
London SW3 1PW

Tel	020 7581 9944
Fax	020 7581 1999
Email	info@parkeshotel.com
Web	www.parkeshotel.com

Searcy's Roof Garden Bedrooms

A one-off, the sort of place you could only find in England. From the street you enter directly a 1927 freight elevator (it's had a face lift), then ascend three floors – by-passing Searcy's, the 160-year-old catering company whose headquarters these are. Step out of the lift and into comfy bedrooms decorated in country-house style – Laura Ashley wallpaper, canopied beds, fresh flowers, a smattering of antiques. Bathrooms can be eccentric – two rooms have baths in the actual bedroom – but most are tucked away snugly and all come with waffle robes, big white towels and Molton Brown treats. Breakfast is brought to you with a complimentary newspaper and is occasionally accompanied by the sound of the Household Cavalry passing below. In summer, you can move outside and scoff croissants on a very pretty roof garden surrounded by pots of colour. Air-conditioning and wireless internet run throughout, dry cleaning can be arranged, and if you want to eat in, local restaurants will deliver. Excellent value close to Harrods, and Hyde Park a short stoll.

Price	£180. Singles £110. Suite £200.
Rooms	10: 7 twins/doubles, 2 singles, 1 family suite.
Meals	Continental breakfast included. 24-hour room service (light meals). Restaurants nearby.
Closed	Christmas & New Year.
Directions	Train: Victoria (to Gatwick). Tube: Knightsbridge (5-minute walk). Bus: 9, 10, 14, 19, 22, 52, 74, 137. Parking: £35 a day, off-street.

Demitrius Neofitidis
30 Pavilion Road, Knightsbridge,
London SW1X 0HJ

Tel	020 7584 4921
Fax	020 7823 8694
Email	rgr@searcys.co.uk
Web	www.30pavilionroad.co.uk

Travel Club Offer: see page 367 for details.

Knightsbridge Green Hotel

This hotel has a battalion of faithful guests who return for the central position, the reasonable prices, the spotless bedrooms and the warm welcome. All things Knightsbridge are on your doorstep – Harrods, Hyde Park and the tube are less than a two-minute stroll – while excursions further afield will lead to the Albert Hall, Piccadilly and the museums of South Kensington. Back at the hotel, you'll find surprisingly big rooms, and while the design may be simple it is also pleasing. There are marble bathrooms, off-white walls, canvas curtains, air-conditioning, flat-screen TVs and WiFi throughout. The hotel doesn't have a bar, but it is licensed and drinks are brought to your room, as is breakfast: croissants, freshly squeezed orange juice, and bacon and sausages from Harrods if you pay the extra. Rooms at the back have been vibrantly decorated to make up for the lack of light in the stairwell and a couple are nicely old-fashioned with warm floral fabrics and big beds (ever-popular with long-standing guests). Zuma, uber-cool Japanese restaurant, is very close. *Children under five free.*

Price	£200. Singles £150. Suites £250.
Rooms	28: 2 twins, 7 doubles, 7 singles, 12 suites.
Meals	Breakfast £5.50–£12.
Closed	Never.
Directions	Train: Victoria (to Gatwick); Paddington (to Heathrow). Tube: Knightsbridge (2-minute walk). Bus: 9, 10, 14, 19, 22, 52, 137. Parking: £30 a day, off-street.

Ardal O'Hanlon
159 Knightsbridge,
London SW1X 7PD

Tel	020 7584 6274
Fax	020 7225 1635
Email	reservations@thekghotel.com
Web	www.thekghotel.co.uk

Miller's

This is Miller's, as in the antique guides, and the collectibles on show in the first-floor drawing room make it one of the loveliest in this book. Continental breakfast is taken around a 1920s walnut table, while at night, cocktails are served on the house, a fire crackles in the carved-wood fireplace and a couple of hundred candles flicker around you. It is an aesthetic overdose, exquisitely ornate, every wall stuffed with gilt-framed pictures. An eclectic collection of regulars include movie moguls, fashion photographers, rock stars, even a professional gambler. An opera singer once gave guests singing lessons at breakfast. Wander at will and find an altar of Tibetan deities (well, their statues), a 1750s old master's chair, busts and sculptures, globes, chandeliers, plinths, rugs, and a three-legged chair stuffed on top of a Regency wardrobe. Things get moved around all the time, so expect the scene to change. Muralled walls in the hall were inspired by the Pope's palace at Avignon. Bedrooms upstairs are equally embellished; some bathrooms are minute. Wild extravagance in cool Notting Hill.

Price	£175–£270.
Rooms	8: 6 doubles, 2 suites.
Meals	Continental breakfast included. Dinner, 3 courses, about £30.
Closed	Never.
Directions	Train: Paddington (to Heathrow). Tube: Notting Hill Gate, Bayswater. Bus: 7, 23, 28, 31, 70. Parking: £25 a day, off-street.

Martin Miller
111a Westbourne Grove,
London W2 4UW

Tel	020 7243 1024
Fax	020 7243 1064
Email	enquiries@millershotel.com
Web	www.millershotel.com

22 York Street

The Callis family live in an 1820s, Georgian-style townhouse in W1 — not your average London residence and one that defies all attempts to pigeonhole. There may be 12 bedrooms but you can still expect the feel of home. Michael keeps things friendly and easy-going, which might explain the salsa dancing lessons that once broke out at breakfast — a meal of great conviviality taken around a curved wooden table in a big, bright kitchen. Here, a weeping ficus tree stands next to the piano, which, of course, you are welcome to play. There's always something to catch your eye, be it the red-lipped oil painting outside the dining room or the old boots on the landing. Wooden floors run throughout. The house has a huge sitting room (original high ceilings, shuttered windows) with sofas, books and backgammon. Bedrooms, spotless and comfy, have Provençal eiderdowns, good beds, country rugs, perhaps a piano or a chaise longue. There's a computer for guests to use, WiFi throughout. Madame Tussaud's, Regent's Park and Lord's are close. A very friendly place.

Price	£120. Singles £89–£100.
Rooms	10: 2 twins, 5 doubles, 3 singles.
Meals	Pubs/restaurants nearby.
Closed	Never.
Directions	Train: Paddington (to Heathrow). Tube: Baker Street (2-minute walk). Bus: 2, 13, 30, 74, 82, 113, 139, 274. Parking: £25 a day, off-street.

Michael & Liz Callis
Marylebone, London W1U 6PX

Tel	020 7224 2990
Fax	020 7224 1990
Email	mc@22yorkstreet.co.uk
Web	www.22yorkstreet.co.uk

Strattons

Nowhere is perfect, but Strattons comes close. It's one of the country's most eco-friendly hotels and if you arrive by public transport, you get a 10% discount on B&B. Silky bantams strut on the lawn, funky classical interiors thrill. Les and Vanessa met at art school and every square inch of their Queen Anne villa is crammed with mosaics and murals, marble busts, cow-hide rugs on stripped wood floors, art packed tight on the wall. It is an informal bohemian country-house bolthole of French inspiration in a small market town. Bedrooms are exquisite: a carved four-poster, a tented bathroom, Indian brocade and stained glass. There's trompe l'œil panelling, bespoke wallpaper and sofas by a log fire. Wonderful food in the candlelit restaurant (turn right by the chaise longue) is all organic, perhaps nettle and barley broth, slow-cooked leg of Papworth lamb, rhubarb and ginger crème brûlée. Les talks you through the cheese board with great panache, and breakfast (toasted stilton, goat's cheese omelette) is equally divine. Don't miss the Brecks for cycle tracks through Thetford forest. *Minimum stay two nights at weekends.*

Price	£150–£175. Singles from £120. Suites from £200.
Rooms	10: 1 twin/double, 4 doubles, 5 suites.
Meals	Dinner, 4 courses, £40.
Closed	One week at Christmas.
Directions	Ash Close runs off north end of market place between W H Brown estate agents & fish & chip restaurant.

Vanessa & Les Scott
4 Ash Close, Swaffham,
Norfolk PE37 7NH

Tel	01760 723845
Fax	01760 720458
Email	enquiries@strattonshotel.com
Web	www.strattonshotel.com

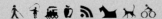 Travel Club Offer: see page 367 for details.

Ethical Collection: Environment; Community; Food. See page 373 for details

Bank House Hotel

In the heart of old King's Lynn, overlooking the Great Ouse river, this exquisite Grade II* townhouse hides a collection of extremely good rooms. The house dates from 1680 and was once owned by Joseph Gurney, father of Elizabeth Fry and founding partner of Barclays Bank; the brasserie at the front was his counting house. Step through the gates, note the statue of Charles I, then slip inside for grand high-ceilinged rooms. There are plush sofas in front of an open fire, old radiators and shuttered windows – but climb the stairs past a fine arched window to discover the real prize: bedrooms that dazzle. Some are big, others are huge, all come in warm colours with Designers Guild fabrics and excellent bathrooms. You may get painted panelling, big armoires, mahogany dressers or a claw-foot bath; in short, luxury. Outside there's much to do. The old quarter of Lynn – medieval with a Georgian face lift – is home to St Margaret's Church, ancient market places and a couple of warehouses that belonged to the Hanseatic League. Sandringham is close, as is the Wash. A treat.

Price	£90–£120. Suites £120–£140. Singles from £80.
Rooms	10: 5 doubles, 3 twins/doubles, 2 suites.
Meals	Lunch from £7.50. Dinner, 3 courses, about £30.
Closed	Never.
Directions	A47, then A1078 for town centre. Under arch & left, signed South Quay. Follow signs to quay, pick up river on left, follow road north. Hotel set back on right in square at top of road.

 Travel Club Offer: see page 367 for details.

Anthony & Jeannette Goodrich
King's Staithe Square, King's Lynn,
Norfolk PE30 1RD

Tel	01553 660492
Email	info@thebankhouse.co.uk
Web	www.thebankhouse.co.uk

Gin Trap Inn

An actor and a lawyer run this old English Inn. Steve and Cindy left London for the quiet life and haven't stopped since, adding a conservatory dining room at the back and giving the garden a haircut. The Gin Trap dates to 1667, while the horse chestnut tree that shades the front took root in the 19th century; a conker championship is in the offing. A smart whitewashed exterior gives way to a beamed locals' bar with a crackling fire and the original dining room in Farrow & Ball hues. Upstairs, you find three delightful bedrooms in smart country style. Two have big bathrooms with claw-foot baths and separate showers, all come with timber frames, cushioned window seats, Jane Churchill fabrics and the odd chandelier; walkers will find great comfort here. Come down for delicious food: Norfolk mussels, local sausages, then poached winter fruits. Ringstead – a pretty village lost in the country – is two miles inland from the coastal road, thus peaceful at night. You're on the Peddars Way, Sandringham is close and fabulous sandy beaches beckon.

Price	£78–£140. Singles from £49.
Rooms	3 doubles.
Meals	Lunch from £7. À la carte dinner from £20.
Closed	2.30pm–6pm. Open all day in summer.
Directions	North from King's Lynn on A149. Ringstead signed right in Heacham. Pub on right in village.

Steve Knowles & Cindy Cook
High Street, Ringstead, Hunstanton,
Norfolk PE36 5JU

Tel	01485 525264
Email	thegintrap@hotmail.co.uk
Web	www.gintrapinn.co.uk

The Neptune

A Shaker-style restaurant with rooms that started life as a smuggler's inn; a tunnel in the cellar leads who knows where. Inside, elegant simplicity is the order of the day, with varnished wood floors, Lloyd Loom furniture, big mirrors to soak up the light and fabulous photography on the walls. There's a small bar for bottled beers or glass of champagne, then an intimate restaurant for ambrosial food. Kevin left his Michelin star on the Isle of Wight to come north and cook for himself, so try crab and rocket risotto, wild sea bass with cucumber spaghetti, then chestnut parfait with almond and honey sorbet. Simple bedrooms above the shop are cosy and nicely priced: comfy beds, crisp linen, woollen blankets, painted bedheads, digital radios, flat-screen TVs and White Company lotions in compact bathrooms. There's a tiny residents' lounge with maps for walkers, so demolish an irreproachable breakfast — local sausage and bacon, boiled eggs and soldiers, homemade croissants and lashings of strong coffee — then sally forth to explore the Norfolk coast. *Minimum stay two nights at weekends in high season.*

Price	£100. Singles from £65.
Rooms	6: 5 doubles, 1 twin.
Meals	Lunch from £15. Sunday lunch £19.50. Dinner, 3 courses, about £35.
Closed	January.
Directions	North from Kings Lynn on A149. Into Old Hunstanton; on left at end of village.

Kevin & Jacki Mangeolles
Old Hunstanton Road,
Old Hunstanton, Norfolk PE36 6HZ
Tel   01485 532122
Email   reservations@theneptune.co.uk
Web   www.theneptune.co.uk

Titchwell Manor

A warmly contemporary hotel, with vast tracts of sandy beach at the end of a one-mile lane. In between is Titchwell's famous RSPB sanctuary; guided tours include the May dawn chorus – stupendous stuff. The hotel, a brick and flint Victorian manor, has a cool and airy colonial feel, with stripped wooden floors and the odd tumbling fern in a gorgeous conservatory dining room. The hotel stands on the road; views from bedrooms at the front drift across fields, then out to sea. Beach towels and picnics can be arranged, so wander down to Brancaster Bay for lazy days, then return for fabulously fresh food in the restaurant: mussels, oysters and lobster straight from the sea, venison from the Houghton estate. Bedrooms are light and airy, nicely uncluttered, with warm colours, crisp linen and padded headboards. Delicious courtyard rooms open onto a parterre herb garden of lavender and rosemary and come with tiled floors, neutral colours, flat screen TVs and super bathrooms; some at the back have French windows onto small terraces. There's a walled garden for afternoon tea and golf all along the coast.

Price	£110–250. Half-board from £95 p.p.
Rooms	25: 7 doubles, 2 twins. Stables: 4 doubles. Herb Garden: 10 doubles, 2 twins/doubles.
Meals	Lunch from £5. Sunday lunch £17. Picnics £10. Dinner, à la carte, about £30.
Closed	Never.
Directions	North from King's Lynn on A149 to Titchwell. Hotel in village on right.

Margaret Snaith
Titchwell, Brancaster, Norfolk PE31 8BB
Tel   01485 210221
Fax   01485 210104
Email margaret@titchwellmanor.com
Web   www.titchwellmanor.com

 Travel Club Offer: see page 367 for details.

The White Horse

You strike gold at The White Horse. For a start, you get one of the best views on the North Norfolk coast – a long, cool sweep over tidal marshes to Scolt Head Island. But it's not just the proximity of the water that elates: the inn, its rooms and the delicious food all score top marks. Follow your nose and find a sunken garden at the front, a local's bar for billiards, a couple of sofas for a game of Scrabble, and a conservatory/dining room for the freshest fish. Best of all is the sun-trapping terrace; eat out here in summer. Walkers pass, sea birds swoop, sail boats glide off into the sunset. At high tide the water laps at the garden edge, at low tide fishermen harvest mussels and oysters from the bay. Inside, the feel is smart without being stuffy: stripped boards, open fires, seaside chic with sunny colours. Beautiful bedrooms in New England style come in duck-egg blue with spotless tongue-and-groove bathrooms. Those in the main house have fabulous views, those in the garden open onto flower-filled terraces. The coastal path passes directly outside. *Minimum stay two nights at weekends.*

Price	£100–£148.
Rooms	15: 11 doubles, 4 twins.
Meals	Lunch from £8.95.
	Dinner, 3 courses, about £25.
Closed	Never.
Directions	Midway between Hunstanton & Wells next the Sea on A149 coast road.

Cliff Nye
Brancaster Staithe, Norfolk PE31 8BY

Tel	01485 210262
Fax	01485 210930
Email	reception@whitehorsebrancaster.co.uk
Web	www.whitehorsebrancaster.co.uk

The Hoste Arms

Nelson was once a local. Now it's farmers, fishermen and film stars who jostle at the bar and roast away on winter evenings in front of a roaring fire. In its 300-year history the Hoste has been a court house, a livestock market, a gallery and a brothel. These days it's more a pleasure dome than an inn and even on a grey February morning it was buzzing with life, the locals in for coffee, the residents polishing off leisurely breakfasts, diligent staff attending a wine tasting. The place has a genius of its own with warm bold colours, armchairs to sink into, panelled walls, its own art gallery. Fabulous food can be eaten anywhere and anytime, so dig into honey-glazed ham hock, fillet of English beef or seared sea bass with fennel. In summer, life spills out onto tables at the front or you can dine on the terrace in the garden at the back. Rooms are all different: a tartan four-poster, a swagged half-tester, leather sleigh beds in the Zulu wing and Fired Earth bathrooms. Burnham Market is gorgeous, the north Norfolk coast is on your doorstep (bring your shrimping net). And don't miss the ladies' loo!

Price	£125–£220. Singles from £95. Suites £166–£270. Half-board from £70 p.p.
Rooms	35: 12 twins/doubles, 4 four-posters, 4 singles, 7 suites. Zulu Wing: 5 doubles, 3 suites.
Meals	Lunch from £10. Dinner from £25.
Closed	Never.
Directions	On B1155 for Burnham Market. By green & church in village centre.

Emma Tagg
The Green, Burnham Market,
Norfolk PE31 8HD

Tel   01328 738777
Fax   01328 730103
Email   reception@hostearms.co.uk
Web   www.hostearms.co.uk

The Victoria at Holkham

A little English whimsy on Norfolk's magical coast. Outside you find a brick-and-flint pub on the Holkham estate (birthplace of the Bowler hat); inside you discover a country-house inn of colonial inspiration. Tom (Viscount) Coke and his wife Polly have renovated from top to toe, so come for stone flags, stripped wood, a buzzing bar and candles everywhere. Flop into deep sofas in front of the fire, slip through Rajasthani doors for supper in the orangery, or head into the garden for a pint on the terrace. Bedrooms upstairs vary in size, but all are grand and gracious with warm colours, silky curtains, country rugs, antique furniture. The four-poster is so high there's a stool to help you up, while those at the front have views over the marshes to a ridge of coastal pine. If you want pure peace escape to fabulous self-catering follies on the estate (The Triumphant Arch is magnificent). An avenue of trees leads down to Holkham's super beach, so hire bikes, grab a picnic, listen to the geese fly overhead. And don't miss the Big Hall in summer. *Minimum stay two nights at weekends.*

Price	£120–£170. Suite £145–£240. Singles from £100. Children in parents' room £15. Lodges £120–£235.
Rooms	10 + 4: 9 doubles, 1 attic suite. 4 self-catering lodges for 2-6.
Meals	Lunch & dinner £15-£40. Bar meals available Mon-Fri and sometimes at weekends.
Closed	Never.
Directions	On A149, 2 miles west of Wells-next-the-Sea.

 Travel Club Offer: see page 367 for details.

Phil Lance
Park Road, Wells-next-the-Sea,
Norfolk NR23 1RG

Tel	01328 711008
Fax	01328 711009
Email	victoria@holkham.co.uk
Web	www.victoriaatholkham.co.uk

The Crown

Nelson was a regular at the bustling Georgian coaching inn overlooking the village green.
He came to catch the London coach and would fortify himself in the bar before setting out;
the journey took four days. Period colours and a jaunty informality now flow throughout.
The bar comes in dining-room red with beamed ceilings, open fires, stripped boards and
three hand pumps to ensure a good pint. There's a restaurant in yellow with contemporary
art on the walls, but a new conservatory stretches out at the back, so dig into super food
wherever you like, perhaps half a dozen Norfolk oysters, fillet of beef with horseradish
cream, velvet chocolate torte. Bedrooms above come in different shapes and sizes. Those
at the front overlook the green, some with high ceilings. Bigger rooms have sofas, a couple
at the back have south-facing roof terraces. All come in airy creams with good beds, crisp
linen, flat-screen TVs and screen prints above the bed. A couple are timber-framed, all have
good tongue-and-groove bathrooms, and there's a DVD library at reception. The coast is a
three-minute stroll. *Minimum stay two nights at weekends.*

Price	£90–£155. Singles from £70. Half-board from £75 p.p.
Rooms	12: 8 doubles, 2 twins, 2 family suites.
Meals	Lunch from £3.95. Dinner, 3 courses, about £25.
Closed	Never.
Directions	Wells-next-the-Sea is on B1105, 10 miles north of Fakenham; pub by the green south of town centre.

Chris Coubrough
The Buttlands, Wells-next-the-Sea,
Norfolk NR23 1EX

Tel   01328 710209
Fax   01328 711432
Email   reception@thecrownhotelwells.co.uk
Web   www.thecrownhotelwells.co.uk

Cley Windmill

The setting here is magical with rushes fluttering in the salt marsh, raised paths leading off to the sea and a vast sky that seemingly starts at your feet. The windmill dates to 1713 and was converted into a house in the 1920s. Square rooms are bigger and suit those who prefer to shuffle, while round rooms in the tower are impossibly romantic (one is for mountaineers only). Six rooms are in the mill and you really want to go for these, though two of the cottages are set up for self-catering and visiting dogs. Inside, you find the loveliest drawing room – low ceiling, open fire, honesty bar, stripped floorboards... and a window seat to beat most others. Bedrooms come in country style with pretty pine, painted wood, colourful walls, super views. Rooms in the tower (with compact shower rooms) get smaller as you rise, but the view improves with every step and the room at the top even has a tiny balcony; there's a viewing platform half way up for all. Meals are taken in a pretty dining room, so drop down for a big breakfast or book for dinner: homemade soups, local-fish pie, sinful puddings. *Minimum stay two nights at weekends.*

Price	£78-£145. Singles from £92. Cottages (min. 2 nights) from £75.
Rooms	7 + 2: 4 doubles, 3 twins/doubles. 2 self-catering cottages.
Meals	Dinner, 3 courses, £24.50.
Closed	Rarely.
Directions	Head east through Cley on A149. Mill signed on left in village.

Charlotte Martin
Cley-next-the-Sea, Holt,
Norfolk NR25 7RP

Tel	01263 740209
Email	info@cleywindmill.co.uk
Web	www.cleywindmill.co.uk

The Wiveton Bell

In deference to the mighty church that soars towards heaven across the green, the Bell refrains from stealing the limelight and crouches respectfully in cottage style. The setting is dreamy – one that has changed over the years. Tidal waters once lapped at the church wall and eight trade ships ploughed the high seas, but the land was reclaimed by Sir Henry Calthorpe in the 17th century and with it went the village's wealth; idyllic views now sweep across the fields to Cley. As for the Bell, it's as good as its setting. Airy interiors shine while old beams, timber frames and stripped boards give a smart rustic feel. You get bright whites, contemporary art and comfy armchairs in front of the wood-burner. Doors open front and back onto terrace and green respectfully. Super-stylish bedrooms are scattered away, one, a suite with a claw-foot bath, in the eaves of the cottage, the others in a converted barn. All come in Farrow & Ball colours with a surfeit of electronic gadgetry and a kitchen in which you make your own breakfast. There's fresh fish and local meat in the restaurant, too. *Minimum stay two nights at weekends.*

Price	£95–£105.
Rooms	2 doubles.
Meals	Continental breakfast included. Lunch from £3.95. Dinner, 3 courses, £20–£25.
Closed	Never.
Directions	Wiveton signed off A149 at Blakeney; pub opposite church.

Berni Morritt & Sandy Butcher
Blakeney Road, Wiveton, Holt,
Norfolk NR25 7TL

Tel	01263 740101
Web	wivetonbell.co.uk

Byfords

A listed deli with rooms in a pretty market town three miles south of the North Norfolk coast. There's a café, too, one that was packed to the gunnels on a Sunday morning in February. Downstairs, labyrinthine interiors weave past red-brick walls and timber-framed alcoves, all of which ooze rustic chic, but it's the bedrooms that take the biscuit: this is 'posh B&B' as the brochure exclaims, without exaggeration. Rooms on the first floor have country rugs on stripped oak boards, Vi-Spring mattresses on half-tester beds, travertine marble bathrooms, Bang & Olufsen TVs. One floor up and you find rooms open to timbered eaves — smaller, but ever so cute and with all the same trappings (speakers in the bathroom ceilings, Egyptian cotton on the beds, vases of lilies liberally displayed, the odd panelled wall). When hunger strikes, drop down to a domed oak restaurant for half a pint of prawns, slow-cooked shoulder of lamb, Knickerbocker Glory. There's a vaulted cellar bar, and in summer life spills onto the pavement. Don't forget to stop at the deli; delicious things wait. *Minimum stay two nights at weekends.*

Price	£130–£150. Singles from £90.
Rooms	16: 3 twins/doubles, 12 doubles, 1 family.
Meals	Lunch & dinner from £8.95.
Closed	Christmas Day.
Directions	A148 for Cromer and into town. On main street (heading east), left after Barclays Bank into car park.

Iain Wilson
1-3 Shirehall Plain, Holt,
Norfolk NR25 6BG

Tel	01263 711400
Email	queries@byfords.org.uk
Web	www.byfords.org.uk

Saracens Head

A country-house pub of old-school splendour lost in the back lanes of deepest Norfolk. Legions of devoted locals wouldn't be seen anywhere else. They come for a pint of ale or a bottle of claret, but it's Robert's epic country cooking that draws the crowd: deep-fried aubergine with garlic mayo, slow-roasted pork with cider and rosemary, treacle tart drenched in double cream – no fusion cooking here! Wander at will and find ancient maps plastered to the walls, logs piled high to feed roaring fires, even the maestro's portrait hangs next to the fox in the front bar. In summer life spills into the walled garden, so explore Norfolk's coast by day, then come home for a leisurely sundowner. Lovely bedrooms, all upstairs, pay heed to comfort rather than fashion. They come in country style with comfy beds, colourful walls, quilted spreads, spotless carpets. Those at the back have long country views, those at the front look onto a rookery. Breakfast is something of a rustic feast. Blickling Hall, a Jacobean pile, is close. One of the best. *Minimum stay two nights & half-board only at weekends.*

Price	£90. Singles £50. Half-board from £70 p.p.
Rooms	6: 5 doubles, 1 twin.
Meals	Bar meals from £4.95. Dinner, 2 courses, about £17. No food Mondays (except bank holidays) or Tuesday lunchtimes.
Closed	Christmas Day.
Directions	From Norwich, A140 past Aylsham, then left, for Erpingham. Don't bear right for Aldborough, go straight through Calthorpe. Over x-roads. On right after about 0.5 miles.

Robert & Rachel Dawson-Smith
Wolterton, Erpingham,
Norfolk NR11 7LZ

Tel	01263 768909
Fax	01263 768993
Email	saracenshead@wolterton.freeserve.co.uk
Web	www.saracenshead-norfolk.co.uk

Fritton House Hotel

A small, chic, country-house hotel on the Somerleyton estate. Walks start from the back door, where paths lead out through sublime parkland and run down to Fritton lake. You can walk round it, row on it or take to the skies above it in a hot-air balloon. The building is 16th-century and was once a smuggler's inn; these days, warmly groovy interiors excite. Come for stripped wood floors, Cole & Son wallpapers, Farrow & Ball paints, sand-blasted beams. There's a smart drawing room at the front with super sofas, old shutters, country rugs and fresh flowers, then an airy bar and restaurant with leather armchairs, exposed brick walls and doors onto a gravelled terrace for views of the estate. Seriously indulging bedrooms flood with light and come with timber-framed walls, padded headboards and mahogany dressers. Beds are dressed in crisp white linen and warmed with Welsh wool blankets, while funky bathrooms have colourful resin floors, deep baths and power showers. Sheep graze in the fields around you, brasserie food keeps you happy and visits to Somerleyton can be arranged. Fabulous. *Minimum stay two nights at weekends in high season.*

Price	£137–£180. Singles from £100. Suite from £200.
Rooms	9: 5 doubles, 2 twins/doubles, 1 family suite.
Meals	Lunch from £8. Dinner, 3 courses, about £27.
Closed	Never.
Directions	From Beccles A143 north for Great Yarmouth. In Fritton, right, signed Fritton Lake. On right before lake.

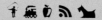 Travel Club Offer: see page 367 for details.

Sarah Winterton
Church Lane, Fritton,
Norfolk NR31 9HA

Tel	01493 484008
Fax	01493 488355
Email	frittonhouse@somerleyton.co.uk
Web	www.frittonhouse.co.uk

Broad House Hotel

A Queen Anne House on Wroxham Broad set in 24 acres of lawn, woodland and paddock. Kingfishers, geese and marsh harriers flock to the water, daffodils, snowdrops and bluebells run riot in spring. Inside, a total renovation has brought grand rooms back to life and warm country-house interiors now flourish. Padded window seats give garden views, facing sofas take the strain, winged armchairs are smartly upholstered, open fires crackle. Wonderful bedrooms are just the ticket with warm colours and thick fabrics; some have four-posters, some claw-foot baths. Bigger rooms on the first floor have fine garden views, while two on the top floor are timber-framed, as are their bathrooms; all come with flat-screen TVs, DVD players, bathrobes and Egyptian linen. A one-acre kitchen garden provides much for the table, so dig into slow-roasted tomato tart with chilli ice cream, fillet of sea bass with saffron mash and vermouth froth, lemon crème brûlée with orange sorbet. Arrive by train and a 1957 Bentley can pick you up. There's an Edwardian launch, too, on which to explore the Broads.

Price	£130–£150. Four-posters & suites £170–£190.
Rooms	9: 3 doubles, 1 twin, 2 four-posters, 3 suites.
Meals	Lunch by arrangement. Dinner, 4 courses, £39.
Closed	Never.
Directions	A47 west of Norwich, then left for Great Plumstead & signs north to Sallhouse. North on B1140, then right, signed Wroxham Broad, just before town. Signed right after 400m.

Philip & Caroline Search
The Avenue, Wroxham,
Norfolk NR12 8TS

Tel	01603 783567
Email	info@broadhousehotel.co.uk
Web	www.broadhousehotel.co.uk

Ethical Collection: Environment; Food.
See page 373 for details

The Mulberry Tree

Attleborough is ancient, mentioned in the Domesday Book. Its weekly market is 800 years old, its monastery suffered at the hands of Henry VIII and a fire swept through in 1559. These days it's a sleepy English country town with a good line in street names: Defunct Passage, Surrogate Precinct and Thieves Lane all bring a smile. It's also well-positioned for Norwich, Thetford Forest and Bury St Edmund's, making the Mulberry Tree a great little base for minor explorations. Airy interiors come in Farrow & Ball colours with stripped floors, big mirrors and contemporary art on the walls. There's a buzzing bar for local ales, a restaurant for super food and a garden that overlooks the bowling green. Best of all are excellent rooms that spoil you rotten: big beds, crisp linen, padded heads, flat-screen TVs. Willow twigs stand six feet high, mirrors lean against the wall, there are cushioned wicker chairs and fabulous tongue-and-groove bathrooms. Back downstairs in the bar, dig into Suffolk ham, free-range eggs and hand-cut chips, or slip into the restaurant for a three-course feast.

Price	£85–£90. Singles from £69.
Rooms	5: 4 doubles, 1 twin/double.
Meals	Continental breakfast included. Full English £7.95. Lunch from £5.45. Dinner, 3 courses, about £25.
Closed	Christmas.
Directions	On one-way system around town centre at junction with Station Road.

Philip & Victoria Milligan
Station Road, Attleborough,
Norfolk NR17 2AS

Tel	01953 452124
Email	relax@the-mulberry-tree.co.uk
Web	www.the-mulberry-tree.co.uk

The Pheasant Inn

A really super little inn, the kind you hope to chance upon. The Kershaws run it with great passion and an instinctive understanding of its traditions. The stone walls hold 100-year-old photos of the local community; from colliery to smithy, a vital record of its past. The bars are wonderful: brass beer taps glow, anything wooden – ceiling, beams, tables – has been polished to perfection and the clock above the fire keeps perfect time. The attention to detail is a delight, the house ales expertly kept: Timothy Taylor's and Northern Kite. Robin cooks with relish, again nothing too fancy, but more than enough to keep a smile on your face – cider-baked gammon, grilled sea bass with herb butter, wicked puddings, Northumbrian cheeses; as for Sunday lunch, *The Observer* voted it the best in the North. Bedrooms in the old hay barn are as you'd expect: simple and cosy, good value for money. You are in the glorious Northumberland National Park – no traffic jams, no rush. Hire bikes and cycle round the lake, canoe or sail on it, or saddle up and take to the hills. *Minimum stay two nights at weekends.*

Price	£85-£90. Singles from £50. Half-board from £76 p.p.
Rooms	8: 4 doubles, 3 twins, 1 family room.
Meals	Bar meals from £8.95. Dinner, 3 courses, £18-£22.
Closed	Mon & Tues November-March.
Directions	From Bellingham follow signs west to Kielder Water & Falstone for 7 miles. Hotel on left, 1 mile short of Kielder Water.

Walter, Irene & Robin Kershaw
Stannersburn, Kielder Water,
Northumberland NE48 1DD

Tel	01434 240382
Fax	01434 240382
Email	stay@thepheasantinn.com
Web	www.thepheasantinn.com

Eshott Hall

Slip into graceful inertia for a weekend, or longer; take the slog out of a drive up to Scotland or ramble and yomp to your heart's content through (some say) the finest countryside in Britain with its dreamy castles and white beaches. Whatever the excuse, you will be indulged in this listed Palladian house. Bedrooms flourish fine linen, thick fabrics, restful colours; warm bathrooms have showers, large baths and grand views over the estate and its medieval woodland. You are only 20 minutes from Newcastle with its variety of shops, restaurants, galleries and theatres, but you are surrounded by wildlife (bats, deer, badgers and red squirrels). Ho and Margaret are passionate conservationists: ceramic floors, working shutters, a rare staircase and a stained-glass window designed by William Morris are just a few of the stunning architectural features. The garden is delightful with rare old trees, a Victorian fernery, a covered pergola and oodles of woodland trails. Enjoy local and seasonal food and vegetables from the walled garden by candlelight in the formal dining room or in the Lost Wing.

Price	£128–£150. Singles £79–£90.
Rooms	6: 4 doubles, 2 twins/doubles.
Meals	Dinner, 3 courses, £35. By arrangement.
Closed	22 December–5 January.
Directions	East off A1, 7 miles north of Morpeth, 9 miles south of Alnwick, at Eshott signpost. Hall gates approx. 1 mile down lane.

Ethical Collection: Environment; Community; Food. See page 373 for details

Ho & Margaret Sanderson
Morpeth,
Northumberland NE65 9EN
Tel   01670 787777
Fax   01670 786000
Email   enquiries@eshotthallestate.co.uk
Web   www.eshotthall.co.uk

No. 1 Sallyport

A boutique hotel that stands a stone's throw from Berwick's Elizabethan ramparts. Tiny lanes and cobbled alleyways sweep up to this 17th-century listed townhouse; step inside and you find seriously funky interiors. Bedrooms are wild – a fire and huge plasma screen in one, cherubs in a bay window in another. Wander at will and find leather sleigh beds, beautifully upholstered armchairs, shimmering Osborne & Little wallpaper, shiny hardwood floors. All rooms come with DVD players (there's a selection of films in a library downstairs) and Bose sound systems (bring some CDs). Super-cool bathrooms, most with deluge showers, come with Fired Earth tiles and waffle bathrobes. There is a restaurant too; Elizabeth used to have her own and will whisk up a feast, perhaps Dublin Bay prawns, leg of lamb casserole, warm orange tart; breakfasts served in a cool dining room are equally seductive. As for medieval Berwick, it was built by an Italian architect from Lucca and is far prettier than you might imagine. *Minimum stay two nights at weekends.*

Price	£110. Suites & cottage £130–£170.
Rooms	7: 2 doubles, 4 suites, 1 cottage.
Meals	Packed lunch £7.50. Early supper £15. Dinner, 3 courses, £39.50.
Closed	Never.
Directions	Leave A1 for A1167. Right at T-junc and over bridge into Berwick. Right into Marygate, right into West St, left into Bridge St and house on right.

Elizabeth Middlemiss
Off Bridge Street, Berwick-upon-Tweed,
Northumberland TD15 1EZ

Tel	01289 308827
Fax	01289 308827
Email	info@sallyport.co.uk
Web	www.sallyport.co.uk

Travel Club Offer: see page 367 for details.

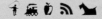

Hart's Nottingham

A small enclave of good things. You're on the smart side of town at the end of a cul-de-sac, thus remarkably quiet. You're also at the top of the hill and close to the castle with exceptional views that sweep south for ten miles; at night, a carpet of light sparkles. Inside, cool lines and travertine marble greet you in reception. Bedrooms are excellent, not huge, but perfectly adequate and extremely well designed. All come with wide-screen TVs, Bose sound systems, super little bathrooms and king-size beds wrapped in Egyptian cotton. Those on the ground floor open onto a fine garden, each with a terrace where you can breakfast in good weather; rooms on higher floors have better views (six overlook the courtyard). A cool little bar, the hub of the hotel, is open for breakfast, lunch and dinner, but Hart's Restaurant across the courtyard offers fabulous food, perhaps pan-fried wood pigeon with blackberries, free-range chicken with wild garlic, tarte tatin with caramel ice cream. There's a private car park for hotel guests and a small gym for those who must.

Price	£120–£170. Suites £220–£260.
Rooms	32: 29 doubles, 1 family, 2 suites.
Meals	Continental breakfast £8.50; full English £13.50. Bar snacks from £3.50. Lunch from £12.95. Dinner, 3 courses, £22.50–£35.
Closed	Never.
Directions	M1, junc. 24, then follow signs for city centre and Nottingham Castle. Let into Park Row from Maid Marion Way. Hotel on left at top of hill.

Paul Fearon
Standard Hill, Park Row, Nottingham,
Nottinghamshire NG1 6GN

Tel	0115 988 1900
Fax	0115 947 7600
Email	reception@hartshotel.co.uk
Web	www.hartsnottingham.co.uk

Langar Hall

Langar Hall is one of the most engaging and delightful places in this book – reason enough to come to Nottinghamshire. Imogen's exquisite style and natural joie de vivre make this a mecca for those in search of a warm, country-house atmosphere. The house sits at the top of a hardly noticeable hill in glorious parkland, bang next door to the church. Imo's family came here over 150 years ago. Much of what fills the house arrived then and it's easy to feel intoxicated by beautiful things: statues and busts, a pillared dining room, ancient tomes in overflowing bookshelves, a good collection of oil paintings. Bedrooms are wonderful, some resplendent with antiques, others with fabrics draped from beams or trompe l'œil panelling. Heavenly food, simply prepared for healthy eating, makes this almost a restaurant with rooms – you'll need to book if you want to enjoy Langar lamb, fish from Brixham, game from Belvoir Castle and garden-grown vegetables. In the grounds: medieval fishponds, canals, a den-like adventure play area and, once a year, Shakespeare on the lawn.

Price	£95–£185. Suite £210. Singles £80–£125.
Rooms	12: 7 doubles, 2 twins, 1 four-poster, 1 suite, 1 chalet for 2.
Meals	Lunch from £14.50. Dinner, 3 courses, £25–£40.
Closed	Never.
Directions	From Nottingham, A52 towards Grantham. Right, signed Cropwell Bishop, then straight on for 5 miles. House next to church on edge of village, signed.

Imogen Skirving
Langar,
Nottinghamshire NG13 9HG

Tel	01949 860559
Fax	01949 861045
Email	info@langarhall.co.uk
Web	www.langarhall.com

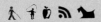 Travel Club Offer: see page 367 for details.

Entry 170   Map 6

Stubton Hall

Remember the name – Stubton Hall; you heard it here first. Kent and Claire – record producer and art historian respectively – have rescued this magnificent Regency mansion from abject ruin and are in the process not simply of restoring former glories but of trumping its original architect, Jeffrey Wyatville (he built parts of Chatsworth and Windsor Castle). The house stands in 25 acres of green and pleasant land, with sprawling lawns, a lake, an arboretum and a terrace that overlooks a strip of water where fountains play; you can even picnic out here. Inside, huge rooms come as standard. You'll find old oils, chandeliers and a roaring fire in the hall, miles of plaster moulding, an informal restaurant that spills onto the terrace and vast shuttered windows. There's a bar, too, for bon viveurs. Bedrooms – some enormous – mix cool wallpapers and beautiful fabrics with the odd four-poster, beautiful art, funky bathrooms and hi-tech gadgets. Stubton is a work in progress; the main house opens at the end of 2008, followed in 2009 by a super-cool spa with treatment rooms galore and a pillared pool. Fabulous.

Price	£120–160. Four-posters £190. Suite £220.
Rooms	40: 35 twins/doubles, 3 four-posters, 2 suites.
Meals	Lunch & dinner £10-£30.
Closed	Never.
Directions	A1 north of Grantham to Claypole. East to Stubton. Left in village & on right.

Travel Club Offer: see page 367 for details.

Claire & Kent Brainard
Stubton, Newark-on-Trent,
Nottinghamshire NG23 5DD
Tel   01636 626187
Email   info@stubtonhall.co.uk
Web   www.stubtonhall.co.uk

The Cherry Tree Inn

A cherry orchard flourished here 400 years ago and farm workers lived in these brick and flint cottages. Five trees survive on the sprawling lawn at the front, so come in spring for the blossom. Beds of lavender lead up to the front door, inside you find ancient stone flagging and low beamed ceilings. It's a real treat, with board games in a cupboard, fairylights in the fireplace and a different colour on the walls in each room. Food is the big draw and on a Sunday in February a fanatical crowd gathered. Huge bowls of mussels flew from the kitchen, then plates of rare roast beef, finally a tarte tatin with a calvados sauce that brought sighs of ecstasy from a lucky diner. Rooms in the next-door barn are super value for money, stylish and private, with walls of colour, creamy carpets, silky red throws and leather headboards. Two have high beamed ceilings, bathrooms with slate floors are just the ticket, and each room has its own thermostat. A breakfast club for locals runs on the first Saturday of each month, so you may have company. Expect kippers, scrambled eggs, the full works.

Price	£95.
Rooms	4 doubles.
Meals	Lunch from £7.50.
	À la carte dinner from £22.50.
Closed	Christmas.
Directions	A4070 north from Reading. After 4 miles, right, through Checkendon, to the village of Stoke Row.

Richard Coates
Stoke Row, Henley-on-Thames,
Oxfordshire RG9 5QA

Tel	01491 680430
Email	info@thecherrytreeinn.com
Web	www.thecherrytreeinn.com

The Miller of Mansfield

Ice-age melt water formed the Goring Gap; 14,000 years later 'cool' is back in town. The Miller, once a sedate red-brick coaching inn, has had a makeover and the results are decidedly groovy. You'll find pink suede beds, Cole & Son wallpaper, leather armchairs in the bar and silver-leaf mirrors above open fires. Beams have been sand blasted, 400-year-old oak panelling brought up from Devon to dress the bar. Expect black suede bar stools, fairy-light chandeliers and candles flickering on the mantelpiece. Bedrooms pack a punch. The chrome four-poster has a leather bedhead, there are cow-hide rugs on white wood floors. You get plasma screens, bathrobes and fluffy towels, while flower-power colours come in pink, orange and electric green. Bathrooms are extravagant, some with monsoon showers, others with free-standing stone baths; one has a Japanese bath for two (two have no door from the bedroom). You get seriously good food and wine in the restaurant, so walk by the Thames, take to the hills, then return to the Miller for a night of carousing. Bells peal at the Norman church. One for the young at heart.

Price	£110–£175. Suites £175–£205.
Rooms	10: 7 doubles, 1 twin, 2 suites.
Meals	Continental breakfast included; full English £9.50. Bar meals available all day. Lunch from £14.95. Dinner from £19.95.
Closed	Never.
Directions	North from Reading on A329. In Streatley right onto B4526. Over bridge; hotel on left.

Travel Club Offer: see page 367 for details.

Miguel Saraiva
High Street, Goring-on-Thames,
Oxfordshire RG8 9AW
Tel   01491 872829
Fax   01491 873100
Email   reservations@millerofmansfield.com
Web   www.millerofmansfield.com

The Trout at Tadpole Bridge

A 17th-century Cotswold inn on the banks of the Thames; pick up a pint, drift into the garden and watch life float by. Gareth and Helen bought the Trout after a two-year search and have cast their fairy dust into every corner: expect super bedrooms, oodles of style, delicious local food. The downstairs is open plan and timber-framed, with stone floors, gilt mirrors, wood-burners and logs piled high in alcoves. Bedrooms at the back are away from the crowd; three open onto a small courtyard where wild roses ramble on creamy stone – but you may prefer to stay put in your room and indulge in unabashed luxury. You get the best of everything: funky fabrics, trim carpets, monsoon showers (one room has a claw-foot bath), DVD players, flat-screen TVs, a library of films. Sleigh beds, brass beds, beautifully upholstered armchairs… one room even has a roof terrace. You can watch boats pass from the breakfast table, feast on local sausages, tuck into homemade marmalade courtesy of Helen's mum. Food is as local as possible, there are maps for walkers to keep you thin. *Minimum stay two nights at weekends May-October.*

Price	£110. Suite £140. Singles from £75.
Rooms	6: 2 doubles, 3 twins/doubles, 1 suite
Meals	Lunch & dinner £5-£30. Not Sunday nights November-April.
Closed	Rarely.
Directions	A420 southwest from Oxford for Swindon. After 13 miles, right for Tadpole Bridge. Pub on right by bridge.

Gareth & Helen Pugh
Buckland Marsh, Faringdon,
Oxfordshire SN7 8RF

Tel	01367 870382
Fax	01367 870912
Email	info@trout-inn.co.uk
Web	www.trout-inn.co.uk

Old Bank Hotel

You're in the heart of old Oxford. Stroll south past Corpus Christi to Christ Church meadows and the Thames, or leave the hotel to the north and find All Souls, the Radcliffe Camera and the Bodleian Library. Back at the Old Bank, a wonderful world of warm contemporary elegance and an important collection of modern art and photography adorning the walls — even in bedrooms. Downstairs, the old tiller's hall is now a vibrant bar/brasserie with fine arched windows giving views onto the high street; come for cocktails before a convivial meal. Bedrooms upstairs are exemplary, with big comfy beds, piles of cushions, Denon CD players, flat-screen TVs. Bigger rooms have sofas, you get robes in super bathrooms and there's free broadband access throughout. Serene service means curtains are pleated, beds are turned down, the daily papers delivered to your door. There's room service, too, and umbrellas in every cupboard. Breakfast is served in the tiller's hall or on the deck in the courtyard in summer. Free off-street parking is priceless.

Price	£135–£325. Singles from £160.
Rooms	42: 10 twins/doubles, 31 doubles, 1 suite.
Meals	Breakfast £10.95–£12.95. Lunch & dinner £10–£30.
Closed	Never.
Directions	Cross Magdalen Bridge for city centre. Straight through 1st set of lights, then left into Merton St. Follow road right; 1st right into Magpie Lane. Car park 2nd right.

Marie Jackson
92–94 High Street, Oxford,
Oxfordshire OX1 4BN

Tel	01865 799599
Fax	01865 799598
Email	info@oldbank-hotel.co.uk
Web	www.oldbank-hotel.co.uk

Old Parsonage Hotel

A country house in the city, with a lively bar for excellent meals, a rooftop terrace for afternoon tea and a hidden garden where you can sit in the shade and listen to the bells of St Giles. Step through an ancient front door to find logs smouldering in the original stone fireplace, the papers spread out beneath an old carved window and a rich collection of classical art emblazoning the walls. Warm stylish bedrooms are scattered all over the place, some at the front (where Oscar Wilde entertained lavishly when he was sent down), others at the back in a sympathetic extension where some suites have French windows onto tiny balconies and a couple of the less-expensive rooms open onto private terraces. Expect Vi-Spring mattresses, flat-screen TVs, crisp white linen, spotless bathrooms and friendly staff on hand to advise. Oxford starts beyond the wall and the hotel owns a couple of bikes that you are free to spin off on. They also have a punt on the Cherwell and will pack you a picnic, so glide effortlessly past spire and meadow, then tie up for lunch.

Price	£150-£225. Suites £250.
Rooms	30: 25 twins/doubles, 4 suites, 1 single.
Meals	Breakfast £12-£14. Lunch & dinner £10-£45.
Closed	Never.
Directions	From A40 ring road, south at Banbury Road r'bout to Summertown city centre. On right next to St Giles church.

Marie Jackson
1 Banbury Road, Oxford,
Oxfordshire OX2 6NN

Tel	01865 310210
Fax	01865 311262
Email	info@oldparsonage-hotel.co.uk
Web	www.oldparsonage-hotel.co.uk

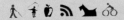

Entry 176   Map 3

The Highway Inn

You can sit out on the high street under the shade of a parasol in summer and watch the shoppers haul their bounty up the hill, but this lovely inn comes complete with a small medieval courtyard where roses, honeysuckle and orange blossom roam on the walls – not a bad spot to escape the crowds. The building itself goes back to 1480 and its carved stone entrance leads into rather lovely interiors where all the architectural gems are on hand: mind-your-head beams, horse hair walls, ancient flagging, mellow golden stone. Tally and Scott, both locals, spent their wedding night here, then returned to renovate, rescuing the inn from 16 years of neglect. They have kept the mood warmly traditional and brought in curios by the truckload: cider flagons, riding boots, vintage luggage, the odd chaise longue. Wander at will and find padded window seats, stripped boards, open fires and a good pint in the front bar. Bedrooms upstairs are all different, all smartly traditional with lots of oak, pretty beds, beams aplenty and sloping floors. Best of all is the welcome – this is a very friendly base. There's jazz on Sundays in summer, too.

Price	£75–£110. Four poster £95–£135. Singles from £65.
Rooms	9: 6 doubles, 1 twin, 1 four-poster, 1 single.
Meals	Lunch from £5. Dinner, 3 courses, £20–£30.
Closed	25 & 26 December.
Directions	A40 west from Oxford to Burford. On right in town, halfway down hill.

Tally & Scott Nelson
117 High Street, Burford,
Oxfordshire OX18 4RG

Tel	01993 823661
Email	enquiries@thehighwayinn.co.uk
Web	www.thehighwayinn.co.uk

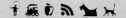

Burford House

Burford was made rich by 14th-century mill owners. Its golden high street slips downhill to the river Windrush, where paths lead out into glorious country, passing a church that dates to Norman times; Cromwell held a band of Levellers here in 1649 and their murals survive inside. Halfway up the hill, this 17th-century timber-framed house stands bang in the middle of town. Interiors sweep you back to the soft elegance of old England: a couple of cosy sitting rooms, a fire that roars, exposed stone walls, a courtyard for summer dining. Slip into the restaurant and find Farrow & Ball colours, freshly cut flowers, rugs on wood boards, theatre posters hanging on the wall. Lunch is offered six days a week – and now dinner at weekends – so try salmon fishcakes, Cotswold lamb, spiced plum cheesecake. Bedrooms are delightful, two across the courtyard in the coach house. Some have oak beams, others a claw-foot bath. All come with super beds, woollen blankets, robes in good bathrooms and those at the back have rooftop views. Wake on Sunday to the sound of pealing bells. Wonderful. *Minimum stay two nights at weekends.*

Price	£150–£170. Singles from £105.
Rooms	8: 3 doubles, 2 twins/doubles, 3 four-posters.
Meals	Light lunch from £4.95 (not Sundays). Dinner (Thurs–Sat) about £30.
Closed	Rarely.
Directions	In centre of Burford, halfway down hill. Free on-street parking, free public car park nearby.

Ian Hawkins & Stewart Dunkley
99 High Street, Burford,
Oxfordshire OX18 4QA

Tel	01993 823151
Fax	01993 823240
Email	stay@burfordhouse.co.uk
Web	www.burfordhouse.co.uk

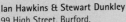 Travel Club Offer: see page 367 for details.

The Kings Head Inn

About as Doctor Dolittle-esque as it gets. Achingly pretty Cotswold stone cottages around a village green with quacking ducks, a pond and a perfect pub with a cobbled courtyard. Archie is young, affable and charming with locals and guests, but Nic is his greatest asset – a milliner, she has done up the bedrooms on a shoestring and they look fabulous. All are different, most have a stunning view, some family furniture mixed in with 'bits' she's picked up, painted wood, great colours and lush fabrics. The bar is lively – not with music but with talk – so choose rooms over the courtyard if you prefer a quiet evening. Breakfast and supper are taken in the pretty flagstoned dining room (exposed stone walls, Farrow & Ball paints, pale wood tables), while you can lunch by the fire in the bar on devilled kidneys, sausage and mash, or perhaps fish pie; there are homemade puds and serious cheeses, too. Lovely unpompous touches like jugs of cow parsley in the loo. There's loads to do, antiques in Stow, golf at Burford, walking and riding in gorgeous country, even a music festival in June.

Price	£70–£125. Singles from £55.
Rooms	12: 10 doubles, 2 twins.
Meals	Lunch & dinner: main courses £9.95–£17.95. Bar meals from £6.
Closed	Christmas Day & Boxing Day.
Directions	East out of Stow-on-the-Wold on A436, then right onto B4450 for Bledington. Pub in village on green.

Archie & Nicola Orr-Ewing
The Green, Bledington,
Oxfordshire OX7 6XQ
Tel   01608 658365
Fax   01608 658902
Email   kingshead@orr-ewing.com
Web   www.kingsheadinn.net

Kings Arms Hotel

Woodstock is the estate village to Blenheim Palace, home to the Dukes of Marlborough, birthplace of Winston Churchill, one of the country's architectural gems. It is open most of the year and there is no better way to arrive than by foot after a good breakfast at a local inn. Cue the King's Arms, a late Georgian hostelry which stands on the corner of Market Place and the Oxford Street. In summer, tables and chairs line up smartly outside, while the wood-burner works overtime in the bar in winter, the logs jammed into alcoves all over the place. Airy, open-plan interiors drift easily from one room to another. You get leather stools at a marble bar, stripped floors in the restaurant, huge hanging lampshades in the breakfast room. There are pots full of lemons, mirrors in driftwood frames, railway sleepers standing on their toes, the odd old settle. Uncluttered bedrooms come in cool colours, many with high ceilings, all with crisp linen, wooden bedheads, black and white photographs and nice little bathrooms. One room is huge with exposed timbers. Posh pub grub waits downstairs... Oxford is close.

Price	£140–£150. Singles from £75.
Rooms	15: 14 doubles, 1 twin.
Meals	Lunch & dinner from £9.95.
Closed	Never.
Directions	On A44 at corner of Market Street in town centre.

David & Sara Sykes
19 Market Street, Woodstock,
Oxfordshire OX20 1SU

Tel	01993 813636
Fax	01993 813737
Email	stay@kingshotelwoodstock.co.uk
Web	www.kings-hotel-woodstock.co.uk

The Kingham Plough

You don't expect to find locals clamouring for a table in a country pub on a cold Tuesday in February, but different rules apply at the Kingham Plough. Emily, once junior sous chef at the famous Fat Duck in Bray, is now doing her own thing and it would seem the locals approve. You eat in the tithe barn, now a splendid dining room, with ceilings open to ancient rafters and excellent art on the walls. Attentive staff bring sublime food. Dig into game broth with pheasant dumplings, fabulous lamb hotpot with crispy kale, and hot chocolate fondant with blood orange sorbet. Interiors elsewhere are equally pretty, all the result of a delightful refurbishment. There's a piano by the fire in the locals' bar, a terrace outside for summer dining, fruit trees, herbs and lavender in the garden. Bedrooms, three of which are small, have honest prices and come with super-comfy beds, flat-screen TVs, smart carpets, white linen, the odd beam; one has a claw-foot bath. Arrive by train, straight from London, to be met by a bus that delivers you to the front door. The Daylesford Organic farm shop/café is close.

Price	£85–£110. Singles from £75.
Rooms	7 twins/doubles.
Meals	Lunch from £10. Dinner, 3 courses, about £30.
Closed	Christmas Day.
Directions	Off B4450 between Chipping Norton & Stow-on-the-Wold, signed.

Emily Watkins & Adam Dorrien-Smith
Kingham, Chipping Norton,
Oxfordshire OX7 6YD
Tel   01608 658327
Email   book@thekinghamplough.co.uk
Web   www.thekinghamplough.co.uk

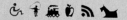

Falkland Arms

In a perfect Cotswold village, the perfect English pub. Five hundred years on and the fire still roars in the stone-flagged bar under a low-slung timbered ceiling that drips with jugs, mugs and tankards. Here, the hop is treated with reverence; ales are changed weekly and old pump clips hang from the bar. Tradition runs deep; they stock endless tins of snuff with great names like Irish High Toast and Crumbs of Comfort. In summer Morris Men jingle in the lane outside, life spills out onto the terrace at the front and into the lovely big garden behind. This lively pub is utterly down-to-earth and in very good hands. Dig into baked Camembert or plates of charcuterie in front of the fire or hop next door to the tiny beamed dining room for home-cooked delights. Bedrooms are cosy, some verging on snug; the attic room is wonderfully private. Brass beds and four-posters, maybe a bit of old oak and an uneven floor; you'll sleep well. The house is blissfully short on modern trappings, nowhere more so than in the bar, where mobile phones meet with swift and decisive action. Very special, book early for weekends.

Price	£80–£110.
Rooms	5 doubles.
Meals	Lunch & dinner: main courses £8–£15. Must book for dinner.
Closed	Never.
Directions	North from Chipping Norton on A361, then right onto B4022, signed Great Tew. Inn by village green.

Paula & James Meredith
Great Tew, Chipping Norton,
Oxfordshire OX7 4DB

Tel	01608 683653
Fax	01608 683656
Email	falklandarms@wadworth.co.uk
Web	www.falklandarms.org.uk

The Olive Branch

A Michelin-starred pub in a sleepy Rutland village, where bridle paths lead out across peaceful fields. The inn dates to the 17th century and is built of Clipsham stone... as are the Houses of Parliament. Inside, a warm, informal rustic chic hits the spot perfectly; come for open fires, old beams, exposed stone walls and choir stalls in the bar. Chalk boards on tables in the restaurant reveal the names of the evening's diners, while the English food – cauliflower soup, roast rib of beef, caramelised lemon tart – elates. As do the hampers of terrine, cheese and homemade pies that you can whisk away for picnics in the country. Bedrooms in Beech House across the lane are impeccable. Three have terraces, one has a free-standing bath, all come with crisp linen, pretty beds, Roberts radios, real coffee. Super breakfasts – smoothies, boiled eggs and soldiers, the full cooked works – are served in a smartly renovated barn, with flames leaping in the wood-burner. The front garden fills in summer, the sloe gin comes from local berries, and Newark is close for the biggest antiques market in Europe. Superb.

Price	£100–£140. Suites £150–£190. Singles from £85.
Rooms	6: 5 doubles, 1 family.
Meals	Lunch from £13.95. Dinner, 3 courses, about £30.
Closed	3pm–6pm. Open all day Sat & Sun.
Directions	2 miles off A1 at Stretton (B668 junction).

Ben Jones & Sean Hope
Main Street, Clipsham,
Rutland LE15 7SH

Tel	01780 410355
Fax	01780 410000
Email	info@theolivebranchpub.com
Web	www.theolivebranchpub.com

Hambleton Hall

A sublime country house, one of the loveliest in England. The position here is matchless. The house stands on a tiny peninsular that juts into Rutland Water. You can sail on it or cycle round it, then come back to the undisputed wonders of Hambleton: sofas by the fire in the panelled hall, a pillared bar in red for cocktails and a Michelin star in the dining room. French windows in the sitting room (beautiful art, fresh flowers, the daily papers) open onto idyllic gardens. Expect clipped lawns and gravel paths, a formal parterre garden that bursts with summer colour and a walled swimming pool with huge views over grazing parkland down to the water. Bedrooms are the very best. Hand-stitched Italian linen, mirrored armoires, mullioned windows, marble bathrooms – and Stefa's eye for fabrics, some of which coat the walls, is faultless; the Croquet Pavilion, a suite with two bedrooms, has its own terrace. Polish the day off with a serious dinner, perhaps scallop ravioli, breast of Goosnargh duck, then poached pear with caramel ice cream. Wonderful. *Minimum stay two nights at weekends.*

Price	£205–£370. Singles from £170. Pavilion £500–£600.
Rooms	17: 15 twins/doubles, 1 four-poster. Pavilion: 1 suite (1 four-poster, 1 twin/double) for 4.
Meals	Continental breakfast included; full English £14.50. Lunch from £21.50. Dinner £40–£70.
Closed	Never.
Directions	From A1, A606 west towards Oakham for about 8 miles, then left, signed Hambleton. In village, bear left and hotel signed right.

Tim & Stefa Hart
Hambleton, Oakham,
Rutland LE15 8TH

Tel	01572 756991
Fax	01572 724721
Email	tim@hambleton.co.uk
Web	www.hambletonhall.com

Entry 184 Map 6

Mr Underhill's at Dinham Weir

A taste of Provence in sleepy Ludlow. You're bang on the water with the river Teme passing serenely in front and Ludlow castle high on the hill behind. Step in off the lane and you find yourself cocooned in a colourful courtyard; you may eat here in summer surrounded by lavender and roses while the river pours over the weir and the odd duck squawks. Glassed arched walls in the airy restaurant bring in the view, so come for a heavenly, seven-course, Michelin-starred tasting menu, highlights of which may include pavé of halibut with lemon grass and ginger broth, slow-roasted forest venison with red wine and thyme, black cherry sponge with cinnamon ice cream, and a plate of delicious cheeses. Everything is made in house, including the croissants at breakfast. Rooms come in whites and creams with crisp linen, flat-screen TVs, bathrobes and handmade mattresses. Those in the main house are small, but overlook river and courtyard, two suites across the lane have proper sitting rooms, and the Shed (some shed!) is a timber-framed palace bang on the water. Wonderful.

Price	£140–£170. Singles from £120. Suites £220–£270.
Rooms	8: 4 doubles, 4 suites.
Meals	Dinner, 7-course tasting menu, £45–£51. Not Monday or Tuesday.
Closed	Occasionally.
Directions	Head to castle in Ludlow centre, take Dinham Road to left of castle; down hill, right at bottom before crossing river. On left, signed.

Chris & Judy Bradley
Dinham Bridge, Ludlow,
Shropshire SY8 1EH
Tel   01584 874431
Web   www.mr-underhills.co.uk

Hotel

Shropshire

Fishmore Hall

Fishmore Hall, once dower house to the Plymouth estate, paddles in the country one mile north of sleepy Ludlow. During the war it housed evacuees, then became a prep school, finally fell into disrepair. With a top-to-toe renovation under its belt, happier days have returned and the hotel now shines in contemporary style. Georgian windows flood rooms with light, varnished wood floors sparkle underfoot, there are fresh flowers, pretty fabrics and old-style radiators to keep you warm in winter. Views from the ivory dining room shoot off across fields to Clee Hill; in summer, French windows open onto a stone terrace for al fresco meals. Bedrooms are fancy with all the bits and bobs: robes and power showers in marble bathrooms, American walnut beds covered in crisp linen. You get flat-screen TVs, contemporary art and rooms at the front have country views. Back downstairs, stop for an aperitif before a meal in the restaurant. Expect big food in the Ludlow tradition, perhaps terrine of rabbit with caramelised figs, Cornish red mullet with crab ravioli, carrot and ginger crème brûlée.

Price	£140–£250. Singles from £100.
Rooms	15 twins/doubles.
Meals	Lunch from £18. Dinner, 3 courses, £46.50. Tasting menu £55.
Closed	Never.
Directions	A4117 into Ludlow. Right at mini roundabout & continue for 1 mile. On right.

Laura Penman
Fishmore Road, Ludlow,
Shropshire SY8 3DP

Tel	01584 875148
Fax	01584 877907
Email	reception@fishmorehall.co.uk
Web	www.fishmorehall.co.uk

 Travel Club Offer: see page 367 for details.

Entry 186 Map 2

The Inn at Grinshill

A ridge of pine soars high above the village; bring the boots and take to Shropshire's wild, wonderful hills. Down at the inn, nothing but good things; this is a wonderfully welcoming bolthole, a top-to-toe renovation which now shines. Wander at will and you find an 18th-century panelled family room with rugs and games, a 19th-century bar with quarry-tiled floors and a crackling fire, and a 21st-century dining room, serene in cream, flooded with light courtesy of glazed coach-house arches. Bedrooms upstairs are just as good, with good beds, piles of pillows, crisp white linen and wispy mohair blankets or shiny quilted eiderdowns. And TVs hidden behind mirrors, DVD players and indulging bathrooms. Back downstairs, ambrosial delights pour from the kitchen – the breast of duck served with an orange and lemon marmalade was faultless. A grand piano gets played on Friday nights and life spills out into the garden in summer. Church bells peal, roses ramble, there's cricket in the village at the weekend and the Shropshire Way passes by outside. Don't miss the magical follies at Hawkstone Park.

Price	From £120. Singles from £60.
Rooms	7: 4 doubles, 2 twins, 1 single.
Meals	Lunch from £10.95; Sunday lunch £16.50. À la carte dinner about £25. Not Sunday evenings or bank holiday evenings.
Closed	Sunday nights and bank holiday evenings unless by prior arrangement.
Directions	A49 north from Shrewsbury. Grinshill signed left after 5 miles.

 Travel Club Offer: see page 367 for details.

Kevin & Victoria Brazier
High Street, Grinshill, Shrewsbury,
Shropshire SY4 3BL

Tel	01939 220410
Fax	01939 220327
Email	info@theinnatgrinshill.co.uk
Web	www.theinnatgrinshill.co.uk

Pen-y-Dyffryn Country Hotel

An old rectory on the side of a blissful hill with long views stretching out across the valley. The church is below, and in Wales (nobody knows when the border was moved). This is a small, welcoming country house with a fire in the sitting room, a terrace for afternoon tea and a good collection of pictures on the walls. Best off all is David Morris's delicious cooking, so head to the dining room for food that's as local as possible, with game from the valley; try spiced parsnip and apple soup, rack of Welsh lamb in a thyme butter sauce, dark chocolate terrine with a cointreau sauce. There are fine organic cheeses, too. Bedrooms are warmly stylish without being grand, most with great views, one with a French sleigh bed; modern bathrooms – one has a two-seater spa bath – come with thick fluffy towels. Four new rooms are more private and have their own patios. There's plenty of space in the house making it ideal for a gathering, with lots of comfortable chairs and sofas to hide in with a good book. Excellent walking from the door and the smoked haddock at breakfast is divine. *Minimum stay two nights at weekends.*

Price	£114–£166. Singles £86.
Rooms	12: 8 doubles, 4 twins.
Meals	Dinner from £35.
Closed	Rarely.
Directions	From A5, head to Oswestry. Leave town on B4580, signed Llansilin. Hotel 3 miles on left just before Rhydycroesau.

Miles & Audrey Hunter
Rhydycroesau, Oswestry,
Shropshire SY10 7JD

Tel	01691 653700
Fax	01978 211004
Email	stay@peny.co.uk
Web	www.peny.co.uk

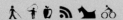 Travel Club Offer: see page 367 for details.

Bellplot House Hotel & Thomas's Restaurant

There are chic inns, there are smart hotels and there's Betty's. This may not be the trendiest place in the book, but what you find comes straight from the heart. With honest prices, quirky interiors and delicious food Bellplot delivers what few others do: a personal world. It's a family affair – Betty greets, her husband Denis pulls the pints, their son Thomas cooks in the kitchen. Step into stripped floors, yellow walls, a pool table in the bar and a dining room in country-house green. This is where you come for dinners with a difference, perhaps green pea soup, Lancashire hot pot, freshly baked lemon meringue pie. This unashamedly old-school menu (every supplier is listed on the back) prompted a visiting New Yorker to declare the food the best he'd tasted in Britain. Bedrooms are sprinkled about. They tend to be large and are furnished in a homely style: warm and spotless, lots of colour, crisp white linen, compact bathrooms. Some have sofas, all come with TVs and WiFi. You're on the high street, but it's quiet at night. Montacute House and Forde Abbey are both close.

Price	£79.50. Family £89.50. Singles £69.50.
Rooms	7: 5 doubles, 1 family, 1 single.
Meals	Breakfast £6–£9.50. Picnic lunch £12. Dinner, 3 courses, £20–£25. Not Sunday.
Closed	Never.
Directions	In centre of Chard, 500 yds from the Guildhall. Car park available.

 Travel Club Offer: see page 367 for details.

	Betty Jones
	High Street, Chard,
	Somerset TA20 1QB
Tel	01460 62600
Fax	01460 62600
Email	info@bellplothouse.co.uk
Web	www.bellplothouse.co.uk

Lord Poulett Arms

In a ravishing village, an idyllic village inn, French at heart and quietly groovy. Part pub, part country house, with walls painted in reds and greens and old rugs covering flagged floors, the Lord Poulett gives a glimpse of a 21st-century dream local, where classical design fuses with earthy rusticity. A fire burns on both sides of the chimney in the dining room; on one side you can sink into leather armchairs, on the other you can eat under beams at antique oak tables while candles flicker. Take refuge with the daily papers on the sofa in the locals' bar or head past a pile of logs at the back door and discover an informal French garden of box and bay trees, with a piste for boules and a creeper-shaded terrace. Bedrooms upstairs come in funky country-house style, with fancy flock wallpaper, perhaps crushed velvet curtains, a small chandelier or a carved-wood bed. Two rooms have slipper baths behind screens in the room; two have claw-foot baths in bathrooms one step across the landing; Roberts radios add to the fun. Delicious food includes summer barbecues, Sunday roasts and the full works at breakfast.

Price	£88. Singles £59.
Rooms	4: 2 doubles, each en suite; 2 doubles, each with separate bath.
Meals	Lunch & dinner: main courses £10–£20.
Closed	Never.
Directions	A303, then A356 south for Crewkerne. Right for West Chinnock. Through village, 1st left for Hinton St George. Pub on right in village.

Steve & Michelle Hill
High Street, Hinton St George,
Crewkerne, Somerset TA17 8SE

Tel	01460 73149
Email	steveandmichelle@lordpoulettarms.com
Web	www.lordpoulettarms.com

Little Barwick House

A dreamy restaurant with rooms lost in the hills three miles south of Yeovil. Tim and Emma rolled west ten years ago and have gathered a legion of fans who come to feast on their ambrosial food. Their stage is this small Georgian country house which stands in three acres of peace. A curtain of trees shields it from the outside world, horses graze in the paddock below and afternoon tea is served in the garden in summer, so sip your Earl Grey accompanied by birdsong. Inside, graceful interiors flood with light courtesy of fine windows that run along the front. There's an open fire in the cosy bar, eclectic reading in the pretty sitting room, and stripped floors in the high-ceilinged dining room. Upstairs, super bedrooms hit the spot with warm colours, crisp linen, silk curtains and a country-house feel. But dinner is the main event, heaven in three courses. Everything is homemade and cooked by Tim and Emma, an equal partnership in the kitchen. Try confit of pork belly roasted with honey, saddle of roe deer with a mushroom risotto, apple strudel with calvados ice cream. A real treat. *Minimum stay two nights at weekends.*

Price	£140–£160. Half-board £95–£115 p.p.
Rooms	6: 4 doubles, 2 twins.
Meals	Lunch £19.95–£25.95 (not Monday & Tuesday). Dinner, 3 courses, £36.95 (not Sunday & Monday).
Closed	Sundays & Mondays. 2 weeks in January.
Directions	From Yeovil, A37 south for Dorchester; left at 1st r'bout. Down hill, past church, left in village and house on left after 200 yds.

Emma & Tim Ford
Barwick Village, Yeovil,
Somerset BA22 9TD

Tel	01935 423902
Fax	01935 420908
Email	reservations@barwick7.fsnet.co.uk
Web	www.littlebarwickhouse.co.uk

The Queen's Arms

In a pretty village blissfully neglected by the rest of the world, a country pub that mixes the best of old and new. You're halfway up a hill with fields soaring to a high ridge on one side, views shooting off across open country on the other, and Wellington boots at the front door; pull on a pair and explore. Return to the pub – rescued from neglect, now shining in relaxed country style – to find a high-ceilinged bar with country rugs on flagstone floors, leather sofas on stripped boards, the odd armchair next to the fire. In summer, life spills onto a sun-trapping courtyard. Bedrooms upstairs are a treat: small chandeliers, contemporary art, beautiful beds, iPod docks and flat-screen TVs, piles of pillows and crisp linen. Super bathrooms come with robes and underfloor heating; one has a copper bath. Back downstairs, dig into delicious country food, much sourced locally, and wash it down with a pint of ale or a bottle of Jim Barry's super Coonawarra shiraz. Breakfast is taken communally: pub-reared pork for your bacon, home-laid eggs. Staff are lovely.

Price	£75–£120. Singles £60–£90.
Rooms	5: 4 doubles, 1 twin.
Meals	Lunch from £5.50.
	Dinner, 3 courses, about £23.
Closed	Rarely.
Directions	From A303 take Chapel Crosse turning, through South Cadbury village. Next left & follow signs to Corton Denham. Pub at end of village, on right.

Rupert & Victoria Reeves
Corton Denham, Somerset DT9 4LR

Tel	01963 220317
Email	relax@thequeensarms.com
Web	www.thequeensarms.com

 Travel Club Offer: see page 367 for details.

The Pilgrim's at Lovington

A slightly eccentric dining pub within striking distance of Wells and Glastonbury. Interiors have a warm, unpretentious, rustic style: timber frames, old flagged floors, panelled walls and painted ceilings. There are alcoves to hide away in or leather armchairs in front of the fire; you'll find games and books, Farrow & Ball colours and photos of New York lined up on the walls. If the bar is earthy, then the rooms are decidedly fancy. They're out at the back in what was the skittle alley, quietly idling away from the road. Three have cathedral ceilings, all come with exposed stone walls, flat-screen TVs, lovely beds wrapped up in good linen, perhaps a faux-leopard-skin chaise longue. As for the bathrooms, expect the best: double-ended baths, separate power showers, fancy tiles and cotton robes. Spin back to the restaurant – fresh flowers, big mirrors, candles galore – and dig into delicious food, perhaps West Country mussels, local lamb, Somerset rhubarb crumble. Breakfast is equally indulging and you can scoff your Gloucester Old Spot sausages on the decked terrace in summer.

Price	£80-£110.
Rooms	5: 4 doubles, 1 twin.
Meals	Lunch from £8.
	Dinner, 3 courses, about £30.
Closed	Never.
Directions	On B3153 between Castle Cary & Somerton. In village by traffic lights.

Julian & Sally Mitchison
Lovington, Castle Cary, Somerset
BA7 7PT

Tel	01963 240597
Email	jools@thepilgrimsatlovington.co.uk
Web	www.thepilgrimsatlovington.co.uk

The Devonshire Arms

A lively English village with a well-kept green; the old school house stands to the south, the church to the east and the post office to the west. The inn (due north) is 400 years old and was once a hunting lodge for the Dukes of Devonshire; a rather smart pillared porch survives at the front. These days open-plan interiors are warmly contemporary with high ceilings, shiny blond floorboards and fresh flowers everywhere. Hop onto brown leather stools at the bar and order a pint of Crop Circle, or sink into sofas in front of the fire and crack open a bottle of wine. In summer, life spills onto the terrace at the front, the courtyard at the back and the lawned garden beyond. Super bedrooms run along at the front; all are a good size, but those at each end are huge. You get low-slung wooden beds, seagrass matting, crisp white linen and freeview TV. One has a purple claw-foot bath, some have compact showers. Delicious food is on tap in the restaurant – chargrilled scallops, slow-cooked lamb, passion fruit crème brûlée – so take to the nearby Somerset levels and walk off your indulgence in style.

Price	£80–£130. Singles from £70.
Rooms	9: 8 doubles, 1 family room.
Meals	Lunch from £5. Dinner from £12.95.
Closed	Rarely.
Directions	A303, then north on B3165, through Martock, to Long Sutton. By village green.

Philip & Sheila Mepham
Long Sutton, Langport, Somerset
TA10 9LP

Tel	01458 241271
Fax	01458 241037
Email	mail@thedevonshirearms.com
Web	www.thedevonshirearms.com

Farmer's Inn

You don't often trek into deepest Somerset and wash up at a deeply groovy inn, but that's what you get at the Farmer's, so brave the narrow country lanes and head to the top of the hill for colour and comfort in equal measure. All the country treats are on hand. Outside, cows in the fields, cockerels crowing and long clean views; inside, friendly natives, open fires and a timber-framed bar. It's all the result of a total renovation, and one airy room now rolls into another giving a sense of space and light. Imagine terracotta-tiled floors and beamed ceilings, yellow-painted tongue-and-groove panelling, old pine dining tables dressed with pots of rosemary and logs piled high in the alcoves. Bedrooms are the best, some big, some huge. They come with off-white walls, seagrass mats on shiny wooden floors, cast-iron beds, power showers or claw-foot baths. One has a daybed, others have sofas, one has a private courtyard. Super food flies from the kitchen — grilled sardines, rib-eye steak, chocolate and mint mousse — and you can eat on the terrace in summer. Great walking, too: bring the boots.

Price	£90–£140.
Rooms	5: 4 doubles, 1 twin.
Meals	Bar meals from £4.50.
	À la carte dinner from £25.
Closed	Rarely.
Directions	M5 junc. 25, then south on A358. Right at Nag's Head pub, up hill for two miles, following signs towards RSPCA. On left.

Debbie Lush
Slough Green, Higher West Hatch,
Taunton, Somerset TA3 5RS

Tel	01823 480480
Email	letsgostay@farmersinnwesthatch.co.uk
Web	www.farmersinnwesthatch.co.uk

Combe House Hotel

A country lane winds up to this hotel, which basks peacefully in the first folds of the Quantocks. Woodlands rise, a stream pours past, paths lead out for uplifting walks. The hotel, an old mill, dates back to the 17th century and couldn't be in better hands: Gareth and Catherine swept in recently and are refurbishing in double-quick time (they polished off the ground floor in a couple of months). Now you find airy interiors, smart carpets, a wood-burner in the inglenook, the odd exposed wall. Sofas take the strain in the sitting room, armchairs do the job in the bar and you eat under beams in the restaurant, where seriously good food does the trick, perhaps crab tian with mango jelly, pan-fried duck breast with roasted chestnuts, white chocolate parfait with apple pie sorbet. Home-grown vegetables, free-range hens and an orchard are all in the pipeline. Some bedrooms have been refurbished, other await their turn; a very pretty country style is emerging with warm colours, silky throws, flat-screen TVs, and robes in super new bathrooms. There are deer on the hill, too.

Price	£125–£150. Suites £175. Singles from £65. Half-board from £80 p.p.
Rooms	16: 11 twins/doubles, 3 singles, 2 suites.
Meals	Lunch from £5. Sunday lunch £15.95–£22.95. Dinner, 3 courses, about £30.
Closed	Never.
Directions	From Bridgwater, A39 to Minehead. At Holford, left in front of Plough Inn; follow lane thro' village. Bear left at fork signed Holford Combe; drive near to end of road on right.

Gareth & Catherine Weed
Butterfly Combe, Holford,
Bridgwater, Somerset TA5 1RZ

Tel	01278 741382
Fax	01278 741322
Email	enquiries@combehouse.co.uk
Web	www.combehouse.co.uk

Travel Club Offer: see page 367 for details.

Bindon Country House Hotel

Bindon is lovely, a big old pile that hides on the edge of woodland where wild flowers flourish. Once derelict, it now shines, and if you want you can take the whole place and have it to yourselves – open fires, tiled entrance hall, stained-glass windows, wall tapestries, plaster-moulded ceilings, galleried staircase and glass-domed roof to boot. Step into the snug panelled bar, past the wrought-iron candlesticks, for coffee served with piping hot milk and delicious homemade biscuits. In summer doors are flung open and you can sit by a magnificent stone balustrade that looks over rose gardens down to an old dovecote. Bright bedrooms come in different sizes: two oval rooms at the front of the house are *huge*, all dusky pink furniture, patterned wallpaper, high brass beds and Victorian baths. The rest are a good size, very comfortable; a couple are warm and cosy up in the eaves. High teas for children, gorgeous food, a small heated pool and a tennis court. In short, a treat, so come to get married or simply to retreat for a day or two. *Minimum stay two nights at weekends.*

Travel Club Offer: see page 367 for details.

Price	£145-£225. Singles £115. Half-board from £95 p.p. (min. 2 nights). Exclusive use £1,250 self-catering (minimum 2 nights).
Rooms	12: 10 twins/doubles, 2 four-posters.
Meals	Dinner, 5 courses, £35.
Closed	Rarely.
Directions	From Wellington, B3187 for 1.5 miles; left at sharp S-bend for Langford Budville; right for Wiveliscombe; 1st right; on right.

Lynn & Mark Jaffa
Langford Budville, Wellington,
Somerset TA21 0RU

Tel	01823 400070
Fax	01823 400071
Email	stay@bindon.com
Web	www.bindon.com

Miller's at Glencot House

An intoxicating country house in a sublime position with lawns that run down to the river Axe and a cricket pitch on the far bank. In summer you can pick up a deckchair, wander down to the water and watch the village team toil in the sun while you dig into afternoon tea. Glencot is a perfect place, a bohemian paradise tucked away in Somerset's leafy lanes. It's all part of Martin Miller's benevolent empire – antique guides, distilled gin, London bolthole, academy of arts, now country retreat. And while England's green and pleasant land encircles this Jacobean mansion, its interiors reveal a thrilling flamboyance that cuts at the establishment grain and shows the designers how to decorate a real country house. Everywhere you go a hundred beautiful things loom into view: busts, bronzes, oils by the truckload, a baby grand in the music room, a pair of peacocks in the drawing room, chandeliers tumbling from ceilings. Bedrooms are immaculate, wildly ornate, rich in colour, with walls of art, draped four-posters, gilt mirrors in tidy bathrooms. Irreverent, exhilarating, magical. One of the best.

Price	£165–£185. Four-posters £240–£265.
Rooms	15: 5 four-posters, 7 doubles, 3 twins/doubles.
Meals	Lunch from £14.95. Sunday lunch £19.95. Dinner, 3 courses, £33.
Closed	Rarely.
Directions	From Wells, follow signs to Wookey Hole. Sharp left at finger post, 100m after pink cottage. House on right in Glencot Lane.

Ben Humber
Glencot Lane, Wells, Somerset BA5 1BH

Tel	01749 677160
Fax	01749 670219
Email	relax@glencothouse.co.uk
Web	www.glencothouse.co.uk

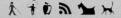

Ounce House

Bury St Edmunds, an ancient English town, is a dream; if you've never been, don't delay. The Romans were here, the barons hatched plans for Magna Carta within the now-crumbled walls of its ancient monastery and its Norman abbey attracted pilgrims by the cartload. The town was made rich by the wool trade in the 1700s and highlights include the cathedral (its exquisite new tower looks hundreds of years old) and the magnificent Abbey Gardens (perfect for summer picnics). Just around the corner Ounce House, a handsome 1870 red-brick townhouse, overflows with creature comforts, so slump into leather armchairs in front of a carved fireplace and gaze at walls of art. You'll also find a snug library, a lawned garden and homely bedrooms packed with books, mahogany furniture and fresh flowers. Princely breakfasts are served on blue-and-white Spode china at one vast table. This is B&B in a grand-ish home, and Jenny and Simon will pick you up from the station or book a table at a local restaurant. Try The Grid (popular with locals) or Maison Bleue (excellent seafood). Don't miss the May arts festival.

Price	£100–£125. Singles £75–£85.
Rooms	5: 4 doubles, 1 twin.
Meals	Restaurants 5-minute walk.
Closed	Rarely.
Directions	A14 north, then central junction for Bury, following signs to historic centre. At 1st r'bout, left into Northgate St. On right at top of hill.

Simon & Jenny Pott
Northgate Street, Bury St Edmunds,
Suffolk IP33 1HP

Tel	01284 761779
Fax	01284 768315
Email	pott@globalnet.co.uk
Web	www.ouncehouse.co.uk

Entry 199   Map 4

The Great House

Lavenham is a Suffolk gem, a showpiece town made prosperous by 14th-century wool merchants, hence the timber-framed houses. The Great House stands across the market place from the Guildhall, its Georgian façade giving way to airy 15th-century interiors which mix timber frames and old beams with contemporary colours and varnished wood floors. The poet Stephen Spender once lived here and the house became a meeting place for artists, but these days it's irresistible French cooking that draws the crowd. Try flash-fried scallops with a goat's cheese sauce, wild Suffolk venison with a red wine jus, Spanish strawberries in champagne with a fennel sorbet; as for the cheese board, it's a work of art. Fabulous bedrooms – all recently refurbished in lavish style – come with Egyptian cotton, suede sofas, coffee machines, and robes in magnificent bathrooms. Four are huge, but even the tiniest is a dream. One has a regal four-poster, another has a 14th-century fireplace in its bathroom. All come with an array of gadgets: hi-fis, surround-sound, flat-screen TVs. *Minimum stay two nights at weekends.*

Price	£99–£180. Singles from £85. Half-board from £92.50 p.p.
Rooms	5: 4 doubles, 1 twin/double.
Meals	Continental breakfast £8.50; full English £12.50. Lunch from £14.95. Dinner from £26.95. Not Sunday nights & Mondays.
Closed	First 3 weeks in January.
Directions	A1141 to Lavenham. At High Street, 1st right after The Swan or up Lady Street into Market Place.

Régis & Martine Crépy
Market Place, Lavenham,
Suffolk CO10 9QZ

Tel	01787 247431
Fax	01787 248007
Email	info@greathouse.co.uk
Web	www.greathouse.co.uk

 Travel Club Offer: see page 367 for details.

The Bildeston Crown

There are flagstones in the locals' bar, warm reds on the walls and sweet-smelling logs smouldering in open fires. The inn dates from 1529, the interior design from 2005. Not that the feel is overly contemporary; ancient beams have been reclaimed from under a thick coat of black paint and varnished wood floors shine like honey. There are gilded mirrors and oils on the walls, candles in the fireplace, happy locals at the bar. An airy open-plan feel runs throughout, with lots of space in the dining room and smart leather chairs tucked under handmade oak tables. You'll also find flowers in the courtyard, old radiators and high-backed settles in the front bar and local Suffolk beers to quench your thirst. Bedrooms come in different sizes, but all are stuffed with luxury. Imagine regal reds and golds, faux-fur blankets, silk curtains, perhaps a bust in a gorgeous bathroom. A hi-tech music system holds 1,000 albums (listen as you soak); and there are flat-screen TVs. Hire bikes from the shop next door and dive into the country, or come for the beer festival in the last week of May.

Price	£120–£180. Singles £70–£120.
Rooms	12: 8 doubles, 3 twins, 1 single.
Meals	Bar meals from £7.
	À la carte dinner from £28;
	8-course tasting menu £65.
Closed	Never.
Directions	A12 junc. 31, then B1070 to Hadleigh.
	A1141 north, then B1115 into village.
	Pub on right.

                Hayley Lee
                Bildeston, Suffolk IP7 7ED

Tel   01449 740510
Fax   01449 741843
Email   info@thebildestoncrown.co.uk
Web   www.thebildestoncrown.co.uk

The White Hart Inn

A beautiful Suffolk village at peace in the folds of Constable country. Those who cross the road to visit St James Church will find one of the great man's paintings hanging on the wall. As for this old coaching inn, it dates from the 15th century and comes with timber frames, ancient flagstones and the odd beamed ceiling, but these days the accent is firmly on food, making this a sparkling restaurant with rooms. A warm relaxing feel runs throughout, with sofas by the bar and a colourful terrace for lunch in summer. It's popular with locals, so beat them to it and dine in style on twice-baked cheese soufflé, rack of lamb Provençal, then banana and rosemary tarte tatin. Bedrooms vary in size but all come in crisp country style: yellow walls, pressed linen, checked fabrics, thick blankets, fresh flowers, sofas or armchairs if there's room. Some have wildly sloping floors, two have vaulted ceilings, one has muralled walls from the hand of Gainsborough's brother (he painted them to pay for a meal, or so the story goes). Beth Chatto's exquisite garden is nearby and open all year.

Price	£96–£129. Singles £76–£108.
Rooms	6: 5 doubles, 1 twin.
Meals	Lunch from £12.90. Dinner, 3 courses, around £30.
Closed	Rarely.
Directions	Nayland signed right 6 miles north of Colchester on the A134 (no access from A12). In village centre.

Christine Altug
High Street, Nayland, Colchester,
Suffolk CO6 4JF

Tel	01206 263382
Fax	01206 263638
Email	nayhart@aol.com
Web	www.whitehart-nayland.co.uk

Travel Club Offer: see page 367 for details.

Chequers

Katie and Mark escaped the London crush, snapped up this 16th-century pub, turned it into a family home, then conjured up three funky rooms in the garden to aide and abet weary escapees from the city. All are divine, two are huge, and while the third is definitively 'snug', it comes with an en suite garden, where breakfast is served in good weather. If you come for a lazy weekend, splash out on the big rooms and revel in style. The Coach House opens onto a gravelled terrace with table and chairs for sunny days; inside you find country rugs on coir matting, Indian wood carvings hung on the wall, faux-fur throws on crisp white linen, and a super bathroom of contemporary splendour. The Hayloft is no less elegant and comes with a decked balcony, mood lighting, an iPod dock and a leather bed from which you can gaze up at Orion's Belt courtesy of a skylight. Wherever you end up, breakfast is bought to you (as are drinks, when required): country eggs, posh local bacon, freshly squeezed juice, pain au chocolat. The gorgeous Suffolk coast is close, don't miss it.
Minimum stay two nights at weekends.

Price	£80–£145. Singles from £70
Rooms	3 doubles.
Meals	Pubs & restaurants nearby.
Closed	Rarely.
Directions	Leave A12 for Wickham Market north of Woodbridge. Through Market Square, down High Street, and opposite Spring Lane.

Katie & Mark Casey
220 High Street, Wickham Market,
Woodbridge, Suffolk IP13 0RF

Tel	01728 746284
Email	info@chequerssuffolk.co.uk
Web	www.chequerssuffolk.co.uk

The Old Rectory

An old country rectory with contemporary interiors; what would the rector think? You get stripped floors in the dining room, a 21st-century orange chaise longue by the honesty bar and windows dressed in fabulous fabrics. Michael and Sally swapped Hong Kong for Suffolk and the odd souvenir came with them: wood carvings from the Orient and framed Burmese chanting bibles. In winter, a fire smoulders at breakfast; in summer, you feast in a huge stone-flagged conservatory where doors open onto two acres of orchard and lawns. A warm country-house informality flows within, so help yourself to a drink, sink into a sofa or spin onto the terrace in search of sun and birdsong. Smart bedrooms are warmly decorated; one is up in the eaves, one overlooks the church, another has a claw-foot bath. Delicious food includes organic sausages and homemade jams at breakfast, perhaps parsnip soup and roast loin of Suffolk pork at dinner, then almond and lemon tart. Sutton Hoo is close as is Snape Maltings (performing opera singers occasionally stay and warm up for work in the bedrooms). A happy house. *Minimum stay two nights at weekends April-October.*

Price	£85-£140. Singles from £75.
Rooms	7: 4 doubles, 1 twins/double, 2 four-posters.
Meals	Dinner, 3 courses, £28. (Not Saturday or Sunday except for parties of 10 or more).
Closed	Occasionally.
Directions	North from Ipswich on A12 for 15 miles, then right onto B1078. In village, over railway line; house on right just before church.

Michael & Sally Ball
Campsea Ashe, Woodbridge,
Suffolk IP13 0PU
Tel   01728 746524
Email   mail@theoldrectorysuffolk.com
Web   www.theoldrectorysuffolk.com

 Travel Club Offer: see page 367 for details.

The Crown and Castle

The road runs out at sleepy Orford, so saddle up and follow cycle tracks or bridle paths into the forest. You can also hop on a boat and chug over to Orfordness, the biggest vegetated shingle spit in the world. In WWII it housed a military research base where Barnes Wallace (bouncing bomb) and Robert Watson-Watt (radar) toiled all day, returning at night to the splendour of the Crown, a Victorian redbrick inn that stands close to a 12th-century castle. Today the feel is light and airy, very comfortable, with stripped wood floors, open fires and eclectic art. A mouthwatering menu (half a pint of Orford prawns, Cornish crab, roasted Suffolk pheasant) caused indecision, but the warm duck salad with spiced pear was exceptional. Rooms in the main house come in pastels, those at the back have long watery views. Garden rooms (dull on the outside, lovely within) are big and airy, with padded headboards, seagrass matting, spotless bathrooms and doors onto a communal garden. All have crisp white linen, TVs and DVDs. Wellington boots wait at the back door, so pull on a pair and discover Suffolk. *Children over 8 welcome.*

Price	£15–£155. Singles from £92. Half-board from £77.50 p.p.
Rooms	19: 16 doubles, 2 twins, 1 suite..
Meals	Lunch from £14.95. À la carte dinner from £24.50.
Closed	Never.
Directions	A12 north from Ipswich to A1152 east of Woodbridge, then B1084 into Orford. Hotel on market square.

 Travel Club Offer: see page 367 for details.

David & Ruth Watson
Orford, Suffolk IP12 2LJ
Tel   01394 450205
Email   info@crownandcastle.co.uk
Web   www.crownandcastle.co.uk

Wentworth Hotel

Come for a little time travel; this stretch of the Suffolk coast will sweep you back to sleepy England at its loveliest: fishing boats on shingle beaches, an estuary for super walks and a music festival in summer. The Wentworth matches the mood perfectly; it's warmly old-fashioned, quietly grand, full of its own traditions. Michael's family have been here since 1920, when scores of fishermen worked the shore; the few that remain haul their boats up onto the beach across from the hotel terrace. Inside you find a warm seaside elegance, nothing too racy; instead, sunshine colours, fresh flowers, flickering coal fires, oils on the walls and shelves of books. Also: delightful sitting rooms, a bar for all seasons, and part of the hotel resembles a grand ocean liner. The restaurant looks out to sea, comes in Georgian red and spills onto the sunken lawn in summer for views of passing boats. Bedrooms (many with sea views) are plush: Zoffany wallpaper, reds and golds, French armoires, comfortable beds. Joyce Grenfell used to stay for the Aldeburgh Festival and has a room named after her. *Minimum stay two nights at weekends.*

Price	£108–£225. Singles from £63. Half-board £57–£125 p.p.
Rooms	35: 24 twins/doubles, 4 singles. Darfield House: 7 doubles.
Meals	Lunch from £7.50. Dinner from £15.
Closed	Never.
Directions	A12 north from Ipswich, then A1094 for Aldeburgh. Past church, down hill, left at x-roads; on right.

Michael Pritt
Wentworth Road, Aldeburgh, Suffolk
IP15 5BD

Tel	01728 452312
Fax	01728 454343
Email	stay@wentworth-aldeburgh.co.uk
Web	www.wentworth-aldeburgh.com

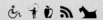

Satis House

Dickens wrote part of *Great Expectations* in this house and gave its name to Mrs Haversham's mansion. Not that you should read too much into this: the house is pristine, the clocks work and the dining tables throng with happy guests. Incredibly, this fine Georgian house was originally built to accommodate servants from Cockfield Hall. Kevin (erstwhile West End musical actor) and David (a rather good cook) have refurbished beautifully in smart contemporary style with Graham & Brown wallpapers in red, gold and charcoal. You'll find original stone flagging in the hall, a pebbled fireplace in the sitting room and a shocking-red bar for cocktails before dinner. The airy restaurant comes with gilt mirrors and smart chandeliers, so drop down for excellent local food: Red Poll beef, Blythburgh pork, Sutton Hoo chicken. Bedrooms are in the grip of a lavish refurbishment; expect lots of colour and style, fancy wallpaper, Egyptian cotton, flat-screen TVs and silky fabrics. One opens onto the walled garden, where wild pheasants roam.

Price	£110–£170. Singles from £75. Half-board from £80.
Rooms	8: 6 doubles, 2 twins.
Meals	Lunch from £14.95 (not Mon/Tues). Dinner, 3 courses, about £35 (not Sun).
Closed	Never.
Directions	A12 north from Woodbridge to Yoxford. Signed left after left-hand bend on northern edge of village.

Travel Club Offer: see page 367 for details.

Kevin Wainwright & David Little
Yoxford, Suffolk IP17 3EX

Tel	01728 668418
Fax	01728 668640
Email	enquiries@satishouse.co.uk
Web	www.satishouse.co.uk

The Westleton Crown

This is one of England's oldest coaching inns, with 800 years of continuous service under its belt. It stands in a village two miles inland from the sea at Dunwich, with Westleton Heath running east towards Minsmere Bird Sanctuary. Inside, you find the best of old and new. A recent refurbishment has introduced Farrow & Ball colours, leather sofas and a tongue-and-groove bar, and they mix harmoniously with panelled walls, stripped floors and ancient beams. Weave around and find nooks and crannies in which to hide, flames flickering in an open fire, a huge map on the wall for walkers. You can eat wherever you want, and a conservatory/breakfast room opens onto a terraced garden for summer barbecues. Fish comes straight off the boats at Lowestoft, local butchers provide local meat. Lovely bedrooms are scattered about and come in cool lime white with comfy beds, Egyptian cotton, flat-screen TVs. Super bathrooms are fitted out in Fired Earth, and some have claw-foot baths. Aldeburgh and Southwold are close by. *Minimum stay two nights at weekends.*

Price	£95–£160. Singles from £85.
Rooms	25: 19 doubles, 2 twins, 3 family rooms, 1 single.
Meals	Lunch & dinner £5–£30.
Closed	24 & 25 December.
Directions	A12 north from Ipswich. Right at Yoxford onto B1122; left for Westleton on B1125. On right in village.

Matt Goodwin
The Street, Westleton, Southwold,
Suffolk IP17 3AD

Tel	01728 648777
Fax	01728 648239
Email	info@westletoncrown.co.uk
Web	www.westletoncrown.co.uk

Travel Club Offer: see page 367 for details.

The George in Rye

Ancient Rye has a big history. It's a reclaimed island, a wealthy Cinque Port which once held its own army yet regularly fell into French hands. Henry James lived here, too, and the oldest working church clock in England chimes in a gracious square at the top of the hill. As for The George, it stands serenely on the cobbled high street. It was built in 1575 from reclaimed ships' timbers and its exposed beams and joists remain on display to this day. A contemporary revamp in classical style trumpets airy interiors, stripped floors, panelled walls and open fires – Jane Austen in the 21st century. There's a huge leather sofa in the bar by the fire, screen prints of The Beatles on the walls in reception, voile curtains and parquet floors in the restaurant. Divine bedrooms come in all shapes and sizes, but fabulous fabrics, Frette linen, flat-screen TVs and Vi-Spring mattresses are standard, as are Aveda soaps by the bath and cashmere covers on hot water bottles. Superb food in the restaurant – seared scallops, Romney Marsh lamb, Seville orange ice cream – can be washed down by local English wines. Exceptional.

Price	£125–£175. Suites £225. Singles from £95.
Rooms	24: 12 doubles, 7 twins/doubles, 5 suites.
Meals	Lunch & dinner £6–£30.
Closed	Never.
Directions	Follow signs up hill into town centre. Through arch; hotel on left, below church. Parking at foot of hill.

Alex & Katie Clarke
98 High Street, Rye, Sussex TN31 7JT

Tel	01797 222114
Fax	01797 224065
Email	stay@thegeorgeinrye.com
Web	www.thegeorgeinrye.com

Jeake's House

Rye, one of the Cinque Ports, is a perfect town for whiling away an afternoon; follow the tidal river, wander past old fishing boats, potter around Church Square, visit a gallery. Jeake's House, on a steep, cobbled street in the heart of it all, has a colourful past as wool store, school and home of American poet Conrad Potter Aiken. Carpeted corridors weave along to cosy bedrooms which come with beams and timber frames. They're generously furnished, excellent value. Some have stunning old chandeliers, others four-posters, one has a telly concealed in the woodburner. A mind-your-head stairway leads up to a generous attic room for views over roof tops and chimneys. The galleried dining room – once an old Baptist chapel, now painted deep red – is full of busts, books, clocks, mirrors and fabric flowers: a fine setting for a full English breakfast. A cosy honesty bar with armchairs, books and papers is a convivial spot for a nightcap, the hearth is lit in winter and musicians will swoon at the working square piano. Jenny, efficient and friendly, has created a lovely atmosphere. *Children over eight welcome.*

Price	£90–£124. Singles £79.
Rooms	11: 7 twins/doubles, 3 four-poster suites, all en suite; 1 double with separate bath.
Meals	Restaurants in Rye.
Closed	Never.
Directions	From centre of Rye on A268, left off High St onto West St, then 1st right into Mermaid St. House on left. Private car park, £3 a day for guests.

Jenny Hadfield
Mermaid Street, Rye, Sussex TN31 7ET

Tel	01797 222828
Fax	01797 222623
Email	stay@jeakeshouse.com
Web	www.jeakeshouse.com

Stone House

One of the bedrooms has a bathroom with enough room for a sofa and two chairs, but does that make it a suite? Jane thought not. The bedroom is also big, has a beautiful four-poster, floods with light and, like all the rooms, has sumptuous furniture and seemingly ancient fabrics. All this is typical of the generosity you find here. Stone House has been in the Dunn family for a mere 500 years and Peter and Jane have kept the feel of home. Downstairs, amid the splendour of the drawing room, there's still space for lots of old family photos; across the hall in the library, logs piled high wait to be tossed on the fire. Weave down a corridor to ancient oak panelling in the dining room for Jane's unbeatable cooking; she's a Master Chef who runs cookery courses that sell out in seconds. She's also a gardener, with a sensational half-acre walled kitchen garden that bursts with fresh produce – they're 99% self-sufficient in summer. There are 1,000 acres to explore and indulgent picnic hampers for Glyndebourne, including chairs and tables, can be arranged. Perfect. *Minimum stay two nights at weekends May-September.*

Travel Club Offer: see page 367 for details.

Price	£135-£255. Singles £110-£135.
Rooms	8: 5 twins/doubles, 2 four-posters, 1 suite.
Meals	Light lunches from May-September. Dinner £28.
Closed	Christmas & New Year.
Directions	From Heathfield, B2096; 4th turning on right, signed Rushlake Green. 2 miles down hill & up into village. 1st left by village green to x-roads; house on far left, signed.

Peter & Jane Dunn
Rushlake Green, Heathfield,
Sussex TN21 9QJ

Tel	01435 830553
Fax	01435 830726
Web	www.stonehousesussex.co.uk

Wingrove House

A lovely house at the end of Alfriston High Street with delightful terraces that give the feel of Provence. A vine runs along an old stone wall, colour bursts from well-kept beds, olive trees shimmer. If the sun shines you can breakfast here with the daily papers, so dig into scrambled eggs and croissants and wash it all down with freshly squeezed juice. This is the last house in a pretty red-brick village; the South Downs Way leads out through wood and field to the cliffs of Beachy Head. If that sounds too energetic, climb up to a lovely first-floor veranda and watch lazily as walkers stride off. Downstairs you find stripped floors and a wood-burner in the bar. In the restaurant, elegant airy interiors give way to the lower terrace where you can eat on warm nights, perhaps pan-fried sweetbreads with toasted brioche, braised blade of beef with mash and green beans, vanilla parfait with a champagne soup. Airy bedrooms are named after wine houses, all found on the wine list. You get good beds, crisp linen, flat-screen TVs and wicker chairs; two open onto the veranda.

Price	£95-£150. Singles from £70.
Rooms	5: 4 doubles, 1 twin.
Meals	Lunch from £10.
	Dinner, 3 courses, about £28.
Closed	Rarely.
Directions	M23, A23, then A27 east from Brighton. Past Berwick, then south at r'about for Alfriston. In village on left.

David & Carry Allcorn
Alfriston, Sussex BN26 5TD

Tel   01323 870276
Fax   01323 871630
Email   info@wingrovehousehotel.com
Web   www.wingrovehousehotel.com

The Griffin Inn

A proper inn, one of the best, a community local that draws a well-heeled and devoted crowd. The occasional touch of scruffiness makes it almost perfect; fancy designers need not apply. The Pullan family run it with huge passion. You get cosy open fires, 400-year-old beams, oak panelling, settles, red carpets, prints on the walls... this inn has aged beautifully. There's a lively bar, a small club room for racing on Saturdays and two cricket teams play in summer. Bedrooms are tremendous value for money and full of uncluttered country-inn elegance: uneven floors, lovely old furniture, soft coloured walls, free-standing Victorian baths, huge shower heads, crisp linen, fluffy bathrobes, handmade soaps. Rooms in the coach house are quieter, those in next-door Griffin House quieter still. Smart seasonal menus include fresh fish from Rye and Fletching lamb. On Sundays in summer they lay on a spit-roast barbecue in the garden, with ten-mile views stretching across Pooh Bear's Ashdown Forest to Sheffield Park. Not to be missed. *Minimum stay two nights bank holiday weekends.*

Price	£85-£145. Singles £60-£80 (Sun-Thur).
Rooms	13: 6 doubles, 7 four-posters.
Meals	Bar lunch & dinner £10-£20. Restaurant £22-£30.
Closed	Christmas Day.
Directions	From East Grinstead, A22 south, right at Nutley for Fletching. On for 2 miles into village.

 Travel Club Offer: see page 367 for details.

Bridget, Nigel & James Pullan
Fletching, Uckfield, Sussex TN22 3SS
Tel   01825 722890
Fax   01825 722810
Email   info@thegriffininn.co.uk
Web   www.thegriffininn.co.uk

Newick Park Hotel

A heavenly country house that thrills at every turn. The setting – 255 acres of parkland, river, lake and gardens – is spectacular; come in winter and you may wake to find a ribbon of mist entangled in a distant ridge of trees. Inside, majestic interiors never fail to elate, be they colour-coded bookshelves in a panelled study, Doric columns in a glittering drawing room or roaring fires in a sofa-strewn hall. You get all the aristocratic fixtures and fittings – grand pianos, plaster mouldings, a bar that sits in an elegant alcove, views from the terrace that run down to a lake. Oils hang on walls, chandeliers dangle above. Country-house bedrooms are the stuff of dreams: lush linen, thick floral fabrics, marble bathrooms with robes and lotions, views to the front of nothing but country; some are the size of a London flat. A two-acre walled garden provides much for the table, so don't miss exceptional food, perhaps foie gras with apple purée, Newick pheasant with chestnut sauce, poached pear with mulled-wine jelly. Peacocks roam outside, Ashdown Forest is close for pooh sticks. *Minimum stay two nights at weekends during Glyndebourne.*

Price	£165-£285. Singles from £125.
Rooms	16 twins/doubles.
Meals	Lunch from £18.50. Dinner around £40.
Closed	31 December-5 January.
Directions	From Newick village turn off the green & follow signs to Newick Park for 1 mile until T-junction. Turn left; after 300 yds, entrance on right.

Michael & Virginia Childs
Newick, Sussex BN8 4SB

Tel	01825 723633
Fax	01825 723969
Email	bookings@newickpark.co.uk
Web	www.newickpark.co.uk

 Travel Club Offer: see page 367 for details.

Burpham Country House

Come for old England in the foothills of the South Downs. Woodpeckers and warblers live in the woods, the church was built in 1167 and when you potter south to Arundel, its magnificent castle looms across the fields. The road runs out in the village and the house stands quietly, with colour tumbling from stone walls and a lawned terrace in front of a Victorian veranda. Originally a Georgian hunting lodge, it served as a vicarage to Tickner Edwardes, the great apiarist, who fought in Gallipoli; John Ruskin knew the house, too. Inside, warmly comfortable interiors are stylish without being style-led. There's an airy sitting-room bar, a panelled restaurant for local food and a brick-and-flint conservatory that opens onto a croquet lawn. Spotless bedrooms are good value for money, some big, some smaller, all with crisp linen, airy colours and flat-screen TVs; most have country views. Collared doves nest in the garden, swans winter on the Arundel wetlands and Alfred the Great extended this ridge 1,200 years ago to defend England from the Vikings. There's cricket in summer, too. *Minimum stay two nights at weekends April-October.*

Price	£80–£140. Singles from £60.
Rooms	10: 6 doubles, 3 twins/doubles, 1 single.
Meals	Lunch from £5 (May-Oct only). Dinner, 3 courses, £20–£25 (not Mon).
Closed	Rarely.
Directions	A27 west from Arundel, past station, then left for Burpham. Straight ahead for 2.5 miles; on left.

 Travel Club Offer: see page 367 for details.

Jacqueline & Steve Penticost
The Street, Burpham, Arundel,
Sussex BN18 9RJ

Tel	01903 882160
Fax	01903 884627
Email	info@burphamcountryhouse.com
Web	www.burphamcountryhouse.com

The Ship Hotel

Admiral Sir George Murray served with Nelson and led the fleet at the Battle of Copenhagen; this grand Georgian townhouse was once his home. The hotel opened in 1939 and Eisenhower came for dinner before D-Day (the menu and guest list is framed on the first-floor landing). More recently, it was rescued from neglect, and a fine furbishment has given Chichester the hotel it deserves. The feel inside is airy and open-plan, while the hall, with its Adam staircase leading up past arches and pillars to a painted ceiling rose, adds a touch of long-lost glamour; at Christmas an enormous tree soars. Downstairs, contemporary interiors shine. Stripped floors in the bar lead past comfy sofas and chattering locals to the brasserie, where fine arched windows look across to Priory Park. Come for fabulous breakfasts, dressed crab at lunch, rib-eye steaks at dinner. Super-comfy bedrooms, all refurbished, have silky curtains, trim carpets, Egyptian cotton, padded headboards. Also: flat-screen TVs, radios, excellent bathrooms. Sand dunes wait at the Witterings. *Minimum stay two nights at weekends.*

Price	£120. Singles £95. Family £155. Suites £175.
Rooms	36: 27 twins/doubles, 5 singles, 2 family, 2 suites.
Meals	Lunch & dinner £5–£25.
Closed	Never.
Directions	A286 south from Midhurst into city. At one-way ring road, straight over (not left); left into North Street. Hotel on left.

Mark Thomas
North Street, Chichester,
Sussex PO10 1NH

Tel	01243 778000
Fax	01243 788000
Email	enquiries@chichester.theplacehotels.co.uk
Web	www.shiphotelchichester.co.uk

The Crab & Lobster

This tiny arrowhead of land south of Chichester is something of a time warp, more 1940s than 21st century. The Crab & Lobster is older still – 350 years at the last count. It sits on Pagham Harbour, a tidal marsh that teems with preening birds. Outside, you find a smart whitewashed exterior and a small garden for dreamy views across grazing fields to the water. Inside, a glittering refurbishment comes in contemporary style with Farrow & Ball colours, flagstone floors, blond wood furniture, suede armchairs and a smouldering fire. Big mirrors reflect the light, candles flicker in the evening. Upstairs, four super rooms come in duck-egg blue with crisp white linen, flat-screen TVs and gorgeous little bathrooms. Three have views of the water, one is up in the eaves and has a telescope to scan the high seas. There's much to explore: Bosham, where King Canute tried to turn back the waves; Fishbourne, for its imperious Roman palace; the Witterings, for sand dunes and miles of beach. Don't forget dinner, perhaps fresh calamari, Barbary duck, marmalade bread and butter pudding. *Minimum stay two nights at weekends.*

Price	£120-£140. Cottage from £180.
Rooms	4 + 1: 4 doubles. 1 cottage for 4.
Meals	Lunch from £5.50. Dinner, 3 courses, about £30.
Closed	Open all day.
Directions	Mill Lane is off B2145 Chichester to Selsey road, just south of Sidlesham. Pub close to Pagham Harbour.

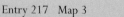 Travel Club Offer: see page 367 for details.

Sam Bakose
Mill Lane, Sidlesham, Chichester,
Sussex PO20 7NB

Tel   01243 641233
Email   enquiries@crab-lobster.co.uk
Web   www.crab-lobster.co.uk

The Royal Oak Inn

There's a cheery wine-bar feel to the Royal Oak; locals and young professionals come with their children and it's all as rural as can be. Inside, a modern-rustic look with traditional touches prevails: stripped floors, exposed brickwork, dark leather sofas, open fires, racing pictures on the walls – the inn was once part of the Goodwood estate. The dining area is big, light and airy, with a conservatory from which you can spill out onto a terrace that's warmed by outdoor lamps on summer nights. Five chefs conjure up delicious salmon and chorizo fishcakes, honey and clove roasted ham, fillet steak. Bedrooms have a contemporary feel. Some are in converted buildings, the rest are at the back of the pub, up the stairs; ask for one with a view. All have CD players, plasma screens, a DVD library and top toiletries – the best of modern – along with excellent lighting, brown leather chairs and big comfy beds. Staff are attentive, breakfasts are good and fresh, a secret garden looks over the South Downs, and you're well-placed for Chichester Theatre and Goodwood.
Minimum stay two nights at weekends.

Price	£90–£180. Singles from £75.
Rooms	8: 4 doubles, 1 twin, 3 cottages.
Meals	Lunch & dinner, à la carte, £12.50–£30.
Closed	Christmas Day & Boxing Day.
Directions	From Chichester A286 for Midhurst. First right at first mini roundabout into E. Lavant. Down hill, pass village green, over bridge, pub 200 yds on left. Car park opposite.

Charles Ullmann
Pook Lane, East Lavant, Chichester,
Sussex PO18 0AX

Tel	01243 527434
Fax	01243 775062
Email	rooms@royaloakeastlavant.co.uk
Web	www.royaloakeastlavant.co.uk

West Stoke House

A sublime country house, an imperious parkland setting, stylish bedrooms that tend to be huge, and a Michelin star in the kitchen – this is some restaurant with rooms. The house dates to 1760 and sits in 14 acres of gardens and paddock that once belonged to the Goodwood estate. These days it's a haven of relaxed informality. An enormous hall doubles as the sitting room, contemporary art adorns the walls, and you eat in the ballroom, where floor-to-ceiling French windows flood the room with light. It's a fittingly grand spot for magnificent food, so come for stuffed saddle of rabbit with a langoustine bisque, slow-braised belly of Sussex pork, then toffee soufflé with banana and lime ice cream. Bedrooms are just as good. Expect high ceilings, old radiators, gilt mirrors, chandeliers. The feel is contemporary with pastel colours to soak up the light. Those at the front have gorgeous views, one has a round bed, all have DVD players, silky curtains, double-ended baths or power showers. Pull yourself away to visit wonderful West Dean; Dali's lobster telephone lives here. *Minimum stay two nights at weekends.*

Price	£140-£215. Singles from £115.
Rooms	8: 7 twins/doubles, 1 suite.
Meals	Lunch £22.50. Dinner, 3 courses, £39.
Closed	Christmas Day & Boxing Day.
Directions	A3 south to Milford, A286 to Lavant. Turn right in Lavant for West Stoke.

 Travel Club Offer: see page 367 for details.

Rowland & Mary Leach
West Stoke, Chichester,
Sussex PO18 9BN

Tel	01243 575226
Fax	01243 574655
Email	info@weststokehouse.co.uk
Web	www.weststokehouse.co.uk

Park House Hotel

Come for the boundless peace of an English country garden. This warm Edwardian house sits in 12 green acres, with croquet on the lawn, a grass tennis court, shrubs and roses in well-kept beds, and a six-hole golf course that slips into the country. Dreamy views from the back shoot off to the South Downs, and there's a swimming pool, too, so snooze in the sun while a tractor works the fields beyond. As for the house, it's as good as the garden: warm, peaceful, utterly spoiling. You get an open fire in the sitting room, flickering candles in the dining room and a snug honesty bar with doors onto the terrace. Super bedrooms come in crisp country style: vintage wallpaper, Farrow & Ball colours, mahogany bedside tables, perhaps a chaise longue in a bay window. The suite has a private terrace and all rooms have lovely touches (good art, fresh flowers, flat-screen TVs). Fancy bathrooms are de rigeur with separate showers and robes. There's an airy conservatory for delicious breakfasts, a terrace for al fresco treats in summer. Walks start from the front door. *Special rates for Goodwood.*

Price	£135–£185. Family £155–£250. Suite/cottage £175–£250.
Rooms	14 + 1: 8 twins/doubles, 4 doubles, 2 family. 1 suite/self-catering cottage.
Meals	Lunch from £5.95. Dinner, 3 courses, £31.95.
Closed	Rarely.
Directions	South from Midhurst on A286. At sharp left bend, right (straight ahead), signed Bepton. On left after 2 miles.

	Rebecca Crowe
	Bepton, Midhurst, Sussex GU29 0JB
Tel	01730 819000
Fax	01730 819099
Email	reservations@parkhousehotel.com
Web	www.parkhousehotel.com

York House Rooms

The South Downs are on your doorstep, but the lures of York House Rooms are legendary, and with two super-stylish suites to hole up in, you may find you don't move very far. The venue for this gentle extravagance is a stone cottage in a peaceful village. Each suite gets half a small house – a sitting room downstairs, a bedroom on the first floor. Expect Farrow & Ball colours, cushioned sofas, DVD players and flat-screen TVs. Vi-Spring beds come wrapped in crisp white linen, there are padded window seats, pillows piled high, fresh flowers, radios and robes in super bathrooms. Felicity and Ian couldn't be kinder and will advise you on where to eat, then book a table. Breakfast is served all over the place – in your suite, in the garden or in the main house if that's what you want; expect platters of fruit, homemade muesli, freshly squeezed orange juice, the full cooked works. There's a fridge in each suite so you can chill your wine or a pub in the village if you want to meet the locals. All this just over an hour from London. Fabulous. *Special rates for Goodwood. Minimum stay two nights at weekends.*

Price	£130-£180. Singles from £100.
Rooms	2 suites.
Meals	Pubs & restaurants nearby.
Closed	Christmas.
Directions	A3 to Hindhead, then A286 south. Down hill approaching Midhurst; left for Tillington & Petworth. Ahead at junction; 1st left at pub; 200 yds on left.

 Travel Club Offer: see page 367 for details.

Felicity & Ian Lock
York House, Easebourne Street,
Easebourne, Midhurst,
Sussex GU29 0AL

Tel   01730 814090
Email   felicity@yorkhouserooms.co.uk
Web   www.yorkhouserooms.co.uk

Fulready Manor

Fulready is majestic, a castle in the fields. It took 12 years to build from 2,000 pieces of hand-cut stone and is designed to last 500 years. It stands in 120 acres of quiet green country, with soothing views at the back over lamb-dotted fields to rippling hills. There's a lake, too, with a rowing boat for excursions to the island. All this you gaze upon dreamily from a glorious drawing room (muralled walls, huge sofas, roaring fire) where mullioned windows from floor to ceiling frame perfect views. Upstairs, bedrooms are just as you'd expect: sublimely decorated. (It helps if your daughter is an interior designer.) Expect Sanderson wallpapers, thick fabrics, mahogany furniture, perhaps an old oak four-poster. One room has tromp l'oeil artwork in the bathroom, another has a sitting room in an en suite turret. Best of all are Michael and Mauveen who pamper you rotten in true B&B fashion with grilled grapefruits and home-laid eggs among myriad breakfast treats. Stratford and Warwick are close and one of Warwickshire's best dining pubs is nearby for tasty dinners.

Price	£110–£150.
Rooms	3: 1 double, 2 four-posters.
Meals	Restaurants within 5 miles.
Closed	Christmas & New Year.
Directions	M40 junc. 11, then A422 west. Left in Pillerton Priors (B4451). Fulready first driveway on left after 0.25 miles.

Michael & Mauveen Spencer
Ettington, Stratford-upon-Avon,
Warwickshire CV37 7PE
Tel   01789 740152
Fax   01789 740247
Email   stay@fulreadymanor.co.uk
Web   www.fulreadymanor.co.uk

 Travel Club Offer: see page 367 for details.

The Howard Arms

The Howard stands on Illmington Green, five miles south of Stratford-upon-Avon; it was built at roughly the same time as Shakespeare wrote *King Lear*. Little has changed since and it's a fabulous country inn, one of the best. All the old fixtures and fittings remain – polished flagstones, heavy beams, mellow stone walls – as logs crackle contentedly on a vast open fire and a blackboard menu scales the wall above. Roast away while you take your pick, then dig into grilled sardines, beef, ale and mustard pie, spicy pear and apple crumble. Elsewhere, you find oils on walls, books on shelves, settles in alcoves, beautiful bay windows. An elegant dining room floods with light, courtesy of fine arched windows that overlook the green. Three gorgeous bedrooms mix period style with modern luxury, but five new rooms are being added behind in warm contemporary style; bathrooms will be fancy. There are maps for walkers, so follow paths through village and field. The church dates back to the 11th century (there are Thompson mice within) and Simon de Montfort owned this land in 1469. *Minimum stay two nights at weekends.*

Price	£130-150. Singles from £90.
Rooms	8: 1 twin, 2 doubles, 5 twins/doubles.
Meals	Lunch from £5.
	Dinner, 3 courses, about £20.
Closed	Christmas Day.
Directions	From Stratford, south on A3400 for 4 miles, right to Wimpstone & Ilmington. Pub in village centre.

Travel Club Offer: see page 367 for details.

Simon Haggon
Lower Green, Ilmington, Stratford-upon-Avon, Warwickshire CV36 4LT

Tel	01608 682226
Fax	01608 682226
Email	info@howardarms.com
Web	www.howardarms.com

Mallory Court Hotel

A super-smart country house which dates to 1910 but looks ancient. It stands in ten acres of formal English gardens with trim lawns, planted beds, a tennis court and sun loungers flanking the pool. Inside, a panelled restaurant, open fires, cavernous sofas, the loveliest staff, a clipped elegance at every turn. Bedrooms in the main house come in grand traditional style. Most are huge, all have big beds dressed in Egyptian cotton, some have bay windows giving views over the grounds or original Art Deco marble bathrooms. One has a muralled ceiling, another has golden wallpaper, all have bowls of fruit, flat-screen TVs and white bathrobes. Simpler rooms in the Knight's Suite have an uncluttered, more contemporary style. A Michelin star in the dining room pulls in the locals and offers rich and irresistible treats, perhaps bisque of shellfish with crab tortellini and Pernod cream, fillet of beef with wild mushrooms and a madeira sauce, and roasted pear with sorbet and a caramel sauce. In summer, you can eat on the terrace by a glorious fig tree with huge views off to distant country.

Price	£185–£255. Suites £325–£385. Singles from £115. Knight's Suite: £145.
Rooms	30: Main house: 6 doubles, 2 twins/doubles, 1 single, 10 suites. Knight's Suite: 6 doubles, 5 twins/doubles.
Meals	Dining room: lunch from £23.50; dinner, 3 courses, £39.50–£55. Brasserie: lunch & dinner £15–£35.
Closed	Never.
Directions	M40 junc. 13; B4087 thro' B. Tachbrook. Right at lights onto A425; on right.

Mark E. Chambers
Harbury Lane, Bishop's Tachbrook,
Leamington Spa, Warwickshire CV33 9QB

Tel	01926 330214
Fax	01926 451714
Email	reception@mallory.co.uk
Web	www.mallory.co.uk

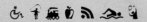

The George

The George began in 1765 and was named after George III, whose granddaughter, Queen Victoria, once stayed. It stands on Shipston's tiny high street, a handsome pile of red bricks. Inside, colour and style shine in equal measure. Airy interiors are easy on the eye and a magnet to locals, who pour in for good food and a lively bar that serves local ales and champagne by the glass (happy hour on Friday is a big hit). The feel is informal, the service is friendly. You get sandblasted beams, stripped floors, cool colours on the walls. There's a sitting room/library with leather armchairs in front of the fire, a private dining room with a jet-black chandelier, a decked terrace for a pint in summer. Colourful bedrooms come with crisp white linen, silky curtains, iPod docks and flat-screen TVs. Some are big, some are smaller, two have fine bay windows, all have super bathrooms (walk-in showers or claw-foot baths). Good food in the restaurant may offer seared scallops, wild sea bass, rhubarb, apple and ginger crumble. You're on the northern flank of the Cotswolds, and Warwick Castle is close. *Minimum stay two nights at weekends.*

Travel Club Offer: see page 367 for details.

Price	£90–£160. Singles from £67.50.
Rooms	15 doubles.
Meals	Bar meals from £4.50. Dinner, 3 courses, £25–£30.
Closed	Never.
Directions	M40 junc. 11, then west on B4035 to Shipston.

Ian Wallace & Ian Fergusson
High Street, Shipston-on-Stour,
Warwickshire CV36 4AJ

Tel	01608 661453
Email	info@thefabulousgeorgehotel.com
Web	www.thefabulousgeorgehotel.com

The Compasses Inn

A 14th-century whitewashed inn, lost down Wiltshire's sleepy lanes. Little has changed in 600 years: flagged floors, stone walls and heavy beams are original; the beams were salvaged from an ancient English naval fleet. Once the haunt of drovers and smugglers, now it's pop stars and famous chefs who jostle with the locals. Duck instinctively into the cosy darkness of this quirky bar to find low ceilings, a roaring fire and small booths divided by rustic cast-offs: a cartwheel here, a stable door there, an old piano at the end of the room. Lanterns glow, the odd pitchfork hangs on the wall and boarded menus entice you with super country cooking, perhaps potted crab, Gressingham duck, and brioche bread and butter pudding. Pretty bedrooms, all above, are a steal. Expect airy interiors, country rugs, wonky ceilings and well-dressed beds. All come with flat-screen TVs and cool little bathrooms, a painted beam here, a window seat there, a French bed. In summer, life spills onto the lawn, flowers tumble from stone troughs. Dogs and children are very welcome. One of the best. *Minimum stay two nights at weekends in summer.*

Price	£85–£90. Singles from £65. Cottage £100–£130.
Rooms	4 + 1: 3 doubles, 1 twin/double. 1 self-catering cottage for 4.
Meals	Lunch from £7.50. À la carte dinner £15–£30.
Closed	25 & 26 December.
Directions	From Salisbury, A30 west, 3rd right after Fovant, signed Lower Chicksgrove, then 1st left down single track lane to village.

Alan & Susie Stoneham
Lower Chicksgrove, Tisbury,
Wiltshire SP3 6NB

Tel	01722 714318
Fax	01722 714318
Email	mail1@thecompassesinn.com
Web	www.thecompassesinn.com

Howard's House

An English village of rare beauty, a wormhole back to the 1700s. The building, Grade-II listed, dates from 1623 and comes with fine gardens, beyond which fields sweep uphill to a ridge of old oak. You can walk straight out, so bring the boots. Inside, find an airy country house with exquisite arched windows, flagstones in reception and the odd beam. Deep sofas, fresh flowers and the morning papers wait in the sitting room, where a fire crackles on cold days and when the sun shines, doors open onto a very pretty terrace; in good weather you can breakfast here. Bedrooms come in country-house style – not overly plush, but more than comfortable – with Laura Ashley wallpaper, mullioned windows, bowls of fruit and a sofa if there's room. Expect padded headboards, floral fabrics, robes in adequate bathrooms. Spin downstairs for dinner – perhaps fillet of sea bass with parsnip purée, Scottish beef with roasted shallots, apple crème caramel with a calvados jelly – then climb back up to find your bed turned down. Salisbury, Stonehenge and the gardens at Stourhead are all close.

Price	£165. Four-poster £185. Singles from £105.
Rooms	9: 6 doubles, 1 twin/double, 1 four-poster, 1 family.
Meals	Lunch £27. Dinner £27.95; à la carte around £45.
Closed	Christmas.
Directions	A30 from Salisbury, B3089 west to Teffont. There, left at sharp right-hand bend, following brown hotel sign. Entrance on right after 0.5 miles.

Noele Thompson
Teffont Evias, Salisbury,
Wiltshire SP3 5RJ

Tel	01722 716392
Fax	01722 716820
Email	enq@howardshousehotel.co.uk
Web	www.howardshousehotel.co.uk

The Lamb at Hindon

The Lamb has been serving ale on Hindon's high street for 800 years, give or take a decade. It is a yard of England's finest cloth, a place where shooting parties come for lunch, where farmers meet to chew the cud. They come for huge oak settles, heavy old beams, deep red walls and roaring fires. A clipped Georgian country elegance lingers; you almost expect Mr Darcy to walk in, give a tormented sigh, then turn on his heels and vanish. You get flagstone floors and stripped wooden boards, window seats and gilded mirrors. Old oils entwined in willow hang on the walls, a bookshelf is stuffed with aged tomes of poetry. At night candles come out, as do some serious whiskies and the odd Cuban cigar, and in the restaurant you can feast on game terrine, Angus rump, then local cheeses. Bedrooms are warm and comfortable, just as they should be, with mahogany furniture, tartan carpets, the odd four-poster, perhaps a sofa. Fishing can be arranged, or you can shoot off to Stonehenge, Stourhead, Salisbury or Bath. Return for a drink on the terrace and watch village life float by.

Price	£99–£135. Singles from £70.
Rooms	14: 6 doubles, 6 twins/doubles, 2 singles.
Meals	Lunch & dinner from £7.50.
Closed	Never.
Directions	M3, A303 & signed left at bottom of steep hill two miles east of junction with A350.

Travel Club Offer: see page 367 for details.

Nathan Evans
High Street, Hindon, Salisbury,
Wiltshire SP3 6DP

Tel	01747 820573
Fax	01747 820605
Email	manager@lambathindon.co.uk
Web	www.lambathindon.co.uk

Entry 228   Map 3

Spread Eagle Inn

Part of the Stourhead estate, the 18th-century inn was built in grand style to accommodate those not deemed worthy of a bed in the big house. More country house than country inn, it stands across the road from the estate's landscaped grounds, a sublime spot to walk off the indulgence of a good lunch. If the exterior is mellow and old-fashioned, then the interior is jaunty, with slate floors and coir matting, Farrow & Ball colours, a wood-burner in a huge inglenook and padded stools at the bar. You can eat here or in the restaurant, which doubles as a sitting room, with red walls, high ceilings and facing sofas in front of the fire. Bedrooms come in traditional style with white linen, the odd antique, Laura Ashley fabrics and delightful views. Bathrooms are not state-of-the-art but perfectly plain – and spotless. Delicious food waits downstairs, perhaps baked camembert, steak and kidney pie, Bramley apple and custard tart. The village is charming – and you can pretend that the stupendous gardens, follies and lake are all yours when the hordes have gone home.

Price	£110. Singles £80.
Rooms	5: 2 doubles, 3 twins/doubles.
Meals	Lunch from £9.95. Dinner, 3 courses, about £25.
Closed	Never.
Directions	Turn off B3092 signed Stourhead Gardens. Spread Eagle is below main car park on left at entrance to garden. Private car park for inn.

 Travel Club Offer: see page 367 for details.

Andrew & Angela Wilson
Stourton, Warminster,
Wiltshire BA12 6QE
Tel   01747 840587
Email   enquiries@spreadeagleinn.com
Web   www.spreadeagleinn.com

The Bath Arms

A 17th-century coaching inn on the Longleat estate in a gorgeous village lost in the country; geese swim in the river, cows laze in the fields and lush woodland wraps around you. At the front the 12 apostles – a dozen pollarded lime trees – shade a gravelled garden, while at the back two large stone terraces, separated by beds of lavender, soak up the sun (you can eat out here in good weather). Inside are the best of old and new: flagstones and boarded floors mix with a stainless steel bar and Farrow & Ball paints. The feel is smart and airy, with a skittle alley that doubles as a sitting room (they show movies here too) and shimmering Cole & Son wallpaper in the dining room. Stop for caramelised onion tart, bavette steak with Lyonnaise potatoes, then Pimms granita. Bedrooms are a real treat, some in the main house, others in a converted barn. Expect lots of colour, big wallpapers, beds dressed in Eygyptian cotton, DVD and CD players; bathrooms come in black slate, some with free-standing baths, others with deluge showers. Longleat is at the bottom of the hill – the walk down is majestic. *Minimum stay two nights at weekends.*

Price	£80–£145. Singles from £60. Lodge £350 (2 nights).
Rooms	15 + 1: 13 doubles, 2 twins. Self-catering lodge for 4.
Meals	Lunch & dinner £5–£30.
Closed	Never.
Directions	A303, then A350 north to Longbridge Deverill. Left for Maiden Bradley; right for Horningsham. Thro' village, on right.

Sara Elston
Longleat Estate, Horningsham,
Warminster, Wiltshire BA12 7LY

Tel   01985 844308
Fax   01985 845187
Email   enquiries@batharms.co.uk
Web   www.batharms.co.uk

The Swan

This graceful town of honey-coloured stone slips downhill to the river Avon, where a 600-year-old bridge spans the water with sublime style. You can pick up riverside paths and follow them eight miles up to Bath, ride your bike, stop at pubs, then hop on a train and come back for supper. The Swan goes back to the 15th century and stands on the main street. Inside, an easy elegance and relaxed informality go hand in hand. Open-plan interiors fill with light, you get stripped boards, flagged floors, high ceilings and country rugs. There's a small terrace for drinks in the sun, a front bar with an open fire and an airy restaurant that fills with locals, so come for great English food – perhaps Devon crab with toast and lemon, fish pie with cheddar mash, lime cheesecake with fresh raspberries. Uncluttered bedrooms are a treat, supremely comfortable with crisp white linen, padded headboards, delicious fabrics and flat-screen TVs. Those at the back on the upper floors overlook the river. All have bold colours on the walls and super little tongue-and-groove bathrooms. *Minimum stay two nights at weekends.*

Price	£95–£140. Singles from £85.
Rooms	12: 8 doubles, 2 twins/doubles, 2 singles.
Meals	Lunch from 4.50. Sunday lunch from £12. Dinner, 3 courses, about £25.
Closed	Never.
Directions	M4 junc. 18, A46 south for Bath. A4 east, A363 south to Bradford. On right in town, car park behind.

 Travel Club Offer: see page 367 for details.

Stephen & Penny Ross
1 Church Street, Bradford-on-Avon,
Wiltshire BA15 1LN

Tel	01225 868686
Fax	01225 868681
Email	theswan-hotel@btconnect.com
Web	www.theswan-hotel.com

The Pear Tree Inn

A super-stylish country inn, a dreamy blend of French inspiration and English whimsy. A cool rustic chic flows effortlessly within. You get all the old favourites: roaring fires, mullioned windows, flagged floors, heavy beams. There are baskets overflowing with logs and smart old rugs on stripped floors in the high-ceilinged restaurant. Wooden scythes, shovels and ladders hang from the walls, candles blaze in the evenings, French windows flood the place with light. In summer, they open up for al fresco suppers on the terrace (there's a boules piste out there, too) so slip down for something tasty, perhaps cauliflower soup with Welsh rarebit, Brixham crab with chive butter, and apple and cinnamon crumble. Exquisite bedrooms come in Farrow & Ball lime white and have suede headboards, wonderfully upholstered armchairs, Bang & Olufsen TVs, funky rugs to add some colour; bathrooms, with robes and creamy tiles, are spoiling. The rooms in the main house are closer to the action than those in the old barn, where sound can travel. Bath is close – head to the spa for some serious pampering.

Price	£120. Family £140.
	Singles £85 (Sun-Thur).
Rooms	8: 6 doubles, 2 family rooms.
Meals	Lunch from £15.
	À la carte dinner about £30.
Closed	Never.
Directions	West from Melksham on A365, then right onto B3353 for Whitley. Through village, then left, signed Purlpit. Pub on right after 400 yards.

Matthew Edwards
Top Lane, Whitley, Melksham,
Wiltshire SN12 8QX

Tel	01225 709131
Fax	01225 702276
Email	peartreeinn@maypolehotels.com
Web	www.maypolehotels.com/peartreeinn

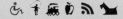

Russell's

A wonderland of beautiful things. First there's Broadway, the prettiest village in the Cotswolds, its golden high street crammed with irresistible shops. Then there's Russell's, bang on the green, a super-stylish restaurant with rooms where locals gather for great food served informally in glittering surrounds. A wall of red wine dominates the inglenook, travertine marble floors brush up against stripped boards, there are sand-blasted beams, exposed stone walls, sun-trapping terraces back and front. Uncluttered bedrooms are simply divine with painted beams, padded bedheads, gorgeous fabrics, excellent bathrooms. You get hi-tech gadgetry, too: flat-screen TVs, DVD players, iPod docks. The four-poster suite is magnificent – a cross-beamed cathedral ceiling, mullioned windows and stone walls – as is its bathroom, where you can soak in front of the telly. Back downstairs, dig into super food (Jay Rayner loved it); there's new season asparagus, sirloin steak with truffle mash, rhubarb mousse and ginger ice cream. Breakfast is just as good: porridge, croissants, the full cooked works. *Minimum stay two nights at weekends.*

Price	£120–£225. Suite £245–£325.
Rooms	7: 3 doubles, 1 twin/double, 2 family, 1 suite.
Meals	Lunch, 2 courses, from £12. Dinner, 3 courses, about £35.
Closed	Rarely.
Directions	A44 from Oxford & Evesham; B4632 from Cheltenham; in centre of Broadway on High Street.

Barry Hancox
The Green, 20 High Street, Broadway,
Worcestershire WR12 7DT

Tel	01386 853555
Fax	01386 853964
Email	info@russellsofbroadway.co.uk
Web	www.russellsofbroadway.co.uk

The Cottage in the Wood

A nine-mile ridge runs above the hotel, where fabulous walks lead through light-dappled trees. There's a terrace for afternoon tea, too, so sip your Earl Grey amid 30-mile views that stretch off to distant Cotswold hills. And while the view is utterly magical, so is this hugely welcoming hotel. The décor is not cutting-edge contemporary, but nor would you want it to be; here is a hotel where old-fashioned values win out. Service is charming, the sort you only get with a passionate family at the helm and a battalion of long-standing staff to back them up. Add to that fabulous food in a restaurant that drinks in the view, and you have a winning combination for those who seek solid comforts rather than fly-by-night fashion. Rooms are split between the main house (simple, traditional), the cottage (cosy low ceilings, warm and snug) and the Pinnacles (hugely pleasing, nice and spacious, super bathrooms, the odd balcony). All have crisp linen and woollen blankets, floral fabrics, flat-screen TVs and DVD players. A pretty garden adds the colour. Wonderful.

Price	£99–£179. Singles £79–£109. Half-board (min. 2 nights) £62–£114 p.p.
Rooms	30: 19 doubles, 9 twins/doubles, 1 four-poster.
Meals	Lunch from £5.45. Sunday lunch £22.95. Dinner, 3 courses, £35–£40. Packed lunch £8.50.
Closed	Never.
Directions	M5 junc. 7; A449 through Gt Malvern. In Malvern Wells, 3rd right after Railway Pub. Signed.

	John & Sue Patin Holywell Road, Malvern Wells, Worcestershire WR14 4LG
Tel	01684 588860
Fax	01684 560662
Email	reception@cottageinthewood.co.uk
Web	www.cottageinthewood.co.uk

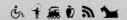

Colwall Park

Jump on a train at Paddington, watch the world pass by; jump off at Colwall and you're 50 paces from the bar. This is the sunny side of the Malvern Hills and paths lead out into blistering country, so walk your socks off then come back for afternoon tea under the old lime tree on the lawn. The hotel was built in 1905 for the owners of Colwall race course. These days it's the players from Malvern Theatre who come; a rogue's gallery of famous faces hangs on a wall. This is a comfortable airy hotel with good prices to match. You find mullioned windows, trim carpets, open fires and fresh flowers. There's a pretty sitting room with cosy sofas and a bar at the front where you can dig into light meals (omelettes, fish pie, local sausages); if you fancy a slap-up dinner, wander into the panelled restaurant and try twice-baked cheese soufflé, roast loin of local venison, pistachio crème brûlée with hot chocolate ice cream. Spotless bedrooms come in pastel colours with padded headboards, good linen and a sofa in the bigger rooms (two are huge). Historic Ledbury town is close. *Minimum stay two nights at weekends.*

Price	£120–£150. Singles £80. Suites £160.
Rooms	22: 17 twins/doubles, 3 singles, 1 suite, 1 family suite.
Meals	Lunch from £7.95. Dinner, à la carte, about £35.
Closed	Rarely.
Directions	M5 junc. 7 or M50 junc. 2. Colwall halfway between Ledbury & Malvern. Colwall Park in centre of village.

 Travel Club Offer: see page 367 for details.

Iain Nesbitt
Colwall, Malvern,
Worcestershire WR13 6QG

Tel	01684 540000
Fax	01684 540847
Email	hotel@colwall.com
Web	www.colwall.co.uk

The Royal Forester Country Inn

The Wyre Forest starts across the road. There are thousands of acres to explore, on foot, on bike, even on horseback; the inn has two stables, so bring your own pony or ride out locally. As for the inn, it looms on the side of the road without attracting much attention, but for those who stop, there's a treat in store. It goes back to 1411, but despite its flagged floors, timber-framed walls and low beamed ceilings, the feel is distinctly contemporary with an open-plan flow. You find stripped floors and sofas in the bar, a bust of Buddha in one of the restaurants and a 1930s photo of the foresters dominating one wall. Super bedrooms upstairs are simply stylish and have extremely attractive prices. You get walls of colour, coir matting, leather beds, crushed velvet throws and flat-screen TVs. And excellent slate bathrooms with coloured glass sinks. Come back down for well-priced bistro-style food, perhaps moules marinières, T-bone steak, and coconut and malibu crème brûlée; there are monthly gourmet nights: three courses, five wines! The River Severn is close. *Minimum stay two nights at weekends.*

Price	£79. Singles £55.
Rooms	7 doubles.
Meals	Lunch from £4.95.
	Dinner, 3 courses, about £25.
Closed	Never.
Directions	West from Kidderminster on A456.
	On left in village.

Sean Mcgahern & Maxine Parker
Callow Hill, Bewdley,
Worcestershire DY14 9XW

Tel	01299 266286
Email	royalforesterinn@btinternet.com
Web	www.royalforesterinn.co.uk

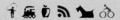

The Weavers Shed Restaurant with Rooms

Sublime simplicity at the top of the hill; the welcome is second to none, the food is some of the best in Yorkshire, and those who make the detour find unbeatable value for money. Wander around outside for a well-kept garden and cobbles in the courtyard, then step inside and discover whitewashed walls, thick stone arches and terracotta-tiled floors. All is bright and breezy – Provence in the Colne Valley! – with menus from around the world framed on the walls. As for the food, Stephen's passion stretches as far as tending a one-acre kitchen garden which supplies most of his needs. You may get duck cooked four ways, calf's liver with a red-onion marmalade, then soufflé of Yorkshire rhubarb with crumble ice cream. Retire to super bedrooms for warm colours, comfy beds, fluffy bathrobes – and pop back down in the morning for a fabulous breakfast: flagons of freshly squeezed orange juice, delicious sausages, homemade marmalades and jams. Take to the glorious Pennines and work off your indulgence or simply climb the hill – *Last of the Summer Wine* is filmed on these streets.

Price	£100–£110. Singles £80–£90.
Rooms	5: 3 doubles, 1 twin/double, 1 four-poster.
Meals	Lunch from £14.95. Dinner, 3 courses, around £45. Restaurant closed Sun/Mon; no lunch Sat.
Closed	Christmas & New Year.
Directions	From Huddersfield A62 west for 2 miles, then right for Milnsbridge & Golcar. Left at Somerfield; signed on right after pub.

Stephen & Tracy Jackson
86–88 Knowl Road, Golcar,
Huddersfield, Yorkshire HD7 4AN

Tel	01484 654284
Fax	01484 650980
Email	info@weaversshed.co.uk
Web	www.weaversshed.co.uk

The Grange Hotel

York Minster is imperious, the oldest Gothic cathedral in northern Europe. It stands less than half a mile from the front door of this extremely comfortable Regency townhouse – a five-minute stroll after bacon and eggs. The streets around it give the feel of Dickensian London and a Roman column stands outside the West Door, but the interior will astound; the Great East Window is the largest piece of medieval stained glass in the world. Back at the hotel, a clipped country-house elegance runs throughout: marble pillars in a flagged entrance hall, an open fire in the panelled morning room and a first-floor drawing room that opens onto a small balcony. Bedrooms come in different shapes and sizes, with smart florals, mahogany dressers, period colours, good bathrooms. Ask for one of the quieter rooms; the more expensive are seriously plush with high beds and swathes of silky curtain. York racecourse brings in a crowd, there are racing prints and murals in a super-smart brasserie, but you can also eat downstairs in the vaulted bar – perhaps baked camembert, grilled bream, apple tarte tatin. *Minimum stay two nights at weekends.*

Price	£130–£198. Four-posters £225. Suite £270. Singles from £117.
Rooms	36: 11 doubles, 18 twins/doubles, 3 four-posters, 3 singles, 1 suite.
Meals	Lunch from £12.50. Dinner, 3 courses, £30–£35.
Closed	Never.
Directions	In centre of town, on A19, 400 yards north of the Minster.

Amie Postings
1 Clifton, York,
Yorkshire YO30 6AA

Tel	01904 644744
Fax	01904 612453
Email	info@grangehotel.co.uk
Web	www.grangehotel.co.uk

The Abbey Inn

Fifty paces from the door, majestic Byland Abbey stands defiant after 900 years. It was one of the first Gothic buildings to rise in the North. Yet in 1536 Henry VIII ordered the dissolution of the monasteries, a fate the abbey could not survive, and over the years locals stripped its roof and looted its stone; still it shines. As for the inn, it dates to 1845 and once served as a farmhouse for the monks of Ampleforth. It's a perfect place with interiors that mix tradition, eccentricity and elegance delightfully. There are busts in alcoves, stone flagged floors, curtains drawn across old doorways, cherubs on the wall. A fire crackles in the bar, the daily papers hang on poles. Bedrooms upstairs sweep you back to long-lost days. Expect beamed ceilings, panelled windows, fancy beds, a sofa if there's room. One has a view straight down the nave, two have ceilings open to the rafters. Breakfast is cooked to order and brought to your room. Downstairs, doors open onto a terrace that gives way to sprawling lawns. Beyond, Wass woods rise, so bring your walking boots.

Price	£95–£165. Suite £199.
Rooms	3: 2 doubles, 1 suite.
Meals	Lunch from £12.50. Dinner, 3 courses, £25–£30. Not Sunday evening, Monday or Tuesday.
Closed	24–26 December, 1 January.
Directions	From A1(M) junc. 49, A168 for Thirsk, then A19 for York. Left for Coxwold after 2 miles. There, left for Byland Abbey. Opposite abbey.

Paul Tatham
Byland Abbey, Coxwold,
Yorkshire YO61 4BD

Tel	01347 868204
Fax	01347 868678
Email	abbeyinn@english-heritage.org.uk
Web	www.bylandabbeyinn.com

Black Swan

The Black Swan stands at the head of Helmsley's square, its three eras of architecture lined up in pristine order: Tudor to the left, Georgian in the middle, Victorian on the right. It stands in the shadow of All Saints Church, thus soundproofing the garden from all but local birds, so come for afternoon tea amid rambling roses and soft stone walls. Inside, timber frames and Farrow & Ball colours rub shoulders with beautifully upholstered sofas and armchairs that wait in front of roaring fires. There's a smart restaurant for sublime food – perhaps ravioli of Whitby crab, Middlewhite pork with apple and vanilla, pear tarte tatin with fromage blanc sorbet – but you'll also find an amazing patisserie at the front. Marco Pierre White and Michel Roux were both smitten, so expect to succumb immediately. Well-priced bedrooms come with neutral colours, beautiful linen, super beds, the usual gadgets; those at the back have garden views. This is the sister hotel to the super-smart Feversham Arms – nip through the churchyard to its magnificent spa and pool and spoil yourself rotten. *Minimum stay two nights at weekends.*

Price	£100–£240. Singles from £80. Half-board £80–£130 p.p.
Rooms	45: 24 doubles, 17 twins, 4 singles.
Meals	Lunch from £5. Dinner, 3 courses, £30–£45.
Closed	Never.
Directions	West from Thirsk on A170 to Helmsley. Hotel at top of square.

Jayne Palliser
Helmsley, Yorkshire YO6 5BJ

Tel	01439 770466
Fax	01439 770174
Email	enquiries@blackswan-helmsley.co.uk
Web	www.blackswan-helmsley.co.uk

Feversham Arms Hotel

Yorkshire may have a slew of grand hotels but you'll be hard pressed to find a more stylish one than this. Simon steered several hotels in the north to prominence and now he's doing it for himself. His 1855 coaching inn seduces the moment you enter. Rich country-house interiors are classically inspired, yet the feel is fresh and contemporary. Wander at will – to find tromp l'oeil wallpaper, huge sofas, wonderful art and fires primed for combustion. There's a snug bar and a sail-shaded conservatory/restaurant, but best of all is a swimming pool courtyard – St Tropez on the Yorkshire Moors. There's a serious spa for just about any treatment you can imagine, while poolside suites circle around with private terraces. Other rooms are equally magical – a night here is a treat wherever you sleep – and a clipped elegance runs throughout; expect fabulous fabrics, beautiful upholstery, perhaps air-blasted beams or a cavernous bath. Beds are turned down, breakfast is brought to your room if that's what you like. Castle Howard is close. Heaven. *Minimum stay two nights at weekends.*

Price	£140-£165. Suites £280-£365. Singles from £130. Half-board from £100 p.p.
Rooms	33: 11 doubles, 22 suites.
Meals	Lunch from £16. Dinner, £35-£45. Tasting menu £47.
Closed	Never.
Directions	West from Thirsk on A170. In Helmsley, left at top of square/car park; hotel on right by church.

Simon Rhatigan
Helmsley, Yorkshire YO62 5AG

Tel	01439 770766
Fax	01439 770346
Email	info@fevershamarmshotel.com
Web	www.fevershamarmshotel.com

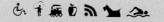

The White Swan Inn

A dreamy old inn that stands on Market Place, where farmers set up shop on the first Thursday of the month. The exterior is 16th century and flower baskets hang from its mellow stone walls. Inside, discover a seriously pretty world: stripped floors, open fires, a tiny bar, beautiful windows. The restaurant is at the back – the heart and soul of the inn – with delicious food flying from the kitchen, perhaps Whitby fishcakes, rack of spring lamb, glazed lemon tart with blood-orange sorbet. Excellent bedrooms are scattered about. Those in the main house have padded bedheads, Egyptian linen, Osborne & Little fabrics and flat-screen TV/DVDs; bathrooms have robes and White Company oils. Rooms in the courtyard tend to be bigger and come in crisp contemporary style with black-and-white screen prints, mohair blankets and York stone bathrooms. You'll also find a cool little residents' sitting room here, with a huge open fire, an honesty bar, a purple pool table and cathedral ceilings. The moors are all around: fabulous walking, Castle Howard and Whitby wait. *Pets £12.50. Minimum stay two nights at weekends.*

Price	£160–£190. Suites £245–£265. Singles from £110.
Rooms	21: 14 doubles, 4 twins/doubles, 3 suites.
Meals	Lunch from £4.95. Dinner, 3 courses, £25–£35.
Closed	Never.
Directions	From North, A170 to Pickering. Entering town, left at traffic lights, then 1st right, Market Place. On left.

Victor & Marion Buchanan
Market Place, Pickering,
Yorkshire YO18 7AA

Tel	01751 472288
Fax	01751 475554
Email	welcome@white-swan.co.uk
Web	www.white-swan.co.uk

Travel Club Offer: see page 367 for details.

Estbek House

A super little find on the Whitby coast. This is a quietly elegant restaurant with rooms ten paces from the beach at Sandsend. It's small, intimate and very welcoming. Tim cooks brilliantly, David pours the drinks and passes on local news. Cliffs rise to the north, the beach runs away to the south, East Beck river passes directly opposite, ducks waddle across the road. There's a terrace at the front for drinks in summer and a small bar on the lower ground; watch Tim at work in his seriously swanky kitchen. Upstairs, two airy dining rooms swim in seaside light and come with stripped floors, painted panelling, old radiators and the odd exposed stone wall, so grab a window seat for watery views and dig into cod fishcakes, duck with slow-roasted figs, Yorkshire rhubarb and stem ginger trifle. Bedrooms above are just the ticket, warmly designed with cast-iron beds, crisp white linen, colourful throws and shuttered windows. Come back down for a delicious breakfast (David's mum makes the marmalade), then walk along cliffs, discover the moors or follow the river upstream to Mulgrave Castle.

Price	£90–£130. Singles from £60.
Rooms	4: 3 doubles, 1 twin.
Meals	Dinner, 3 courses, about £30.
Closed	Occasionally.
Directions	North from Whitby on A174 to Sansend. On left in village by bridge.

David Cross & Tim Lawrence
Eastrow, Sandsend, Whitby,
Yorkshire YO21 3SU

Tel	01947 893424
Fax	01947 893625
Email	info@estbekhouse.co.uk
Web	www.estbekhouse.co.uk

Restaurant with rooms   Yorkshire

The Endeavour

Captain Cook – whose famous ship was built down the road at Whitby – spent his apprenticeship in this fishing village and little has changed since. This quirky restaurant with rooms has squeezed itself into four storeys of an old cottage and you eat surrounded by modern art, with windows looking onto a narrow cobbled street that plunges down towards the harbour. For 2009, the restaurant proper is only open on Fridays and Saturdays (though DBB is available to residents through the week), while twice a month 'catch and cook' courses run for three nights, the idea being that you board a boat, head out to sea, drop in a line and catch your own dinner. After that you then return to the kitchen and learn how to prepare and cook what you've caught before sitting down to eat in style. Finally, retire to comfortable, colourful bedrooms. One looks out to sea, all have local art, and libraries for the telly. Breakfast starts at 9.15am, so lie in, then walk to Cook's museum or round the pretty harbour; waves crash, seagulls screech. Honest, passionate, unpretentious. *Private parking for guests.*

Price	£80-£95. Half-board from £135 per room (min. 2 nights).
Rooms	4 doubles.
Meals	Lunch by arrangement. Dinner £29-£32 (Friday & Saturday only).
Closed	December-April.
Directions	From Whitby, A174 for 8 miles, right for Staithes. Down hill into old village. Parking opposite Staithes art gallery.

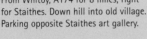

Charlotte Willoughby & Brian Kay
1 High Street, Staithes,
Yorkshire TS13 5BH
Tel   01947 840825
Email   endeavour.restaurant@virgin.net
Web   www.endeavour-restaurant.co.uk

Waterford House

In a lively village dominated by Middleham Castle – northern stronghold of Richard III – is this very pretty Georgian house, now a small hotel. Martin and Anne are exceptional hosts, easy and delightful, their house full of beautiful things. Settle into sofas for drinks and canapés in the cosiest drawing room, then amble across to the red dining room for a memorable meal and ambrosial wines. On summer evenings dine alfresco in the small garden with its summerhouse and trickling stream. Bedrooms, up narrow – in parts steep – stairs, have bags of old-fashioned comfort: wrought-iron beds, William Morris wallpaper, pictures, books, sherry, homemade cakes. The panelled four-poster with blue bedspread and bolsters is a treat. Middleham is a racing village and has 14 stable yards; horses clop by in the morning on their way to the gallops. Breakfast, served on white linen, is a feast of local produce. Linger as long as you like – it's that sort of place – then grab a rod and fish the Ure or pull on your hiking boots and unravel the Dales. Leyburn, for the biggest auction house in the north, is close.

Price	£90–£120. Singles £75–£90.
Rooms	5: 2 doubles, 1 twin/double, 2 four-posters.
Meals	Dinner, 4 courses, £33 (not Sunday).
Closed	Rarely.
Directions	Southbound from A1 at Scotch Corner via Richmond & Leyburn. Northbound from A1 on B6267 via Masham. House in northern corner of square.

Martin Cade & Anne Parkinson Cade
19 Kirkgate, Middleham,
Yorkshire DL8 4PG

Tel	01969 622090
Fax	01969 624020
Email	info@waterfordhousehotel.co.uk
Web	www.waterfordhousehotel.co.uk

The Old Deanery

This mellow pile of golden stone dates back to 1625 and stands in the graceful shadow of Ripon's wonderful cathedral (don't miss the 6th-century crypt). Step in to airy interiors that are full of good things: high ceilings, varnished boards, old oak stairs, a log fire in winter. Fine glass doors sweep you into the bar (leather sofas, beautiful art, painted panelling), beyond which beckons a big restaurant decked out with chandeliers, an original fireplace and fabulous windows. It's all very relaxed and convivial, with locals piling in for sustenance day and night. Most surprising of all is the idyllic garden with its sprawling lawns and curtain of oak and willow; you can eat here serenaded by birdsong in good weather. Spotless bedrooms upstairs are uncluttered, stylish, good value for money. All have comfy beds, pretty linen, lovely bathrooms and views of cathedral or garden. You might find shuttered windows, beams in the eaves, a sparkly four-poster or a slipper bath. Dive down for dinner, perhaps lobster risotto, loin of spring lamb, apple terrine with Granny Smith sorbet. *Minimum stay two nights at weekends.*

Price	£110–£125. Four-posters £150. Half-board from £77.50 p.p.
Rooms	11: 9 doubles, 2 four-posters.
Meals	Lunch from £9.50. Dinner £24.50–£28.50. Sunday lunch from £12.75.
Closed	Rarely.
Directions	From outskirts of Ripon on all sides, follow signs to Cathedral. Hotel to north directly opposite.

Linda & Peter Whitehouse
Minster Road, Ripon,
Yorkshire HG4 1QS

Tel	01765 600003
Fax	01765 600027
Email	reception@theolddeanery.co.uk
Web	www.theolddeanery.co.uk

Entry 246   Map 6

Hob Green

A super country house happily lingering in a quirky past, with a fire smouldering merrily in the hall and ancient wallpaper hanging on the walls. Hob Green is a much-needed antidote to the contemporary world. It sits in absolute peace on an 800-acre estate with exquisite views from the lawned terrace of hill, wood and paddock. Roses climb, birds sing, hanging baskets burst with colour, a huge kitchen garden employs two full-time gardeners, who grow flowers for the house and much of the food that ends up on the table. Inside, the drawing room and dining room both look the right way, there are warm colours, comfortable sofas, open fires and oils on the walls. Bedrooms – all different, all super value for money – are plush without being grand: country-cosy, floral fabrics, white sheets and blankets, new tiles to brighten up bathrooms. Those at the back have gorgeous views. Staff, many long-serving, couldn't be kinder and guests return for the personal touch. Dinner pays little heed to modern trends: devilled kidneys, lemon sole, crème caramel. York and the Dales wait. *Minimum stay two nights at weekends.*

Price	£115–£125. Four-poster £135. Suite £140. Singles from £95. Half-board £80–£95 p.p.
Rooms	12: 4 doubles, 4 twins/doubles, 2 twins, 1 four-poster, 1 suite.
Meals	Lunch from £13.99. Dinner, 3 courses, £27.50. Sunday lunch £21.95.
Closed	Never.
Directions	A61 north from Ripon, then left for Markington in Wormald Green. Straight through Markington; on left.

Christopher Ashby
Markington, Harrowgate,
Yorkshire HG3 3PJ

Tel	01423 770031
Fax	01423 771589
Email	info@hobgreen.com
Web	www.hobgreen.com

Gallon House

A bespoke B&B that clings to the side of an impossibly steep hill with a medieval castle tottering on one side, a grand Victorian railway bridge passing on the other and the serene river sparkling below. Ancient steps lead gently down, you can follow the Nidd into the country or hire a boat and mess about on it. Climb back up to this magical house, where walls of glass bring in the view. There's Lloyd Loom wicker in the small conservatory, an open fire in the panelled sitting room, stripped floors and delicious communal breakfasts in the dining room. Best of all is the sun terrace for one of Yorkshire's best views, with parasols and pots of colour, and deckchairs to take the strain. Bedrooms are warmly stylish, not too big, but spoiling nonetheless, with bathrobes and white towels, crisp linen and soft colours, videos and CD players. Two have the view, two have showers in the actual room. As for dinner, Rick, a chef, is a maestro in the kitchen (Marco Pierre White learnt at his shoulder). So come down for something tasty, perhaps salmon fish cakes, rack of lamb, pear and almond tart. A great little place.

Price	£110. Singles £85.
Rooms	3: 2 doubles, 1 twin.
Meals	Dinner, 3 courses, £27.50, by arrangement.
Closed	Christmas & New Year.
Directions	A1(M) junc. 46, A59 west for 3 miles. Climb hill into Knaresborough. Left into Market Place at Barclays bank; 1st right into Kirkgate; on left.

Sue & Rick Hodgson
47 Kirkgate, Knaresborough,
Yorkshire HG5 8BZ

Tel	01423 862102
Email	gallon-house@ntlworld.com
Web	www.gallon-house.co.uk

The Bijou

Great prices, an easy style and ever-present owners are the hallmarks of this smart B&B hotel close to the centre of town. Outside, a small, manicured garden leads up to a Victorian stone townhouse; inside, a clean contemporary feel runs throughout. Gill and Stephen (he's ex-Hotel du Vin) renovated completely; out with the woodchip and swirly carpets, in with stripped boards and faux-zebra-skin rugs. There's a cool little sitting room with an open fire, a computer for guests to use, and an honesty bar on tap all day. Bedrooms mix leather bedheads, airy colours, Cole & Son wallpaper and orange stools. Excellent bathrooms, most compact, have smart creamy ceramics, you get waffle robes, hot water bottles, flat-screen TVs and double glazing (the house is set back from the road). Two rooms in the coach house are good for small groups. Breakfast is a leisurely feast: freshly squeezed orange juice, eggs and bacon from a local farm, homemade breads and muesli. Don't miss the Stray (the vast common that wraps up the town) or Betty's for afternoon tea. Good restaurants wait, too.

Price	£85–£105. Singles from £75.
Rooms	10: 8 doubles, 2 twins.
Meals	Restaurants within walking distance.
Closed	Never.
Directions	A61 north into town, following signs for Ripon. Past Betty's Teashop, down hill, back up, past Cairn Hotel. Signed on left.

Stephen & Gill Watson
17 Ripon Road, Harrogate,
Yorkshire HG1 2JL

Tel	01423 567974
Fax	01423 566200
Email	info@thebijou.co.uk
Web	www.thebijou.co.uk

The Yorke Arms

An ancient inn on the village green surrounded by nothing but hills and peace. Spin across to the main door and you find a cobbled terrace behind clipped yew hedging, a perfect spot for lunch in summer. Inside, a sublime slice of old England, a country-house dining inn that's been lovingly restored in grand style. You get stone walls, old beams, roaring fires and flagged floors sealed beneath bitumen that are washed and polished every day. The cellars date to the 11th century, the interior design to the 21st. Guests snooze in sofas in the sitting room, a mirrored restaurant floods with light, cricket memorabilia hangs on the wall in the panelled snug. Michelin-starred cooking is a joy: perhaps crispy duck with orange and basil, saddle of venison in a juniper sauce, Grand Marnier and chocolate soufflé. Airy bedrooms are predictably lovely. Expect the best fabrics, gorgeous bathrooms, gilt mirrors, flat-screen TVs, bathrobes and silky curtains. There are home-laid eggs at breakfast and wonderful walking all around.

Price	£180–£240. Singles from £100. Half-board (obligatory on Saturdays) £150–£190 p.p.
Rooms	14: 3 twins/doubles, 7 doubles, 1 four-poster, 3 singles.
Meals	Lunch, 3 courses, from £25. Dinner, 3 courses, about £45. 6-course tasting menu £65 (not Sunday eves).
Closed	Rarely.
Directions	From Ripley, B6165 to Pateley Bridge. Over bridge at bottom of High St; 1st right into Low Wath Road to Ramsgill (4 miles).

Bill & Frances Atkins
Ramsgill-in-Nidderdale, Harrogate,
Yorkshire HG3 5RL

Tel	01423 755243
Fax	01423 755330
Email	enquiries@yorke-arms.co.uk
Web	www.yorke-arms.co.uk

The Red Lion & Manor House at Burnsall

A very pretty village in the middle of the Dales; fells rise all around, there's cricket on the green in summer and the river Wharfe flows past the garden. Family-run and family-friendly, The Red Lion is an inn for all ages, full of old-world charm. Elizabeth still keeps a matriarchal eye on things but her daughters have taken the helm, their husbands by their sides; Robert farms, providing much for the kitchen, Jim and Olivier cook seriously good food. The net result is a cosy, happy, comfortable inn that hums with contented locals. Expect coal fires, books in the sitting room, a good supply of well-kept ales and pink roses rambling across the mellow stone exterior. Bedrooms above aren't huge but have bags of character: low beamed ceilings, big brass beds, fancy compact bathrooms, fluffy white robes. Rooms next door in the Manor House come in sleek contemporary style. Eat under pear blossom on the terrace while walkers pass, following the Dales Way along the river. August's Fell Race — eight minutes up, four minutes down — starts from the front door. *Minimum stay two nights at weekends.*

Price	£130-£150. Singles from £65. Manor House: £82.50-£97.50.
Rooms	25: Red Lion: 7 doubles, 5 twins/doubles, 1 family, 1 single. Manor House: 11 twins/doubles.
Meals	Brasserie lunch & dinner from £7.50. Dinner in restaurant about £30.
Closed	Never.
Directions	From Harrogate, A59 west to Bolton Bridge; B6160 to Burnsall. Hotel next to bridge.

Elizabeth & Andrew Grayshon
Burnsall, Skipton, Yorkshire BD23 6BU

Tel	01756 720204
Fax	01756 720292
Email	redlion@daelnet.co.uk
Web	www.redlion.co.uk

The Devonshire Fell

You're high on the hill with huge views of Wharfdale: mountains rise, the river roars and in summer you can watch the cricket team toil on the pitch below. Up at this rather cool hotel there's a plant-festooned terrace and a trim lawn for sunbathing (people do). Inside, funky interiors are the order of the day. A lilac bar comes with halogen lighting and leather sofas; wander on and find stripped floors, Designers Guild fabrics and a wood-burner to keep you warm. There's a sense of space, too, with one room flowing into another, the bar, bistro and conservatory united by an open-plan feel. Bedrooms upstairs are equally flamboyant, those at the front with stupendous views. Expect lots of colour, padded bedheads and beautiful upholstery. You get big TVs, DVD players, iPod docks, a sofa if there's room; tongue-and-groove bathrooms come with robes and fluffy towels. Back downstairs, delicious food is served informally in the bistro, perhaps twice-baked cheese soufflé, roast rump of lamb, sticky toffee pudding. There are movie nights, the odd game of poker; the walking is heavenly.

Price	£145–£192. Suites £215. Singles from £110. Half-board from £97.50 p.p.
Rooms	12: 6 doubles, 4 twins, 2 suites.
Meals	Lunch & dinner £5–£30.
Closed	Never.
Directions	From Harrogate, A59 west for 15 miles, then right onto B6160, signed Burnsall & Bolton Abbey. Hotel in village.

	Stephane Leyreloup
	Burnsall, Yorkshire BD23 6BT
Tel	01756 729000
Fax	01756 729009
Email	res@devonshirehotels.co.uk
Web	www.devonshirefell.com

The Devonshire Arms

It is quite impossible to do justice to this fabulous hotel in the space allotted below, so take it as read that this is one of the loveliest places to stay in the country, and with a level of service that surpasses most others. Follow your nose and find everything you'd hope to see in a hotel. Fires roar, staff swoop on luggage, old beams hang overhead, there's a piano in the cocktail bar, a sitting room that welcomes dogs, a dining room for serious food and a conservatory for sunny breakfasts. Across the road is a pool in the spa – and a small kitchen garden with a bench by the stream, a great place to hide away in summer. Beautiful gardens abound, but if you want to walk, follow the Dales Way past Bolton Abbey up to Burnsall. Country-house bedrooms are predictably sublime, some with high four-posters, others with magnificent bathrooms. All come with robes, gadgets and the crispest linen. Eat like a king in the restaurant, perhaps braised pork belly, sea bass with artichokes, chocolate mayhem; if you want something simpler, the whitewashed brasserie will deliver. *Minimum stay two nights at weekends.*

Travel Club Offer: see page 367 for details.

Price	£225-£315. Four-posters £320-£370. Suites £410. Half-board from £135 p.p.
Rooms	40: 23 doubles, 8 twins/doubles, 7 four-posters, 2 suites.
Meals	Lunch £35. Dinner £58. Tasting menu £65. Gourmand menu £75 (not Monday night). Lunch & dinner in brasserie £5-£30.
Closed	Never.
Directions	A59 to Bolton Bridge, then north for Bolton Abbey on B6160. Hotel on right in village.

Brian van Ousten
Bolton Abbey, Skipton,
Yorkshire BD23 6AJ

Tel   01756 710441
Fax   01756 710564
Email   res@devonshirehotels.co.uk
Web   www.thedevonshirearms.co.uk

The Angel Inn

The Angel has it all – a perfect English inn. It stands in the middle of a tiny hamlet surrounded by lush grazing land with Rylstone Fell rising behind. You can drop by for a pint of Black Sheep in the half-panelled bar, pop a bottle of champagne on the flower-festooned terrace or seek out the restaurant for a fabulous meal. All the ancient trimmings are here – mullioned windows, beamed ceilings, exposed stone walls, a working Yorkshire range – yet the feel is bright and breezy, especially in the dining rooms, of which there are several to satisfy the legions of fans who come for Bruce Elsworth's delicious concoctions (smoked local trout with horseradish mousse, Yorkshire beef with truffle sauce, cinnamon brioche perdue with deep-fried ice cream). Juliet's son runs a wine cave over the road, above which you find exquisite bedrooms, the lap of luxury. All are different, you may get a French armoire, a brass bed, a claw-foot bath. One is partly muralled, another has an icon in an alcove. Expect the best fabrics, pretty colours, flat-screen TVs. Jazz bands play at summer barbecues. Wonderful.

Price	£130–£155. Suites £155–£180.
Rooms	5: 2 doubles, 3 suites.
Meals	Bar meals from £9.50. Sunday lunch £24. À la carte dinner about £25.
Closed	Christmas Day.
Directions	North from Skipton on B6265. Left at Rylstone for Hetton. In village.

Juliet Watkins
Hetton, Skipton,
Yorkshire BD23 6LT
Tel   01756 730263
Fax   01756 730363
Email   info@angelhetton.co.uk
Web   www.angelhetton.co.uk

Travel Club Offer: see page 367 for details.

The Tempest Arms

A 16th-century ale house three miles west of Skipton with great prices, friendly staff and an easy style. Inside you find stone walls and open fires, six ales on tap at the bar and a smart beamed restaurant. An airy open-plan feel runs throughout with sofas and armchairs strategically placed in front of a fire that burns on both sides. Delicious traditional food is a big draw – the inn was packed for lunch on a Tuesday in April. You can eat wherever you want, so grab a seat and dig into Yorkshire puddings with a rich onion gravy, cottage pie with a Wensleydale crust, treacle tart with pink grapefruit sorbet. Bedrooms are just as good. Those in the main house are slightly simpler, but most are ten paces beyond in two newly built stone houses and they're rather indulging. You get crisp linen, neutral colours, slate bathrooms and flat-screen TVs. Those at the back have views of the fells, suites are large and worth the money, a couple have decks with hot tubs to soak in. The Dales are on your doorstep, this is a great base for walkers. Skipton, a proper Yorkshire market town, is worth a look.

Price	£80. Suites £95-£110.
	Singles from £60.
Rooms	21: 9 twins/doubles, 12 suites.
Meals	Lunch & dinner £5-£25.
Closed	Never.
Directions	A56 west from Skipton.
	Signed left after two miles.

Martin & Veronica Clarkson
Elslack, Skipton, Yorkshire BD23 3AY
Tel   01282 842450
Fax   01282 843331
Email   info@tempestarms.co.uk
Web   www.tempestarms.co.uk

The Austwick Traddock

Friendly, unpretentious and full of traditional comforts, this family-run hotel is a terrific base for walkers – the Three Peaks are at the door. The house is Georgian with Victorian additions and its name originates from horse sales that took place in next door's paddock. Open fires smoulder on winter days, deckchairs dot the garden in summer. Country-house bedrooms have bags of charm: antique dressing tables, quilted beds, perhaps a bergère headboard or a claw-foot bath. Those on the second floor have a cosy attic feel, all have fresh fruit, flat-screen TVs, homemade shortbread and Dales views. You eat in the first hotel restaurant in the north of England to be certified 100% organic by the Soil Association, so dig into seared scallops, wild venison, lemon soufflé with a Yorkshire curd sorbet. There's a cheerful William Morris feel to it all – polished brass in front of the fire, a panelled breakfast room, beds of lavender in the garden – and the village, with two clapper bridges, is a gem. Don't miss the caves at Ingleborough, or Settle for antiques.
Minimum stay two nights at weekends May-September.

Price	£140-£180. Singles £80-£100. Half-board from £85 p.p.
Rooms	10: 7 doubles, 1 twin/double, 1 family, 1 single.
Meals	Lunch £13-£20. Dinner, 3 courses, about £35.
Closed	Rarely.
Directions	0.75 miles off the A65, midway between Kirkby Lonsdale & Skipton, 4 miles north-west of Settle.

Bruce Reynolds
Austwick, Settle, Yorkshire LA2 8BY

Tel	01524 251224
Fax	01524 251796
Email	info@austwicktraddock.co.uk
Web	www.austwicktraddock.co.uk

Ethical Collection: Community; Food.
See page 373 for details

Austwick Hall

This grand old manor house has a Tudor door, a Georgian porch and may have started life as a 12th-century pele tower. Today it is either a grand B&B or a small, intimate hotel. Whatever it is, it's rather lovely, with 12 acres of mature woodland, terraced gardens and herbaceous borders occasionally open to the public. You enter a delightful hall: seven rugs on a flagstone floor, a couple of sofas in front of the wood-burner, a vase of flowers on a rosewood table, a butterfly staircase that leads to rather grand rooms. There's lots of colour, exceptional art and a half-panelled dining room where you may feast on wild rocket soufflé, chilled watercress soup, local venison with red wine and blackcurrants, brandy parfait with Earl Grey syrup. Bedrooms are either big or huge, the simplest quite divine, with a golden four-poster and garden views. One is enormous, as is its bathroom (large sofa, claw-foot bath); another has a crowned half-tester with rugs on stripped floors. All have robes, flat-screen TVs and gorgeous linen. The Dales are on your doorstep, Settle is close for antiques. *Minimum stay two nights at weekends.*

Price	£95–£125. Suite £155.
Rooms	4: 2 doubles, 1 four-poster, 1 suite.
Meals	Dinner, 5 courses, £30. By arrangement.
Closed	Never.
Directions	1 mile off A65, midway between Kendal & Skipton. Follow sign for Austwick, through village. House on left halfway up hill towards the moors (marked 'No Through Road').

 Travel Club Offer: see page 367 for details.

Michael Pearson & Eric Culley
Austwick, Settle, Yorkshire LA2 8BS
Tel   01524 251794
Email   austwickhall@austwick.org
Web   www.austwickhall.co.uk

White House Hotel

A coastal path rings idyllic Herm; you'll find high cliffs to the south, sandy beaches to the north and cattle grazing in the hills between. You get fabulous views at every turn – shimmering islands, pristine waters, yachts and ferries zipping about – while the pace of life is wonderfully lazy, so stop at the grocery store, gather a picnic, find a meadow and bask in the sun. There are beach cafés, succulent gardens, an ancient church, even a tavern. Herm's owners are eminently benign; Pennie was born here, Adrian migrated from Guernsey, together they've kept things blissfully simple: no cars, no TVs, just an old-fashioned England that kids love (the self-catering cottages are extremely popular with families). As for the hotel, it's exceptionally comfortable with one toe lingering in an elegant past; come for open fires, delicious four-course dinners, a tennis court with watery views and a pool to keep you cool. Bedrooms are scattered around, some in the village's colour-washed cottages, others with balconies in the hotel. Expect warm colours, padded headboards, and spotless bathrooms.

Price	Half-board £80–£120 p.p.
Rooms	40: 12 twins/doubles, 5 family rooms. Cottages (some self-catering): 16 twins/doubles, 5 family rooms, 2 singles.
Meals	Half-board only. Lunch from £7. Dinner for non-residents, £25.
Closed	5 October–29 March.
Directions	Via Guernsey. Trident ferries leave from the harbour at St Peter Port 8 times a day in summer (£9.50 return).

Adrian & Pennie Heyworth
Herm, Channel Islands GY1 3HR

Tel	01481 722159
Fax	01481 710066
Email	hotel@herm-island.com
Web	www.herm-island.com

Wales

Neuadd Lwyd

Tudor kings came from this village, their forefathers buried in the tiny church that stands beyond the garden gate. Six sublime acres wrap around you, sheep graze in the fields, views shoot off to a distant Snowdon. The house, an 1871 rectory cloaked in wisteria, has been refurbished in lavish style and smart Victorian interiors shine. The drawing room floods with morning light, has deep sofas, polished wood floors, loads of books and a crackling fire; French windows open onto the south-facing terrace for sunny afternoons. High-ceilinged bedrooms are immaculate and full of beautiful things: cut-glass Venetian mirrors, ornate marble fireplaces, beautifully upholstered armchairs, Provençal eiderdowns; the two front rooms have slipper baths. Best of all is the cooking. Susannah trained at Ballymaloe and whatever can be is homemade; delicious breads, fabulous oat cakes, jams, compotes, sorbets, ice creams. You may get Gorau Glas cheese soufflé, rack of Anglesey lamb with minted pea purée, warm pear and frangipane tarte, a plate of Welsh cheeses. Coastal paths will help you atone.

Price	£120–£190. Singles £100–£170. Half-board from £97.50 p.p.
Rooms	4: 3 doubles, 1 twin.
Meals	Dinner, 4 courses, £37–£50.
Closed	Sundays, Mondays & Tuesdays.
Directions	A55 north over Britannia Bridge. 2nd exit (A5025) for Amlwch, then left for Llangefni (B5420). After 2 miles, right signed St Gredifael's Church. 1 mile up lane; on right.

 Travel Club Offer: see page 367 for details.

Susannah & Peter Woods
Penmynydd, Anglesey LL61 5BX

Tel	01248 715005
Fax	01248 715005
Email	post@neuaddlwyd.co.uk
Web	www.neuaddlwyd.co.uk

Jolyon's Boutique Hotel

Down in Butetown, the captain's house stands on Cardiff Bay's oldest residential street. Bang opposite, the regenerated docks are home to the Welsh Assembly, the Norwegian Church and the Millennium Centre. At Jolyon's, a boutique B&B hotel run in the Mediterranean style, you get quietly groovy interiors. Bedrooms start on the ground floor and work their way skywards to the one at the top with a private roof terrace. The higher you go, the better the view. In the basement is a bar made from reclaimed 1840 timbers encased in stainless steel; stop for an espresso, a trappist beer or a glass of pear and strawberry cider. An old harmonium rests against an exposed stone wall; sink into red leather sofas and gaze at contemporary art. Spotless bedrooms aren't huge, but nor are they small, and light floods in so none feel cramped. You find Moroccan lanterns, French armoires, Dutch marble, Canadian oak, Indian teak, Philippe Starck loos in airy bathrooms (you can watch TV while you soak in a couple). Drop down to the bar for fresh pizzas cooked on a log fire every night. Dr Who is filmed locally. Perfect.

Price	£89–£150.
Rooms	8: 6 doubles, 2 twins.
Meals	From £5.50.
Closed	Never.
Directions	M4 junc. 29, then A48(M) for Cardiff. Take exit marked 'Docks and Bay'. Straight ahead, past Millenium Centre & 1st left.

	Jolyon Joseph
	5 Bute Crescent, Cardiff CF10 5AN
Tel	02920 488775
Fax	02920 488775
Email	info@jolyons.co.uk
Web	www.jolyons.co.uk

Travel Club Offer: see page 367 for details.

Hurst House on the Marsh

As you roll down the hill and glide across the marshes you may well overlook the whitewashed farmhouse that looms splendidly to your left. You may wonder where the fancy hotel is, or step out of your car to behold the vast sky that has suddenly appeared above you. But, when you find no other building to call at, you will return to the farmhouse, and smile. Inside, beyond the exquisitely understated exterior, is a pleasure dome of colour and style that does nothing but elate. Expect a close approximation to perfection, a 21st-century canvas in a 17th-century frame. Fires roar, stone glistens, a statue of Buddha sits in an alcove, beautifully upholstered armchairs wait in a glass bar. Bedrooms – many in renovated outbuildings that form an almost monastic courtyard – are an A-Z of luxury, with Frette linen, Bang & Olufsen media centres, Jocelyn Warner wallpaper and Farrow & Ball colours. There's a cinema, a pool and a jacuzzi with a view, but stretch your legs across the marshes and find miles of sand and a woodland path that leads up to Dylan Thomas's boat house on the estuary. Magnificent.

Price	£265-£285.
	Cottage & penthouse £350.
Rooms	18: 16 suites, 1 penthouse, 1 cottage.
Meals	Lunch from £12.95.
	Dinner, 3 courses, £32.95.
Closed	Never.
Directions	South from St Clears on A4066 for Pendine. Through villages of Laugharne & Broadway, then signed left after 0.5 miles. Down hill and onto marshes and left again, signed.

Matt Roberts
East Marsh, Laugharne,
Carmarthenshire SA33 4RS

Tel	01994 427417
Fax	01994 427840
Email	reservations@hurst-house.co.uk
Web	www.hurst-house.co.uk

Harbourmaster Aberaeron

The harbour at Aberaeron was created by an Act of Parliament in 1807. Shipbuilding flourished and the harbourmaster got his house on the quay with big views over Cardigan Bay. Step in to find that winning combination of seductive good looks, informal but attentive service and a menu overflowing with fresh local produce. The airy open-plan dining room/bar has stripped floors and a horseshoe bar for good beers and wines, with harbour views looming through the windows. Wind up the staircase to super little bedrooms that come with shuttered windows, loads of colour and quietly funky bathrooms. You get Frette linen, Welsh wool blankets and a hot water bottle on every bed in winter. There are flat-screen TVs and DVD players, watery views and tide books. Come down for supper and try fishcakes with lime mayonnaise, rack of lamb with sweet potato chips, and poached pear with honey ice cream. There are bikes to borrow, cycle tracks that spin off into the hills, coastal paths lead north and south. Sunsets are fabulous, too. *Minimum stay two nights at weekends.*

Price	£110–£190. Suite £190–£250.
	Singles £65. Half-board from £80 p.p.
Rooms	13: 11 doubles, 2 singles.
Meals	Lunch from £10.50.
	Dinner, 3 courses, around £30.
Closed	Christmas Day.
Directions	A487 south from Aberystwyth.
	In Aberaeron, right, for the harbour.
	Hotel on waterfront.

Glyn & Menna Heulyn
Pen Cei, Aberaeron,
Ceredigion SA46 0BA

Tel	01545 570755
Email	info@harbour-master.com
Web	www.harbour-master.com

Gwesty Cymru Hotel & Restaurant

A seafront gem, newly refurbished, with magnificent bathrooms that take some beating. Beth and Huw worked for the BBC in Cardiff before upping sticks to renovate this terraced house that overlooks the bay, the pier and Constitution Hill (train up, stroll down). Inside, white walls, Welsh art and Blaenau slate combine to give a fresh contemporary feel. There's a mirrored bar and a cool little restaurant, which was packed for lunch in early March. A big window brings in the light, a glass door leads onto the terrace. Bedrooms are warmly stylish and very good value for money, so splash out on those at the front: leather armchairs face out to sea, giving box seats for imperious sunsets. You also get handmade European oak furniture, crisp white linen, piles of pillows and silky bed throws that match the colour of the art. Bathrooms are magnificent. Expect Italian stone, enormous power showers, double-ended baths (two overlook the bay) and towelling bathrobes. Pop down for dinner and try the best of Wales, perhaps roasted mushrooms, cannon of valley lamb, espresso panna cotta.

Price	£85–£105. Suite £115. Singles from £65.
Rooms	8: 4 doubles, 3 twins/doubles, 1 single.
Meals	Lunch from £7. Dinner, 3 courses, about £30.
Closed	Never.
Directions	On sea front in town close to pier. On-street parking only.

Huw & Beth Roberts
19 Marine Terrace, Aberystwyth,
Ceredigion SY23 2AZ
Tel   01970 612252
Fax   01970 623348
Email   info@gwestycymru.com
Web   www.gwestycymru.com

The Kinmel Arms

The Kinmel Arms stands halfway up a hill, yards from the gates of the estate it once served. These days it's thrown off its bonds and basks in a new-found freedom. Better still, it's remained in local hands. Lovely Lynn grew up in the village and returned with Tim to transform the old place into a sparkling restaurant with rooms. The results are delightful. Outside, the scent of woodsmoke hangs in the air; inside, the wood-burner pumps out the heat. It's warmly stylish with leather sofas, a solid slate bar, stripped wood floors and palms in the conservatory. Walls are covered with Tim's excellent art, there are local ales, wines by the glass and food to keep you smiling, perhaps Menai mussels, Welsh lamb, a plate of Snowdonia cheeses. Bedrooms are divine, all hidden away, thus quiet and private. Expect huge beds, gorgeous linen, warm yellows, the very best bathrooms. There are flat-screen TVs with DVD players, sofas to sink into and hidden kitchens, where a continental breakfast is left the night before; your lie-in is assured. Great walks start from the front door.

Price	£135–£175.
Rooms	4 suites.
Meals	Continental breakfast only. Lunch from £6.95. Dinner, 3 courses, about £30.
Closed	Sundays & Mondays.
Directions	A55, junc. 24A from Chester; left; 0.25 miles to top of Primrose Hill.

Tim Watson & Lynn Cunnah-Watson
The Village, St George, Abergele,
Conwy LL22 9BP

Tel	01745 832207
Fax	01745 822044
Email	info@thekinmelarms.co.uk
Web	www.thekinmelarms.co.uk

Entry 264 Map 5

Escape Boutique B&B

Llandudno is a holiday town, built by Victorians as a place to take the air. It is the Welsh equivalent of Brighton and Bill Bryson loved it – the unspoilt front with its bright white hotels, the two-mile beach and its 1878 pier, the bustling shops and restaurants behind. Away from the crowds (but not the seagulls!), Escape stands high on the hill with its ornate carved fireplaces, stained-glass windows and wrought-iron veranda still intact. Not that you should expect Victoriana. Interiors have been transformed into a contemporary world of wooden floors, neutral colours, Italian leather and glass chandeliers. Bedrooms – some big, some smaller – come with pillow-top mattresses, goose-down duvets, crisp linen and Farrow & Ball colours. Those at the front have views over the town, but all have buckets of style and good little bathrooms (one has a roll-top tub). Also: flat-screen TVs, DVD players and a PlayStation if you ask for it. There's an honesty bar and an open fire in the sitting room, while breakfast is a feast: Java coffee, the full Welsh works. *Minimum stay two nights at weekends.*

Price	£85–£125.
Rooms	9: 8 doubles, 1 twin/double.
Meals	Restaurants & pubs within walking distance.
Closed	23-27 December.
Directions	A55, junc. 19, then A470 for Llandudno. On promenade, head west hugging the coast, then left at Belmont Hotel and house on right.

Sam Nayar
48 Church Walks, Llandudno,
Conwy LL30 2HL

Tel	01492 877776
Fax	01492 878777
Email	info@escapebandb.co.uk
Web	www.escapebandb.co.uk

The Lion Inn

A simple inn lost in the hills of North Wales. You are more likely to hear birdsong, bleating sheep or a rumbling tractor than a car. The village was the setting for the first Cadfael novel, which is partly based on fact; St Winifred was buried at the priory here. In summer you can sit at colourful tables on the pavement and watch buzzards circle high in the sky, in winter you can sip your pint by a fire that burns on both sides in the bar. Downstairs, there are blue carpets and sprigs of hawthorn decorate stone walls. Upstairs, bedrooms are an unexpected tonic, warm and cosy, nicely stylish, super value for money. There are Farrow & Ball paints on old stone walls and Canadian pitch pine furniture, rustic wooden beds with crisp white linen and Welsh wool blankets, spotless bathrooms, flat-screen TVs and DVD players too. Big breakfasts set you up for the day – porridge, croissants, free-range eggs – so burn off the excess on Snowdon or ride your bike through local forests. The mobile library passes once a month. Portmerion and Anglesey are both close. *Minimum stay two nights at weekends.*

Price	£79. Singles from £49. Family from £91.
Rooms	5: 2 doubles, 1 twin, 1 single, 1 family room.
Meals	Packed lunches £5. Dinner, 3 courses, about £20.
Closed	Christmas Day.
Directions	A55 to Abergele; A544 south to Llansannan; B5384 west to Gwytherin. In village.

Dai Richardson & Rose James
Gwytherin, Betws-y-Coed,
Conwy LL22 8UU

Tel	01745 860123
Fax	01745 860556
Email	info@thelioninn.net
Web	www.thelioninn.net

Travel Club Offer: see page 367 for details.

Manorhaus

It's a little like rural France here – an old country town that climbs a hill with a sea of lush country all around. Wash up at Manorhaus and you discover a perfect little townhouse retreat. It's Georgian on the outside, distinctly groovy within, the hotel doubling as a gallery with fine contemporary art on every wall; it's all for sale and each bedroom shows the work of a different artist. Downstairs: a sitting room in white and blue, a restaurant with stripped wood floors and a small cinema in the Tudor basement. Upstairs you find a library for books, maps, CDs, DVDs, then a sauna and steam room to help you recover after a day in the hills. Keep going and you come to a sweep of funky bedrooms. Some are bigger than others but all have super bathrooms, oodles of character and style and king-size beds with crisp white linen and goose-down bedding. One has a freestanding bath, another has huge views off to a distant ridge. Delicious food is fresh and local: Menai mussels, Welsh beef, warm treacle tart. Mountain biking can be arranged, Offa's Dyke is close for walkers. *Minimum stay two nights at weekends.*

Price	£95–£125. Suite £150. Half-board £72.50–£95 p.p.
Rooms	8: 7 doubles, 1 suite.
Meals	Dinner, 3 courses, about £27.50.
Closed	24–30 December.
Directions	M56; A55; A494 to Ruthin. Follow signs to town centre, up hill; Well Street on left when entering square.

 Travel Club Offer: see page 367 for details.

Christopher Frost & Gavin Harris
Well Street, Ruthin,
Denbighshire LL15 1AH
Tel   01824 704830
Fax   01824 707333
Email   cjf@manorhaus.com
Web   www.manorhaus.com

Tyddyn Llan

A small pocket of heaven blissfully lost in imperious country. Everything here is a treat – house, staff, garden and bedrooms – but best of all is Bryan's food, which draws a devoted crowd. The house stands in three acres of formal gardens, with banks of daffodils in spring and huge views of field and mountain all around. Inside, warm country-house interiors abound. There's a cavernous sitting room with a roaring fire, eccentric collections of menus and matchboxes framed in the bar and a wisteria-entwined veranda, where you can dine in good weather. Ambrosial delights await in the candlelit restaurant, so take to the hills and earn your indulgence, then tumble back down and dig into smoked salmon terrine with horseradish cream, Gressingham duck with cider and apples, grilled pineapple with chilli syrup and coconut sorbet; breakfast is equally sinful. Bedrooms are lovely, some are seriously swanky, and even the simpler rooms elate, so don't feel you have to splash out. Bala, Snowdon and the coast all close; stay for a week and explore this magical land.

Price	£110–£200. Suite £260. Half-board from £100 p.p.
Rooms	12: 8 doubles, 3 twins, 1 suite.
Meals	Lunch (Fri & Sat) £21–£28. Dinner £38–£45. Tasting menu £65. Sunday lunch £27.
Closed	Occasionally.
Directions	From A5 west of Corwen, left on B4401 to Llandrillo. Go through village, entrance signed right after tight bend.

Bryan & Susan Webb
Llandrillo, Corwen,
Denbighshire LL21 0ST

Tel	01490 440264
Fax	01490 440414
Email	tyddynllan@compuserve.com
Web	www.tyddynllan.co.uk

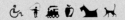

The Hand at Llanarmon

Single-track lanes plunge you into the middle of nowhere. Lush valleys rise and fall, so pull on your boots and scale a mountain or find a river and jump into a canoe. Back at The Hand, a 16th-century drovers' inn, the pleasures of a country local are hard to miss. A coal fire burns on the range in reception, a wood fire crackles under brass in the front bar and a wood-burner warms the lofty dining room. Expect exposed stone walls, low beamed ceilings, old pine settles and candles on the mantelpiece. There's a games room for darts and pool, a quiet sitting room for maps and books. Delicious food is popular with locals, so grab a table and enjoy seasonal menus – perhaps game broth, lamb casserole, and orange and coriander sponge served warm with a cointreau syrup. Bedrooms are just as they should be: not too fancy, cosy and warm, spotlessly clean and with crisp white linen. A very friendly place. Martin and Gaynor are full of quiet enthusiasm and have made their home warmly welcoming. John Ceiriog Hughes, the Welsh Shakespeare, came from these hills. Special indeed.

Price	£80–£120. Singles from from £40.
Rooms	13: 8 doubles, 4 twins, 1 suite.
Meals	Lunch from £6. Sunday lunch £20. Dinner £10–£30.
Closed	24–26 December.
Directions	Leave A5 south of Chirk for B4500. Llanarmon 11 miles on.

Gaynor & Martin De Luchi
Llanarmon Dyffryn Ceiriog, Llangollen,
Denbighshire LL20 7LD

Tel	01691 600666
Fax	01691 600262
Email	reception@thehandhotel.co.uk
Web	www.thehandhotel.co.uk

Holm House

A glittering hotel down by the sea: stylish, intimate and hugely spoiling. A two-year renovation has covered every square inch with something lovely, so step into this grand Edwardian house and find half-panelled walls, vintage wallpaper and a mirrored bar that doubles as a sitting room. Interiors mix Art Deco touches with contemporary flair. Downstairs, doors everywhere open onto a balustraded terrace with formal gardens below and a sparkling sea beyond; on a good day you're on the Côte d'Azur. Slip into the airy restaurant for delicious comfort food, perhaps chicken liver pâté, fillet of lamb, chocolate tart with orange confit. Beautiful bedrooms come with Frette linen, super beds, designer fabrics and Italian ceramics in smart bathrooms. Rooms at the back look out to sea, one has a TV embedded in the bathroom wall, another comes in creamy leather; two have balconies. There are loungers on a first-floor sun terrace, a spa for treatments and a hydrotherapy pool. Cardiff is close. Heaven. *Minimum stay two nights at weekends.*

Price	£145-£355. Half-board (obligatory Thursday-Saturday) £100-£202.50 p.p.
Rooms	12: 4 suites, 6 doubles, 2 twins.
Meals	Lunch from £12.50. Dinner, 3 courses, £31.50-£41.50.
Closed	Never.
Directions	M4 junc. 33, then A4232 south. Follow signs to Penarth town centre (not marina). Along seafront, up hill, 1st right; 4th house on right.

Susan Sessions
Marine Parade, Penarth,
Glamorgan CF64 3BG

Tel	02920 701572
Fax	02920 709875
Email	info@holmhouse.co.uk
Web	www.holmhouse.co.uk

 Travel Club Offer: see page 367 for details.

Rhiwafallen Restaurant with Rooms

North Wales may be a touch far flung, but its star shines brightly these days and ever-growing numbers are flocking in to explore its magical landscapes. Luckily, a smattering of stylish hotels has mushroomed to look after the lucky souls who venture forth; this intimate restaurant with rooms is one of the best. Roll up the drive to find old stone walls, ducks on the pond and a pebbled terrace overlooking the fields. Inside, cool interiors are warm and restful with candles in the fireplace and the odd bust of an eastern deity, but it's the bedrooms that take the biscuit, each one brimming with understated grace. The style is crisply contemporary: Egyptian cotton and goose-down duvets, modern art and flat-screen TVs, fancy bathrooms and fluffy cotton bathrobes. One has a claw-foot bath in the room itself, another has its own balcony. Pull yourself away for Rob's glorious food, perhaps local crab, Welsh lamb, raspberry and lemon grass trifle. You eat in a canvas-shaded conservatory with doors that open onto the terrace in summer. Snowdon is close, as are wild beaches for seaside walks.

Price	£100–£150. Singles from £80.
Rooms	5 doubles.
Meals	Sunday lunch £19.50. Dinner, 3 courses, £29.50. Not Sunday or Monday.
Closed	Rarely.
Directions	South from Caernarfon on A487. Right onto A499 for Llandwrog. Through village and on left after 0.5 miles.

Rob & Kate John
Llandwrog, Caernarfon,
Gwynedd LL54 5SW

Tel	01286 830172
Web	www.rhiwafallen.co.uk

Plas Bodegroes

Close to the end of the world and worth every second it takes to get here. Chris and Gunna are inspirational, their home a temple of cool elegance, the food possibly the best in Wales. Fronted by an avenue of 200-year-old beech trees, this Georgian manor house is wrapped in climbing roses, wildly roaming wisteria and ferns. The veranda circles the house, as do long French windows that lighten every room; open one up, grab a book and pull up a chair. Not a formal place – come to relax and be yourself. Bedrooms are wonderful, the courtyard rooms especially good; exposed wooden ceilings and a crisp clean style give the feel of a smart Scandinavian forest hideaway. Best of all is the dining room, almost a work of art in itself, cool and crisp with exceptional art on the walls – a great place to eat Chris's Michelin-starred food. How about French onion soup, roast mountain lamb with rosemary jus, and apricot and ginger parfait with pistachio praline? Tear yourself away and explore the Lleyn peninsula: sandy beaches, towering cliffs and country walks all wait. Snowdon is close, too.

Price	£110–£175. Singles £50–£99. Half-board from £95 p.p.
Rooms	11: 7 doubles, 2 twins, 1 four-poster, 1 single.
Meals	Sunday lunch £18.50. Dinner £42.50. Not Sunday evenings.
Closed	December–February; Sunday & Monday.
Directions	From Pwllheli, A497 towards Nefyn. House on left after 1 mile, signed.

Chris & Gunna Chown
Pwllheli, Gwynedd LL53 5TH

Tel	01758 612363
Fax	01758 701247
Email	gunna@bodegroes.co.uk
Web	www.bodegroes.co.uk

Plas Tan-yr-allt

A sublime country house on the side of a hill with majestic views from the terrace stretching for miles across land and sea. There's history, too. The poet Shelley lived here in 1812, fleeing to Ireland after a ghost shot at him in the middle of the night; the event inspired Mary Shelley to dream up Frankenstein. These days you find nothing but relaxed country life; an honesty bar and a fire in the drawing room, the daily papers and fine art in the library, and lively communal dinner parties in the dining room each night. Nick and Michael receive with warmth and humour – this is a country-house B&B, not a hotel – and parties are welcome to take the whole place over. Airy bedrooms are predictably divine. Expect padded window seats, thick fabrics, Farrow & Ball colours, perhaps a sofa at the end of your bed. Also: crisp linen, fancy bathrooms and fresh flowers. You're in 47 acres of garden and hillside, you can climb to the top of the rock that soars behind and gaze down the Welsh coast. Snowdon, Anglesey and Portmerion are close. This one is hard to leave. *Minimum stay two nights at weekends.*

Price	£120-£175. Singles £100-£140. Half-board from £82.50 p.p.
Rooms	6: 3 doubles, 1 twin, 2 four-posters.
Meals	Dinner, 3 courses, £38.
Closed	2 weeks in January/February.
Directions	Leave Tremadog on A498 for Beddgelert. Signed on left after 0.5 miles. House at top of hill.

Michael Bewick & Nick Golding
Tremadog, Porthmadog,
Gwynedd LL49 9RG

Tel	01766 514545
Email	info@tanyrallt.co.uk
Web	www.tanyrallt.co.uk

Penmaenuchaf Hall

The gardens are amazing – woodlands strewn with daffodils in spring, topiary on the upper lawn, a walled garden of tumbling colour. The position high on the hill is equally sublime, with the Mawdacch estuary carving imperiously through the valley below. The house has attitude, too – built in 1865 for a Bolton cotton merchant. The smell of woodsmoke greets you at the front door. Step inside to find an open fire crackling in the half-panelled hall, where armchairs take the strain. The drawing room is even better with mullioned windows to frame the view, a grand piano and cavernous sofas, country rugs on original wood floors. Steps illuminated by fairy lights lead up to the airy conservatory/dining room, where French windows open onto to a terrace for alfresco dining in good weather. Bedrooms come in traditional country-house style with warm florals, ornamental fireplaces, padded window seats and comfy beds. Some rooms are huge, one has a balcony, all have bathrooms that are more than adequate. There are 13 miles of river to fish, while Snowdon, Bala and Portmeirion are close.

Price	£140-£210. Singles from £90.
Rooms	14: 7 doubles, 5 twins/doubles, 1 four-poster, 1 family.
Meals	Lunch from £6. Afternoon tea from £6. Dinner, 3 courses, £40.
Closed	Rarely.
Directions	From Dolgellau, A493 west for about 1.5 miles. Entrance on left.

Mark Watson & Lorraine Fielding
Penmaenpool, Dolgellau,
Gwynedd LL40 1YB

Tel	01341 422129
Fax	01341 422787
Email	relax@penhall.co.uk
Web	www.penhall.co.uk

Travel Club Offer: see page 367 for details.

Ffynnon

A seriously indulging boutique B&B hidden away in the backstreets of this old market town. By day, you try valiantly to leave your luxurious room to explore the majesty of North Wales (many fail). Cycle tracks lead over forested hills, white beaches stretch for miles, there are rivers to ride, castles to visit, even Snowdon to climb. If you fail to budge, make do with luxury. The exterior of this former rectory may be a touch stern, but interiors sparkle with abandon. You find open fires, Farrow & Ball colours, fancy chandeliers and rugs on stripped floors. Breakfast is served communally in an elegant dining room, there's an honesty bar in the airy sitting room and doors fly open in summer to a lawned garden complete with standing stone. Bedrooms upstairs are magnificent, those at the front have views over the town. Expect Egyptian linen on beautiful beds, high ceilings and elegant fabrics, flat-screen TVs and DVD players. Faultless bathrooms are somewhat addictive, so expect to go home smelling of roses. Kids are very welcome, good restaurants wait in town, Steve and Debra couldn't be nicer. Don't miss it.

Price	£120–£150. Singles from £80.
Rooms	4: 3 doubles, 1 twin/double.
Meals	Restaurants within walking distance. Room service (6pm–10pm) from £4.50.
Closed	Occasionally.
Directions	Leave A470 for Dolgellau, over bridge, into town. At T-junction, right then 1st left. Straight across Springfield Road & 2nd right into Bryn Teg. Entrance at end of road.

Debra Harris & Steve Holt
Brynffynnon, Love Lane, Dolgellau,
Gwynedd LL40 1RR

Tel	01341 421774
Fax	01341 421779
Email	info@ffynnontownhouse.com
Web	www.ffynnontownhouse.com

Llety Bodfor

Super-stylish interiors are stuffed with contemporary flair, but it's the views from the bedrooms that take the breath – a cool sweep across the Dyfi estuary as it spills into Cardigan Bay. The house stands on the main street in town with five miles of sandy beach heading north 50 paces from the front door. Inside, you find a boutique hotel that's joined at the hip to an interior design company. Downstairs, sitting room, dining room and bar are all rolled into one, with Gareth's old record collection for guests to dip into, seaside colours to soak up the light, big chunky tables for delicious communal breakfasts. Upstairs, enormous rooms at the front have sofas that face the right way and come beautifully attired with crisp linen, Welsh wool blankets, and cool colours to soak up the light. Exceptional bathrooms have double-ended baths, separate power showers, waffle robes, big white towels. There are nibbles and drinks in the fridge and movies downstairs for your DVD player, so don't expect to move too much. Ann's ground-floor shop waits, crammed with beautiful things. *Minimum stay two nights at weekends.*

Price	£118. Suites £148. Singles from £60. Apartment £125.
Rooms	8 + 1: 2 doubles, 2 singles, 4 suites. 1 self-catering apartment.
Meals	Restaurants within walking distance. Snacks from £4.50.
Closed	23-27 December.
Directions	A493 west from Machynlleth. Opposite car park on far side of village before railway bridge.

	Ann & Gareth Hughes
	Bodfor Terrace, Aberdyfi,
	Gwynedd LL35 0EA
Tel	01654 767475
Fax	01654 767836
Email	info@lletybodfor.co.uk
Web	www.lletybodfor.co.uk

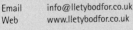

The Crown at Whitebrook

An unbeatable combination of attentive service, sublime food and impeccable style make this a real find for those in search of affordable luxury. The Crown is a small restaurant with rooms in a tiny village that's wrapped up in the Wye Valley. Forest rises all around, goats graze in fields, deer amble by in summer. Walks start from the front door, so climb to the ridge for imperious views or head south to Tintern Abbey. Don't stray too far. Bedrooms are a real treat, seriously comfortable, with crisp linen, pretty colours, decanters of sherry and fluffy white bathrobes. The smaller rooms are exceptional value, but splash out on bigger ones for sofas, armchairs and a little more space, huge walk-in showers, sparkling deep baths, perhaps a four-poster bed; all come with an astonishing array of hi-tech gadgetry including a movie library and internet access through the TV. As for the food, it's Michelin-starred and utterly delicious, perhaps seared langoustine and crab risotto, chargrilled loin of wild venison, then confit of rhubarb with apple sorbet. Whatever can be is homemade and flavour floods from every bite.

Price	£115–£140. Singles from £75.
Rooms	8: 6 doubles, 2 twins/doubles.
Meals	Lunch (Wed–Sun) from £25. Dinner (Wed–Sat), 3 courses, £45.
Closed	Late December to early January.
Directions	M4 junc. 24, A449/A40 north to Monmouth, then B4293 south. Up hill. After 2.7 miles left for Whitebook. On right after two miles.

David Hennigan
Whitebrook, Monmouth,
Monmouthshire NP25 4TX

Tel	01600 860254
Fax	01600 860607
Email	info@crownatwhitebrook.co.uk
Web	www.crownatwhitebrook.co.uk

Entry 277   Map 2

The Bell at Skenfrith

The Bell stands by an ancient stone bridge in a much-ignored valley with hugely beautiful hills rising behind and a Norman castle paddling in the river a hundred yards from the front door. A sublime spot – and the inn is as good. It dates to the 17th century, but its crisply designed interiors ooze a cool country chic. In the locals' bar you find slate floors, open fires, plump-cushioned armchairs and polished oak. In summer, doors fly open and life decants onto the terrace at the back; views of wood and hill are interrupted only by the odd chef pottering past on his way to a rather productive kitchen garden. Stripped boards in the restaurant give an airy feel, so stop for delicious food served by young, attentive staff, perhaps roasted red pepper soup, breast of local duck and fig tarte tatin with lemon and thyme ice cream. Bedrooms above are as you'd expect: dressed in fine fabrics, uncluttered and elegant, brimming with light, some beamed, others overlooking the river. Idyllic circular walks start from the front door and sweep you into blissful country. A perfect place. *Minimum stay two nights at weekends.*

Price	£110–£220. Singles from £75 (Monday-Friday).
Rooms	11: 7 doubles, 4 suites.
Meals	Bar lunch from £14. Sunday lunch £21.50. Dinner, à la carte, about £30.
Closed	Open all day. Closed Mondays November-March.
Directions	From Monmouth, B4233 to Rockfield; B4347 for 5 miles; right on B4521, Skenfrith 1 mile.

William & Janet Hutchings
Skenfrith, Monmouthshire NP7 8UH

Tel	01600 750235
Fax	01600 750525
Email	enquiries@skenfrith.co.uk
Web	www.skenfrith.co.uk

Penally Abbey

A fabulous position up on the hill with a ridge of sycamore and ash towering above and huge views of Carmarthen Bay to the front. Caldy Island lies to the east, the road ends at the village green, a quick stride across the golf course leads to the beach. Up at the house, a fine arched window by the grand piano frames the view perfectly, so sink into a chesterfield in front of the fire and gaze out to sea. The house dates to 1790 and was once an abbey; you'll also find St Deiniol's, a ruined 13th-century church that's lit up at night. Sprawling lawns are yours to roam, bluebells carpet the wood in May. Bedrooms are all different: grand four-posters and wild flock wallpaper in the main house; a simpler cottage feel in the coach house; warm contemporary luxury in St Deiniol's Lodge. Steve's gentle, unflappable manner is infectious and hugely relaxing; don't expect to feel rushed. Elleen cooks in the French style, much of it picked up in the kitchen of a château many years ago; her Tenby sea bass is exquisite. The Pembrokeshire coastal path passes by outside; don't miss it. *Minimum stay two nights at weekends.*

Price	£148–£240. Half-board from £105 p.p.
Rooms	17: 6 doubles, 1 twin all en suite; 1 double with separate bath. Coach house: 4 doubles. Lodge: 5 twins/doubles.
Meals	Lunch by arrangement. Dinner, 3 courses, £36.50.
Closed	Never.
Directions	From Tenby, A4139 for Pembroke. Right into Penally after 1.5 miles. Hotel signed at village green. Train station 5 mins walk.

Steve & Elleen Warren
Penally, Tenby, Pembrokeshire
SA70 7PY

Tel	01834 843033
Fax	01834 844714
Email	info@penally-abbey.com
Web	www.penally-abbey.com

Stackpole Inn

This friendly inn is hard to fault. It sits in a quiet village drenched in honeysuckle with a fine garden at the front, a perfect spot for a drop of Welsh ale in summer. Wander further afield and you come to the sea at Barafundle Bay – a Pembrokeshire glory – where you can pick up the coastal path and follow it west past Stackpole Head to St Gorvan's Chapel. Stride back up to the inn and find interiors worthy of a country pub. There are smart red carpets, whitewashed walls, a hard-working wood-burner and obligatory beamed ceilings. Locals and visitors mingle in harmony, there are four hand pumps at the slate bar and tasty rustic cooking in the restaurant, perhaps deep-fried whitebait, rack of lamb, fresh raspberry brûlée. Super bedrooms are tremendous value for money and quietly positioned in a converted outbuilding. Two have sofabeds, two have velux windows for star gazing. All come in seaside colours with tongue-and-groove panelling, stripped floors, comfy beds, crisp linen and excellent bathrooms. Don't miss Pembroke Castle or the beach at Freshwater West.

Price	£70–£80. Singles from £45.
Rooms	4: 2 twins/doubles, 2 family rooms.
Meals	Lunch from £5. Dinner, 3 courses, £20–£25 (not Sun eves October–March).
Closed	Rarely.
Directions	B4319 south of Pembroke for 3 miles, then left for Stackpole. Through Stackpole Cheriton, up hill, right at T-junc. On right.

Gary & Becky Evans
Stackpole, Pembroke, Pembrokeshire
SA71 5DF

Tel	01646 672324
Email	info@stackpoleinn.co.uk
Web	www.stackpoleinn.co.uk

Stone Hall

A magical house lost in sublime country. If you want to hide out in glorious hills, do it here. There are ten acres of enchanted gardens with trim lawns, specimen rhododendrons, thousands of bluebells, even a handkerchief tree. As for the house, it dates from the 13th century and its heavy beams and stone floors are all original. More recent additions include Nina Campbell wallpaper, pillars, wood carvings and a rather good bar, where stone walls come in Venetian Red. Bedrooms are simpler and pay no heed to prevailing fashions, but they're more than comfortable and filled with pretty things, perhaps a mirrored armoire, a padded headboard or floral fabrics. What's more, they are very well priced. Roast away in front of a crackling fire or potter about in the sublime walled garden that provides much for the table. Martine serves delicious French food, perhaps crab soufflé with a sweet chilli sauce, roasted duck breast with a pear compote, hazelnut meringue with a raspberry coulis. The Pembrokeshire coast is on your doorstep, fabulous walking abounds.

Price	£105. Singles £75.
Rooms	4: 3 doubles, 1 twin.
Meals	Dinner, 3 courses, £30-£35 (not Sunday or Monday).
Closed	Occasionally.
Directions	A40 north from Haverfordwest. Left for Welsh Hook after Wolf's Castle. Keep left, under railway, over river, past church. Left up hill, signed.

Martine Watson
Welsh Hook, Haverfordwest,
Pembrokeshire SA62 5NS

Tel	01348 840212
Email	m.watson5@btconnect.com
Web	www.stonehall-mansion.co.uk

Cnapan

Cnapan is a way of life – a family affair with three generations at work in harmony. Eluned makes the preserves, Judith excels in the kitchen, Michael looks after the bar and Oliver, the newest recruit, serves a mean breakfast. It is a very friendly place with locals popping in to book tables and guests chatting in the bar before dinner. As for the house, it's warm and cosy, charmingly home-spun, with whitewashed stone walls and old pine settles in the dining room, comfy sofas and a wood-burner in the sitting room, and a tiny telly in the bar for the odd game of rugby (the game of cnapan, rugby's precursor, originated in the town). There are maps for walkers, bird books, flower books, the daily papers, too. Spill into the garden in summer for pre-dinner drinks under the weeping willow, then slip back in for Judith's delicious food, perhaps parsnip soup, breast of Gressingham duck, honey ice cream. Comfy bedrooms, warmly simple, are super value for money. You're in the Pembrokeshire National Park here; beaches and clifftop coastal walks beckon. *Minimum stay two nights at weekends.*

Price	£80. Singles £50.
Rooms	5: 1 double, 3 twins, 1 family. Extra bath available.
Meals	Dinner from £28. Not Tuesday evenings from Easter to October.
Closed	Christmas, January & February.
Directions	From Cardigan, A487 to Newport. 1st pink house on right.

Eluned Lloyd & Michael & Judith Cooper
East Street, Newport, Fishguard,
Pembrokeshire SA42 0SY

Tel	01239 820575
Fax	01239 820878
Email	enquiry@cnapan.co.uk
Web	www.cnapan.co.uk

Entry 282   Map 1

Llys Meddyg

This quirky restaurant with rooms has a bit of everything: rooms that pack a designer punch, super food in a sparkling restaurant, a cellar bar for drinks before dinner, a fabulous garden for summer treats. The house – the town's old doctor's surgery – is built of pretty stone upon which a trim Virginia creeper now roams. Inside, Victorian interiors have a warm contemporary finish. In the restaurant, where candles burn serenely under a teardrop chandelier, there's mussel and saffron soup, rump of lamb with cucumber noodles, raspberry soufflé with bitter chocolate ice cream. Excellent bedrooms are split between the main house (high ceilings) and the one behind (quieter). All have the same fresh style: Farrow & Ball colours, good art, oak beds with crisp linen, fancy bathrooms with fluffy robes. Three have computers stuffed with music and film, others have flat-screen TVs and DVD players, one has a super-cool bathroom in Jerusalem stone. Best of all is a lush garden with a mountain-fed stream pouring past. By day it becomes an open-air café. There's even a small sofa-clad marquee for cocktails before dinner.

Price	£90-£120. Suites £130-£150. Singles from £75.
Rooms	8: 2 doubles, 2 twin/double, 4 suites.
Meals	Lunch from £7 (June to mid-Sept). Dinner, 3 courses, about £35. Not Sunday/Monday in winter.
Closed	Never.
Directions	East from Fishguard on A487. On left in Newport towards eastern edge of town.

Louise & Edward Sykes
East Street, Newport,
Pembrokeshire SA42 0SY

Tel	01239 820008
Email	contact@llysmeddyg.com
Web	www.llysmeddyg.com

Gliffaes Hotel

A matchless country house that towers majestically above the river Usk as it pours through the valley below. It is a view to feed the soul, so sit on the stone terrace and drink it in; people do. Pull yourself away and find 33 acres of formal lawns and woodland that ensure nothing but silence. Interiors pack a grand punch. Afternoon tea is laid out in a sitting room of panelled walls, shiny wood floors and family portraits, while logs crackle in a magnificent carved fireplace. Fishermen gather in the bar for tall stories and a quick drink before supper, then spin through to the restaurant for local, seasonal food (the hotel is part of the Slow Food Movement). Elsewhere, country-house bedrooms do the trick. Several have river views, one has a claw-foot bath that overlooks the front lawn, all come with thick fabrics, crisp linen, antique furniture, a sofa if there's room. As you may have deduced, Gliffaes is a fishing hotel, one of the finest in the land, so come to cast a fly while red kite circle above. Packed lunches in brown paper bags keep you going through the day. *Minimum stay two nights at weekends.*

Price	£92.50–£225. Singles from £84. Half-board from £80 p.p.
Rooms	23: 3 doubles, 15 twins/doubles, 5 singles.
Meals	Light lunches from £5. Dinner, 3 courses, £34. Sunday lunch £18–£24.
Closed	First 4 weeks in January.
Directions	From Crickhowell, A40 west for 2.5 miles. Entrance on left, signed. Hotel 1 mile up windy hill.

James & Susie Suter
Crickhowell, Powys NP8 1RH

Tel	01874 730371
Fax	01874 730463
Email	calls@gliffaeshotel.com
Web	www.gliffaeshotel.com

Travel Club Offer: see page 367 for details.

Ethical Collection: Environment; Food.
See page 373 for details

The Felin Fach Griffin

Delicious food, a friendly bar and honest prices make the Griffin a must for those in search of a welcoming billet close to the mountains. It's quirky, homespun, utterly intoxicating and thrives on a mix of relaxed informality and colourful style. The timber-framed bar resembles the sitting room of a small hip country house, with sofas in front of a fire that burns on both sides and backgammon waiting to be played. Painted stone walls throughout come in blocks of colour. An open-plan feel sweeps you through to the restaurant, where stock pots simmer on an Aga; try roasted scallops, Welsh lamb, vanilla crème brûlée with pina colada. Bedrooms above are warmly simple with comfy beds wrapped in crisp linen, framed photography on the walls, good books and the odd piece of mahogany furniture (but no TVs unless you ask); tongue-and-groove bathrooms have White Company lotions. A road passes outside, quietly at night, lanes lead into the hills, and a small organic kitchen garden provides much for the table. The Beacons are close, so walk, ride, bike, canoe – or head to Hay for books galore.

Price	£100–£140. Singles from £75.
Rooms	7: 2 doubles, 2 twins/doubles, 3 four-posters.
Meals	Lunch £15.90–£18.90. Dinner £21.50–£34. Not Monday lunchtimes.
Closed	25 & 26 December.
Directions	From Brecon, A470 north to Felin Fach (4.5 miles). On left.

 Travel Club Offer: see page 367 for details.

Charles & Edmund Inkin
Felin Fach, Brecon, Powys LD3 0UB
Tel   01874 620111
Email   enquiries@felinfachgriffin.co.uk
Web   www.felinfachgriffin.co.uk

The Lake Country House & Spa

Deep in the silence of Wales, a country house intent on pampering you rotten. Fifty acres of lawns, lake and ancient woodland sweep you clean of city cobwebs, and if that's not enough a spa has been added, with an indoor pool, treatment rooms and a tennis court by the lake. Sit in a hot tub and watch guests fish for their supper, try your luck on the nine-hole golf course, or saddle up nearby and take to the hills. Come home to afternoon tea in the drawing room, where beautiful rugs warm a brightly polished wooden floor and chandeliers hang from the ceiling. The hotel opened over 100 years ago and the leather-bound fishing logs go back to 1894. A feel of the 1920s lingers. Fires come to life in front of your eyes, grand pianos and grandfather clocks sing their songs, snooker balls crash about in the distance. Dress for a delicious dinner – the food and wines deserve it – then retire to cosseting bedrooms. Most are suites: those in the house are warmly traditional, those in the lodge are softly contemporary. The London train takes four hours and stops in the village. Resident geese waddle. Marvellous.

Price	£170–£220. Singles from £115–£155. Suites £250–£300. Half-board £105–£150 p.p.
Rooms	30: 6 twins/doubles, 12 suites. Lodge: 12 suites.
Meals	Lunch, 3 courses, £21.50. Dinner, 3 courses, £42.50.
Closed	Rarely.
Directions	From Builth Wells, A483 west for 7 miles to Garth. Signed from village.

Jean-Pierre Mifsud
Llangammarch Wells, Powys LD4 4BS

Tel	01591 620202
Fax	01591 620457
Email	info@lakecountryhouse.co.uk
Web	www.lakecountryhouse.co.uk

Milebrook House Hotel

An old-school country hotel with three acres of fabulous gardens that run down to the river Teme. You'll find Wales on one bank and England on the other, so bring your wellies and wade across; the walking is magnificent. The house, once home to writer Wilfred Thesiger, is run in informal style by three generations of the Marsden family with Beryl and Rodney leading the way. Step inside and enter a world that's rooted in a delightful past: clocks tick, cats snooze, fires crackle, the odd champagne cork escapes its bondage. Beautiful art hangs on the walls, the sitting room is stuffed with books, the bar comes in country-house style and there's food to reckon with in the wonderful dining room – perhaps Cornish scallops with a pea purée, rack of Welsh lamb with dauphinoise potatoes, ginger crème brûlée with poached rhubarb. A kitchen garden supplies much for the table, you can fish for trout, spot deer in the woods, play croquet on the lawn. Red kite, moorhens, kingfishers and herons live in the valley. Homely bedrooms are more than comfortable, so don't delay. *Minimum stay two nights at weekends.*

Price	£103–£142.50 Singles from £60. Half-board (min. 2 nights) from £72.50 p.p.
Rooms	10: 5 doubles, 4 twins, 1 family.
Meals	Lunch from £9.95. Dinner, 3 courses, £31.95. Not Monday lunchtimes.
Closed	Never.
Directions	From Ludlow, A49 north, then left at Bromfield on A4113 towards Knighton for 10 miles. Hotel on right.

Travel Club Offer: see page 367 for details.

Rodney & Beryl Marsden
Milebrook, Knighton, Powys LD7 1LT
Tel   01547 528632
Fax   01547 520509
Email   hotel@milebrook.kc3ltd.co.uk
Web   www.milebrookhouse.co.uk

The Trewythen Hotel

A small pretty provincial town lost in the hills of mid-Wales, a good place to escape the world. With its classical exterior and jaunty interior, The Trewythen – which stands opposite the town hall – gives the best of both worlds: a little style and lots of comfort. A blue plaque on the front wall marks the scene of Chartist riots in 1770, but these days all is calm, so wander the streets and find the market hall, the odd antique shop, old woollen mills down by the river. Inside, all is spic and span, newly refurbished in neutral colours, with leather sofas and colourful art in the sitting room, and fine windows and gilt mirrors in the restaurant. Airy bedrooms are very well priced and those at the front on the first floor are huge, so splash out if you can. All have the same style: wooden beds, oatmeal carpets, white walls, good linen. You get flat-screen TVs and excellent bathrooms (most have showers). Food in the restaurant is fairly simple – pizzas for lunch, a good steak for dinner, hot apple pie. There's a secure cellar for bicycles, fantastic walking, even rally driving in the mountains – come to try your hand.

Price	£75-£95. Singles from £55.
Rooms	7: 4 doubles, 1 twin, 2 family.
Meals	Lunch from £2.35.
	Dinner, 3 courses, £17.50.
	Sunday lunch £14.95.
Closed	Never.
Directions	In centre of town, opposite clock tower.

Huw Griffiths
Great Oak Street, Llanidloes,
Powys SY18 6BW

Tel	01686 411333
Email	reservations@trewythen.co.uk
Web	www.trewythen.co.uk

Lake Vyrnwy Hotel

A blissful pocket of rural Wales. The lake – cradled by high hills of forest and grazing land – was excavated by hand in 1891 and took two years to fill; it now provides Liverpool's water. The hotel was built shortly afterwards so civic dignitaries could come to fish the 400,000 trout that were released into the water. The view is *stupendous*, the lake stretching five miles into the distance, home to rolling mists and sunbursts. You can walk or cycle round it, canoe, sail or fish on it, and birdwatchers will be in heaven. Country-house comforts prevail at the hotel, where all reception rooms look the right way – a plush drawing room, an armchaired library, a pretty conservatory, a terraced bar and an award-winning restaurant for fresh local produce. Some rooms in the house are seriously grand (in one you can soak in a claw-foot bath while gazing down the lake), others are snug in the eaves and come in warm country colours; 14 new rooms have private balconies. There's a spa and thermal suite, too, with long views down the lake and treatments galore. *Minimum stay two nights at weekends.*

Price	£105–£210. Singles from £95. Half-board £70–£120 p.p.
Rooms	52: 49 twins/doubles, 2 four-posters, 1 suite.
Meals	Lunch from £8.50. Bar meals from £8. Dinner, 5 courses, £37.50.
Closed	Rarely.
Directions	A490 from Welshpool; B4393 to Lake Vyrnwy. Brown signs from A5 at Shrewsbury as well.

Travel Club Offer: see page 367 for details.

The Bisiker Family
Llanwddyn, Powys SY10 0LY

Tel	01691 870692
Fax	01691 870259
Email	res@lakevyrnwy.com
Web	www.lakevyrnwyhotel.co.uk

Fairyhill

The Gower peninsula has legions of fans who come for its glorious heathland, its rugged coastline and some of the best beaches in the country. Fairyhill is bang in the middle of it all, but just to ensure absolute silence it is wrapped in 24 acres of its own. Follow your nose and discover a stream-fed lake, an ancient orchard, a walled garden with asparagus beds and, somewhere, a family of Muscovy ducks. Inside, an informal house-party feel comes courtesy of Andrew and Paul, who've been here since 1992. Most bedrooms are big and fancy, a couple are smaller and simpler. The plush ones have painted beams, striking stripes, bold colours, immaculate bathrooms. Mattresses are Vi-Spring, but if that's not enough you'll find a treatment room, so book a massage. There's croquet on the lawn in summer and seriously good food all year round. Lamb, poultry, beef and cheese come from Gower, so tuck into duck eggs with white asparagus mousse, grilled lemon sole with beurre noisette, twice-glazed lemon tart with sour-apple ice cream. Fabulous walking, too.

Price	£165–£275. Singles from £145. Half-board from £110 p.p.
Rooms	8: 3 doubles, 5 twins/doubles.
Meals	Lunch from £15.95. Dinner £30–£40.
Closed	First 3 weeks in January.
Directions	M4 junc. 47; A483 south; A484 west to Gowerton; B4295 to Llanrhidian; through Oldwalls & 1 mile up on left.

Andrew Hetherington & Paul Davies
Reynoldston, Gower, Swansea SA3 1BS

Tel	01792 390139
Fax	01792 391358
Email	postbox@fairyhill.net
Web	www.fairyhill.net

Scotland

Photo: istockphoto.com

Darroch Learg

The country here is glorious – river, forest, mountain, sky – so walk by Loch Muick, climb Lochnagar, fish the Dee or drop down to Braemar and the Highland Games. Swing back to Darroch Learg to find nothing but good things. This is a smart, family-run hotel firmly rooted in a graceful past, an old country house with roaring fires, polished brass, Zoffany wallpaper and ambrosial food in a much-admired restaurant. Ever-present Nigel and Fiona look after guests with great aplomb; many return. Everything is just as it should be: tartan fabrics on the walls in the hall, Canadian pitch pine windows and doors, fabulous views sweeping south across Balmoral forest. Bedrooms upstairs come in different shapes and sizes; all have warmth and comfort in spades. Big grand rooms at the front thrill with padded window seats, wallpapered bathrooms, old oak furniture, perhaps a four-poster. Spotlessly cosy rooms in the eaves are equally lovely, just not quite as big. You get warm colours, pretty furniture, crisp white linen and bathrobes to pad about in. A perfect highland retreat.

Price	£140–£210. Half-board (obligatory May–Sept, & Saturdays all year) £110–£140 p.p.
Rooms	12: 10 twins/doubles, 2 four-posters.
Meals	Sunday lunch £24. Dinner, à la carte, about £45. 7-course tasting menu £55.
Closed	Christmas week & last 3 weeks in January.
Directions	From Perth, A93 north to Ballater. Entering village, hotel 1st building on left above road.

Nigel & Fiona Franks
Braemar Road, Ballater,
Aberdeenshire AB35 5UX

Tel	01339 755443
Fax	01339 755252
Email	enquiries@darrochlearg.co.uk
Web	www.darrochlearg.co.uk

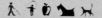

The Lime Tree

The Lime Tree is unique – an art gallery with rooms. The house, a Mackintosh manse, dates back to 1850, while the tree itself, sublime on the front lawn, was planted in 1700, the year the town was settled. Inside you find a small, intimate, stylish world – stripped floors in the hall, bold colours on the walls, open fires scattered around, beautiful windows for views of Loch Linnhe. David – a mountain guide/stuntman who also paints – has a fabulous map room, but if you want to do more than walk, you've come to the right place; climbing, cragging, mountain biking, kayaking and diving can all be arranged. Airy bedrooms are delightful – oatmeal carpets, crisp white linen, good art and flat-screen TVs. You get super little bathrooms, white walls to soak up the light and those at the front have watery views. Downstairs, drift through to the gallery and see what's on (when the Royal Geographical Society came, they had a full-scale copy of Ernest Shackleton's boat on the front lawn). There's a rustic bistro, too: homemade soups, slow-cooked lamb, hot chocolate fondant pudding. Ben Nevis is close.

Price	£80–£110. Singles from £60.
Rooms	9: 4 doubles, 5 family.
Meals	Lunch, 3 courses, £10. Dinner, 3 courses, £25.
Closed	November.
Directions	North to Fort William on A82. Hotel on right at 1st roundabout in town.

David Wilson
Achintore Road, Fort William,
Argyll & Bute PH33 6RQ

Tel	01397 701806
Fax	01397 701806
Email	info@limetreefortwilliam.co.uk
Web	www.limetreefortwilliam.co.uk

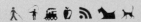

Entry 292   Map 8

The Airds Hotel & Restaurant

Faultless service, ambrosial food and warmly cosy interiors make this one of Scotland's most indulging country-house hotels. Views from the front slide down to Loch Linnhe, sweep over Lismore Island and cross to the towering mountains of Ardnamurchan beyond. A small conservatory, candlelit at night, frames the view perfectly, but in good weather you can slip across the lane to discover a lawned garden of rainbow colours decked out with tables and parasols. Pre-dinner drinks are taken in the sitting rooms – open fires, elegant sofas, fresh flowers, lots of books – after which you're whisked off to the dining room where four delicious courses are served on Limoges china. Whatever can be is homemade, so expect the best, maybe baked goat's cheese with onion confit, cream of cauliflower and mustard soup, seared fillet of brill in a citrus butter sauce, hot chocolate fondant with pistachio ice cream. Retire to smart country-house bedrooms (crisp florals, soft colours, Frette linen, Italian bathrobes) and find your bed turned down, the curtains drawn. There's pink grapefruit and campari sorbet for breakfast, too.

Price	Half-board £245–£415 for two. Cottage £560–£1,600 per week (inc. breakfast).
Rooms	11 + 1: 4 doubles, 4 twins, 3 suites. 1 self-catering cottage for 2-4.
Meals	Half-board only (except cottage). Lunch £5–£25. Dinner for non-residents, £49.50.
Closed	2 days a week, November–February.
Directions	A82 north for Fort William, then A828 south for Oban. Right for Port Appin after 12 miles. On left after 2 miles.

Travel Club Offer: see page 367 for details.

Shaun & Jenny McKivragan
Port Appin, Appin,
Argyll & Bute PA38 4DF
Tel   01631 730236
Fax   01631 730535
Email   airds@airds-hotel.com
Web   www.airds-hotel.com

Lerags House

A spectacular drive down a single-track road through lochs and gentle mountains to this lovely house by the water. Built in 1815, the rooms are large and light with high ceilings and sash windows. Cool interiors mix natural colours and pretty pine with comfy sofas, straight lines, fresh flowers and bold pictures. Charlie and Bella are part of the new generation of hoteliers: more style, less formality, good prices, great service and Bella's exceptional food – perhaps smoked-salmon fish cakes, twice-baked Gressingham duck, chocolate amaretti fudge with vanilla cream… Bedrooms are lovely: pale earthy colours, big beds with Italian linen. The suite has a view to the loch and its own sitting area, bathrooms are warm and the towels are big. The delightful garden runs down to tidal mud flats; watch the ebb and flow from the dining room while you breakfast on proper porridge. At the end of the road – a short mile – is a beach for uninterrupted walks or a constitutional dip. Day trips to Mull, Crinan and Glencoe are all easy, all wonderful. The Glasgow–Oban sea plane now flies daily. *Arrival after 4pm.*

Price	Half-board £90–£100 p.p. Singles from £110.
Rooms	6: 4 doubles, 1 twin/double, 1 suite.
Meals	Half-board only. Packed lunch £8.
Closed	Christmas.
Directions	From Oban, south on A816 for 2 miles, then right, signed Lerags for 2.5 miles. House on left, signed.

Charlie & Bella Miller
Lerags, Oban, Argyll & Bute PA34 4SE

Tel	01631 563381
Email	stay@leragshouse.com
Web	www.leragshouse.com

The Manor House

A 1780 dower house for the Dukes of Argyll – their cottage by the sea – built of local stone, high on the hill, with long views over Oban harbour to the Isle of Mull. A smart and proper place, not one to bow to the fads of fashion: sea views from the lawn, cherry trees in the courtyard garden, a fire roaring in the drawing room, a beautiful tiled floor in the entrance hall and an elegant bay window in the dining room that catches the eye. Bedrooms tend to be small, but they're also rather pretty and come in warm colours – blues, reds, yellows, greens – with fresh flowers, crisp linen, bowls of fruit and piles of towels in good bathrooms; those that look seaward have binoculars with which to scour the horizon. Try Loch Fyne kippers for breakfast, salmon for lunch and, if you've room, rack of lamb for supper; there's excellent home baking, too. Ferries leave for the islands from the bottom of the hill – see them depart from the hotel garden. At the top, overlooking Oban, watch the day's close from McCaig's Folly; sunsets here are really special. *Children over 12 welcome.*

Price	£115–£185.
	Half-board £87.50–£122.50 p.p.
Rooms	11: 9 doubles, 2 twins.
Meals	Lunch from £8.50.
	Dinner, 5 courses, £36.
Closed	Christmas.
Directions	In Oban, follow signs to ferry. Hotel on right 0.5 miles after ferry turn-off, signed.

Ann MacEachen
Gallanach Road, Oban,
Argyll & Bute PA34 4LS

Tel	01631 562087
Fax	01631 563053
Email	info@manorhouseoban.com
Web	www.manorhouseoban.com

Ardanaiseig

You're lost to the world, ten miles down a track that winds past giant rhododendrons before petering out at this baronial mansion. Beyond, Loch Awe rules supreme, 30 miles of deep blue water on which to sail or fish. In one of the loveliest hotel drawing rooms you are ever likely to see (gold leaf panelling, Doric columns rising gleefully) an enormous window frames the view and a single sofa waits for those lucky enough to have it. Elsewhere there are Wellington boots lined up in the hall, roaring fires wherever you go, eccentric art on the dining room wall and a lawned terrace that runs down to the loch. You're in 200 acres of private grounds, in May bluebells riddle the woods. Country-house bedrooms are the real thing (old armoires, feather boa lamp shades, the odd four-poster), but five external rooms are soon to be built in a natural amphitheatre with watery views. To prove the point the boat house (below) has been converted into a funky suite with a wall of glass that opens onto a decked terrace. Dinner is a seven-course feast — as one might expect of this rather flamboyant hotel.

Price	£122–£404. Boathouse £252–£404. Singles from £91. Half-board £108–£233 p.p.
Rooms	18: 8 twins/doubles, 7 doubles, 2 four-posters, 1 boathouse suite.
Meals	Light lunch from £4. Afternoon tea £2–£10. Dinner, 7 courses, £45.
Closed	2 January–8 February.
Directions	A85 to Taynuilt. Left onto B845 for Kilchrenan. Then left at Kilchrenan pub; down track for 4 miles.

Peter Webster
Kilchrenan, Taynuilt,
Argyll & Bute PA35 1HE

Tel	01866 833333
Fax	01866 833222
Email	info@ardanaiseig.com
Web	www.ardanaiseig.com

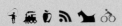 Travel Club Offer: see page 367 for details.

Culzean Castle

Culzean (pronounced 'Cullane') is one of Scotland's grandest buildings, a Robert Adam castle built into solid rock a couple of hundred feet above crashing waves. When the Marquess of Ailsa presented the castle to the Scottish people in 1945, General Eisenhower was given the top-floor suite, Scotland's thank you for his contribution to the war effort. You stay on the same floor – or even in his apartment – where rooms are either big or huge and where a country-house style infuses every corner. You'll find glowing fires, cashmere throws, twinkling chandeliers, thrilling sea views (the most splendid rooms overlook the gardens). Bathrooms are grandly traditional, service is courteous and thoughtful, the rest is awe-inspiring: hundreds of portraits crammed on the walls, a sublime drawing room that juts out over the sea, a central oval staircase with 12 Corinthian columns, an armoury of 716 flintlock pistols and 400 swords. Americans in search of ancestors will love it. You can tour the castle before the tourists invade, take a stirring cliff-top walk, wander 560 idyllic acres.

Price	£225–£375. Singles from £140. Whole floor £1,700 per night. Afternoon tea included.
Rooms	6: 1 double, 3 twins/doubles, 1 four-poster, all en suite; 1 twin/double with separate bath.
Meals	Dinner, 3 courses, £35. By arrangement.
Closed	Rarely.
Directions	From A77 in Maybole, A719 for 4 miles, signed.

Fi McClelland
The National Trust for Scotland,
Maybole, Ayrshire KA19 8LE

Tel	01655 884455
Fax	01655 884503
Email	culzean@nts.org.uk
Web	www.culzeanexperience.org

Hotel

Dumfries & Galloway

Knockinaam Lodge

Lawns run down to the Irish sea, sunsets streak the sky red, roe deer amble down to eat the roses. An exceptional 1869 shooting lodge with unremitting luxuries: a Michelin star in the dining room, 150 malts in the bar and a level of service you might not expect in such far-flung corners of the realm. And history. Churchill once stayed and you can sleep in his big elegant room, where copies of his books wait to be read and where you need steps to climb into an ancient bath. It remains very much a country house: plump cushions on a Queen Anne sofa in an immaculate morning room where the scent of flowers mixes with the smell of burnt wood, invigorating cliff walks, curlews to lull you to sleep, nesting peregrine falcons, and a rock pool where David keeps lobsters for the pot. In storms, waves crash all around. Trees stand guard high on the hill, their branches buffeted by the wind, bluebells come out by the thousand in spring. Remote, beguiling, utterly spoiling – Knockinaam is worth the detour. John Buchan knew the house and described it in *The Thirty-Nine Steps* as the house to which Hannay fled.

Price	Half-board £95-£200 p.p. Singles from £165.
Rooms	10: 3 doubles, 6 twins/doubles, 1 suite.
Meals	Half-board only. Lunch, by arrangement, £25-£37.50. Dinner, 5 courses, included; non-residents £50.
Closed	Never.
Directions	From A77 or A75, signs for Portpatrick. 2 miles west of Lochans, left at smokehouse. Signed for 3 miles.

David & Sian Ibbotson
Portpatrick,
Dumfries & Galloway DG9 9AD

Tel	01776 810471
Fax	01776 810435
Email	reservations@knockinaamlodge.com
Web	www.knockinaamlodge.com

Travel Club Offer: see page 367 for details.

Cavens

A very welcoming country house, with views from the front door that stretch across a quilt of fields to the imperious Solway Firth. The house, a 1753 shooting lodge, stands in six acres of native wood and sweeping lawns. Inside, quietly elegant interiors flood with light making this a very pleasant place to linger. You get busts and oils, seagrass matting, golden sofas and smouldering fires. Cavens is popular among local hoteliers who come to escape for a day or two. They come in part for the food that Angus whisks up single-handedly (perhaps scallops with lime and vermouth, sea bass with roasted fennel, raspberry tartlets, local cheeses). Country-house bedrooms all have garden views. Some are snug, others palatial. You get smart florals, pretty linen, mahogany dressers, bowls of fruit. One has an en suite sunroom, another comes in wild tangerine. Lose yourself in beautiful country: follow the Solway coast, come in November for millions of birds, play golf at spectacular Southerness. Afternoon tea can be eaten in the garden. A treat.

Price	£100–£160. Singles from £80.
Rooms	6: 5 doubles, 1 twin.
Meals	Dinner, 3 courses, £30. Packed lunch available.
Closed	House parties only December–February.
Directions	From Dumfries, A710 to Kirkbean (12 miles). Hotel signed in village, on left.

Travel Club Offer: see page 367 for details.

Jane & Angus Fordyce
Kirkbean,
Dumfries & Galloway DG2 8AA

Tel	01387 880234
Fax	01387 880467
Email	enquiries@cavens.com
Web	www.cavens.com

Trigony House Hotel

A super little hotel – warm, stylish and extremely welcoming. Adam and Jan are doing their own thing wonderfully: expect delicious food, pretty rooms and a lovely garden. The house dates back to 1700, a shooting lodge for the local castle. Inside: Japanese oak panelling in the hall, leather sofas in the sitting room and an open fire in the dining room, where doors open onto the terrace for al fresco dinners in summer. Adam cooks delicious rustic fare, perhaps crab, saffron and lemon tart, loin of roe venison with a juniper jus, rhubarb and port jelly with a citrus sorbet; there's a vegetable garden that provides much in summer. Bedrooms are excellent value for money (many are dog friendly) and come with floral fabrics, summer colours, padded bedheads, golden throws. One has its own conservatory/sitting room which opens onto a private lawn, but even the simpler rooms are attractive and all have flat-screen TV/DVDs; there's a film library downstairs. Falconry, riding and fishing can all be arranged, even vintage car hire. Drumlanrig Castle is close and worth a peek. Marvellous.

Price	£90–£120. Suite £140. Single from £45. Half-board from £70 p.p.
Rooms	10: 8 twins/doubles, 1 single, 1 suite.
Meals	Lunch from £5. Dinner, 3 courses, £25.
Closed	24–26 & 31 December.
Directions	North from Dumfries on A76 through Closeburn. Signed left after 1 mile.

Adam and Jan Moore
Closeburn, Thornhill,
Dumfries & Galloway DG3 5EZ
Tel   01848 331211
Email   info@trigonyhotel.co.uk
Web   www.countryhousehotelsscotland.com

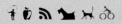

The Inn at Lathones

You don't have to be a golfer to fall in love with this inn, but the hallowed fairways of St Andrews are five miles west and after shooting three under par into the wind, your body will thank you for organising a night of luxury to follow. Here you find a whitewashed stone inn that dates to 1603. A super expansion in 2007 has added stylish suites with terraces or balconies overlooking the fields, sparkling bathrooms for an indulging soak, and bedrooms laden with technological excess. Goose-down duvets are wrapped in crisp white linen, scatter cushions and local art add colour. Spin across to the inn and find stone walls, timber frames, painted panelling and a wood-burner in the sitting room. Best of all is the food. Nick loves the stuff and has brought in 'trilogy' cooking from France: each course offers three micro-courses built around a central theme – perhaps soups for starters, lamb for main course, a trio of ices for pudding. It's all rather fun and helps you prepare for golf the next day; Scotland's four oldest courses are on your doorstep. *Minimum stay two nights at weekends.*

Price	£180–£245. Suites £295.
Rooms	21: 19 twins/doubles, 2 suites.
Meals	Lunch £14.50–£17.40.
	Dinner, à la carte, about £40.
	Packed lunch from £12.
Closed	Christmas & 2 weeks in January.
Directions	From Kirkcaldy, or St Andrews, A915 to Largoward. Inn 1 mile north on roadside.

Nick White
Lathones, St Andrews, Fife KY9 1JE
Tel	01334 840494
Fax	01334 840694
Email	lathones@theinn.co.uk
Web	www.theinn.co.uk

The Colonsay

Another fabulous Hebridean island, a perfect place to do nothing at all. Wander at will and find wild flowers in the machair, a golf course tended by sheep and huge sandy beaches across which cows roam. Wildlife is ever present, from a small colony of wild goats to a rich migratory bird population; the odd golden eagle passes overhead, too. At low tide the sands of the south give access to Oronsay. The island's 14th-century priory was one of Scotland's finest and amid impressive ruins its ornate stone cross still stands. As for the hotel, it's a splendid island base and brims with an easy style – airy interiors, stripped floors, fires everywhere, friendly staff. There's a locals' bar for a pint (and a brewery on the island), a pretty sitting room packed with books, a dining room for super food and a decked terrace for drinks in the sun. Recently refurbished bedrooms have local art, warm colours, lovely fabrics and the best beds; those at the front have sea views, all have neat little bathrooms. Fish for brown trout, search for standing stones, lie in the sun and stare at the sky. Wonderful.

Price	£95-£145. Singles from £60.
Rooms	9: 4 doubles, 3 twins, 1 single, 1 family.
Meals	Lunch from £4.50. Packed lunch £7. Bar meals from £7.50. Dinner, 3 courses, about £25.
Closed	November & February.
Directions	Calmac ferries from Oban or Kennacraig (not Tue or Sat) or Highland Airways (Tue and Thur). Hotel on right, half a mile up road from jetty.

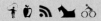 Travel Club Offer: see page 367 for details.

Scott & Becky Omar
Scalasaig, Isle of Colonsay PA61 7YP
Tel   01951 200316
Fax   01951 200353
Email   reception@thecolonsay.com
Web   www.thecolonsay.com

Hotel

Minmore House

In 1822 George IV tasted Glenlivet whisky for the first time. It swiftly became his favourite tipple and was used in all royal toasts thereafter. Minmore was built four years later by George Smith, whose whisky the king so admired, and the house became the family home of one of Scotland's most famous whisky men. These days it's a comfortable country house with a carved bar in a panelled sitting room that pays due homage to the wee dram; there are over a hundred malts to boggle the mind and books to help you choose. Elsewhere: roaring fires, comfy sofas, terraced gardens dripping with colour and 40 free-range hens. Windows at the front frame views of the Ladder Hills, but it's Victor's cooking that holds your attention; a four-course dinner may offer hand-dived scallops, minted pea soup, rack of Highland lamb, apple and calvados soufflé. Bedrooms span the scale, some warmly cosy, others lavishly over-the-top. One has a bath with views down the valley, all have crisp linen, trim carpets, fancy bathrobes and a drop of whisky. Highland safaris can be arranged. *Minimum stay two nights at weekends in summer.*

Price	£110-£152. Suites £162-£204. Singles from £70. Half-board from £96 p.p.
Rooms	9: 3 doubles, 4 twins, 2 suites.
Meals	Light lunch £15. Dinner, 4 courses, £41. Full picnic £15.
Closed	26 November-28 December.
Directions	From Aviemore, A95 north to Bridge of Avon; south on B9008 to Glenlivet. At top of hill, 400 yds before distillery.

Victor & Lynne Janssen
Glenlivet, Banffshire AB37 9DB

Tel	01807 590378
Fax	01807 590472
Email	enquiries@minmorehousehotel.com
Web	www.minmorehousehotel.com

The Pines

The pines in question rise in the garden and mark the entrance to the wild woods of Anagach, so spin through the gate and meet the locals: roe deer, woodpeckers and red squirrels live within. Circular walks are easy to follow, and if you keep going for a mile or two you'll come to the banks of the beautiful Spey. Gwen (a whiz in the kitchen) and Michael (charming, chatty, debonair) make you feel immediately at home. Inside: a fire in the sitting room, a conservatory with garden views, and smartly clothed tables in the red dining room; best of all is the first-floor drawing room where big sofas wait in front of the fire, and beautiful art crams the walls. Bedrooms have a traditional country style: sheets and blankets, fresh flowers, polished wood and bowls of fruit; nip down to dinner and return to find your bed turned down. Expect delicious food (menus are discussed in advance), perhaps pork and apple terrine, fillet of sea bass with a lime vinaigrette, lemon parfait, a plate of cheese. Squirrel boxes and bird feeders in the garden offer entertainment at breakfast. A very cosseting place.

Price	£130. Singles £65. Half-board £100 p.p.
Rooms	5: 4 twins/doubles, 1 double.
Meals	Dinner, 4 courses, £34. Packed lunch available.
Closed	Mid-October-mid-March.
Directions	A95 north to Grantown. Right in town at 1st traffic lights on A939 for Tomintoul, 1st right into Woodside Ave. 500 yds on left.

Michael & Gwen Stewart
Woodside Avenue, Grantown-on-Spey,
Moray PH26 3JR

Tel	01479 872092
Email	info@thepinesgrantown.co.uk
Web	www.thepinesgrantown.co.uk

Woodwick House

This Northern outpost of the Sawday realm stands 200 yards up from the sea, with views across the Sound of Gairsay to a small archipelago. The house, once home to the local laird, stands in its own grounds with almost every tree on the island flanking a burn that tumbles over slabs of rock on its way to the sea; in May, bluebells in their millions join the fray. Inside, you find an extraordinary little place, not fancy for a moment, but the spirit here is second to none. Imagine the country house of a friend who doesn't have the money to pack it with smart antiques, so paints the walls, fits fresh carpets and fills it with the feel of home. Colourful bedrooms are simple and spotless, there's a fire in the sitting room, big views from the sunroom, a small dining room for delicious home cooking, a music room for the occasional concert, a library for good books and a TV room stacked with videos in case it rains. James is the star; he loves the Orkneys, has no airs and graces, and your trip to these extraordinary islands will be richer because of him. History, wildlife and vast skies wait.

Price	£68-£110. Singles £34-£75.
Rooms	7: 3 doubles, 1 twin, all en suite; 1 double, 1 twin, 1 single, with basins, all sharing bathroom.
Meals	Dinner, 3 courses, £26. Packed lunch £7, by arrangement.
Closed	Rarely.
Directions	From Kirkwall, A965 to Finstown, then right onto A966 for Evie. After 7 miles, 1st right after turning for Tingwall ferry. Left down track to house.

James Bryan
Evie, Orkney KW17 2PQ

Tel	01856 751330
Fax	01856 751383
Email	mail@woodwickhouse.co.uk
Web	www.woodwickhouse.co.uk

Killiecrankie House Hotel

Henrietta receives with great panache – no Highland fling would be complete without a night or two at her extremely welcoming hotel. Outside, gardens galore: one for roses, another for vegetables and a fine herbaceous border. Venture further afield and you find much to entertain your eyes – Loch Tummel, Rannoch Moor and magnificent Glenshee, over which you tumble for the Highland Games at Braemar. Return to a warm world of airy interiors with a little tartan in the dining room, 52 malts at the bar and views at breakfast of red squirrels climbing garden trees. There's a snug sitting room where a fire burns in winter, while doors open in summer for croquet on the lawn. Homely bedrooms come in different shapes and sizes. All are immensely comfortable and have a smart country style: pretty linen, warm colours, good fabrics, lovely views. Spin down to the restaurant for delicious country fare, perhaps carrot and coriander soup, Highland venison, sticky toffee pudding. There's porridge with cream and brown sugar for breakfast. A super little place.

Price	Half-board £94–£114 p.p.
Rooms	10: 4 doubles, 4 twins/doubles, 2 singles.
Meals	Half-board only. Lunch from £3.50. Dinner for non-residents, £38.
Closed	January & February.
Directions	A9 north of Pitlochry, then B8079, signed Killiecrankie. Straight ahead for 2 miles. Hotel on right, signed.

Henrietta Fergusson
Killiecrankie, Pitlochry, Perth PH16 5LG
Tel   01796 473220
Fax   01796 472451
Email   enquiries@killiecrankiehotel.co.uk
Web   www.killiecrankiehotel.co.uk

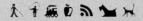

Craigatin House & Courtyard

Pitlochry – gateway to the Highlands – is a vibrant town with a famous theatre festival, castles and mountains, lochs and forests, even skiing over at Glenshee. This handsome old doctor's house – now a chic B&B – is perfectly situated to explore it all. It stands peacefully in two acres of manicured gardens on the northern shores of town; good restaurants are a short stroll. The formality of a smart stone exterior gives way to warmly contemporary interiors. Beautiful windows flood the rooms with light, there are shutters in the breakfast room and Lloyd Loom wicker in the conservatory, where French windows open onto a terrace for sun loungers and parasols in summer. Big uncluttered bedrooms – some in the main house, others in converted stables – are super value for money. Expect Farrow & Ball colours, comfy beds, crisp white linen, padded bedheads and pretty shower rooms. Breakfast offers the full cooked works and tempting alternatives: creamy omelettes or apple pancakes with grilled bacon and maple syrup. You're on the Whisky Trail, too. *Minimum stay two nights at weekends.*

Price	£60–£90. Suite £100. Singles from £70.
Rooms	13: 10 doubles, 2 twins, 1 suite.
Meals	Restaurants in town.
Closed	Christmas.
Directions	A9 north to Pitlochry. Take 1st turn-off for town, up main street, past shops and signed on left.

 Travel Club Offer: see page 367 for details.

	Martin & Andrea Anderson
	165 Atholl Road, Pitlochry,
	Perth & Kinross PH16 5QL
Tel	01796 472478
Email	enquiries@craigatinhouse.co.uk
Web	www.craigatinhouse.co.uk

The Ardeonaig Hotel & Restaurant

A little bit of heaven on the quiet side of Loch Tay. This is a seriously spoiling hotel, the epitome of 21st-century deep country chic. Whitewashed walls and hanging baskets give way to a courtyard where stone flowerbeds tumble with colour. Best of all is the first-floor library in varnished pine with its enormous window framing imperious views of field, loch and mountain. There are plump sofas, leather armchairs, books and maps, binoculars, too. Elsewhere, a snug bar in tartan, a peat fire in a sparkling sitting room, and views of a tumbling burn through dining room windows. Pete, a South African, had Fish Hoek in London and made a splash cooking up fabulous things, so expect seriously good food, perhaps smoked salmon salad, roast saddle of local hare, purple figs with honey and ginger. Stylish, uncluttered bedrooms are blissfully free of TVs and come in creams and browns, with good art, halogen lighting and cedarwood blinds. Those at the back have exquisite views. Stroll down to the water and find a flotilla of fishing boats; the hotel has rights, so bring your rod. *Minimum stay two nights at weekends.*

Price	£180–£300. Singles from £90. Lodges & suites from £350.
Rooms	27: 20 doubles, 5 lodges, 2 suites.
Meals	Bistro meals from £6.50. Dinner £26.50–£40. Tasting menu £49.50.
Closed	Never.
Directions	A9, then A827 to Kenmore via Aberfeldy. In Kenmore take south side road along Loch Tay for 10 miles. On right.

Pete Gottgens
Loch Tay, Killin, Perth & Kinross
FK21 8SU

Tel	01567 820400
Fax	01567 820282
Email	info@ardeonaighotel.co.uk
Web	www.ardeonaighotel.co.uk

 Travel Club Offer: see page 367 for details.

Monachyle Mhor

Twenty-five years of evolution has turned this 17th-century farmhouse into one of Scotland's coolest hotels. It's a family affair set in 2,000 acres of silence, with the Trossachs circling around you and Loch Voil shimming below. Dick farms, Melanie designs her magical rooms and Tom cooks some of the best food in Scotland. You're close to the end of the track with only the sheep and the birds to disturb you; lawns roll past a boules pitch towards the water. Step inside and find a slim restaurant behind a wall of glass, a small candlelit bar and an open fire in the sitting room. Bedrooms — most in a courtyard of converted stone outbuildings — are dreamy: big beds, crisp linen, cool colours, designer fabrics, hi-tech gadgets. Bathrooms can be out of this world: a deluge shower in a granite steam room, claw-foot baths that gaze upon the glen. Those in the main house are smaller, while suites in loft-house style are enormous. Walk, sail, fish, ride a bike through the forest. Dinner is five courses of unbridled heaven — with beef, lamb, pork and venison all off the farm. *Minimum stay two nights at weekends.*

Price	£105–£190. Singles from £95. Suites £180–£245. Half-board from £98.50 p.p.
Rooms	14: 3 doubles, 2 twins, 9 suites.
Meals	Sunday lunch £31. Dinner £46.
Closed	January.
Directions	M9 junc. 11, then B824 and A84 north. 6 miles north of Callander, turn right for Balquhidder. 5 miles west along road & Loch Voil. Hotel on right up drive, signed.

Tom Lewis
Balquhidder, Lochearnhead,
Perth & Kinross FK19 8PQ

Tel	01877 384622
Fax	01877 384305
Email	monachyle@mhor.net
Web	www.mhor.net

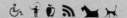

Creagan House

Where else can you sit in a baronial dining room and read a small tract on the iconography of the toast rack while waiting for your bacon and eggs? Creagan is a delight – a small and intimate restaurant with rooms run with great passion by Gordon and Cherry. At its heart is Gordon's kitchen, from which flies ambrosial food, perhaps hand-dived scallops with langoustine and lemon grass, Gressingham duck with honey and cloves, squidgy spiced apple cake. Food is sourced locally – meat and game from Perthshire, seafood from west-coast boats – and served on Skye pottery. There's a snug sitting room which doubles as a bar where you'll find a good wine list and 50 malt whiskies; if you like a dram, you'll be in heaven, and there's a guide to help you choose. Bedrooms fit the bill: warm and comfortable with smart carpets, wood and florals, flat-screen TVs, a sofa if there's room. No airs and graces, just the sort of attention you only get in small owner-run places. Bag a munro, too; let the walking sticks at the front door help you up Beinn An T-Sidhein. A perfect wee retreat.

Price	£120–£130. Singles £70–£85.
Rooms	5: 1 four-poster, 3 doubles, 1 twin.
Meals	Dinner, 3 courses, £29.50–£34.50.
Closed	Wednesdays, Thursdays & February.
Directions	From Stirling, A84 north through Callander to Strathyre. Hotel 0.25 miles north of village on right.

Travel Club Offer: see page 367 for details.

Gordon & Cherry Gunn
Strathyre, Callander,
Perth & Kinross FK18 8ND

Tel	01877 384638
Fax	01877 384319
Email	eatandstay@creaganhouse.co.uk
Web	www.creaganhouse.co.uk

The Royal Hotel

The Royal is lovely – softly grand, intimate and welcoming, a country house in the middle of town. Queen Victoria once stayed, hence the name. It stands on the river Earn – the eponymous loch glistens majestically five miles up stream – but you're brilliantly placed to strike out in all directions: Loch Tay, Pitlochry, The Trossachs and Perth are all on your doorstep, even Edinburgh is easy to get to. Those who linger fare rather well. Two fires burn side by side in a wonderful sitting room, newspapers hang on poles, logs tumble from wicker baskets, sofas and armchairs are impeccably upholstered. There's a grandfather clock in the hall, rugs to cover stripped floors in the bar, and walls festooned with beautiful art. You eat all over the place, with leather armchairs in the bar, Lloyd Loom furniture in the conservatory/brasserie or at smartly dressed tables in a warm and elegant dining room. Spotless rooms above are just what you'd want: padded bedheads, crisp white linen, mahogany dressers, gilt-framed mirrors. Bathrooms come with fluffy robes, one four-poster has a log fire. Fabulous.

Travel Club Offer: see page 367 for details.

Price	£140. Four-posters £160. Singles from £85. Half-board £90–£110 p.p. Self-catering from £320 (2 nights).
Rooms	11 + 1: 5 doubles, 3 twins, 3 four-posters. 1 self-catering townhouse for 4.
Meals	Bar meals from £6.95. Dinner, 3 courses, £26.50.
Closed	Occasionally.
Directions	A9 north of Dunblane, then A822 through Braco & left onto B827. Left for centre of town, over bridge & hotel on square.

Teresa Milsom
Melville Square, Comrie,
Perthshire PH6 2DN

Tel	01764 679200
Fax	01764 679219
Email	reception@royalhotel.co.uk
Web	www.royalhotel.co.uk

An Lochan

This is one of Scotland's most famous inns. It was run for years by a Yorkshireman who decided to treat the Scots to an English inn; remarkably, the locals liked it. These days it's safely back in Scottish hands – with a Scottish name to boot – and a quick wander through delightful rooms confirms that a Scot has trumped the old enemy and made the place better. Simplicity is the virtue. You get slate floors covered in hessian, logs piled high in the fireplace, panelled walls, roaring fires, old beams running above. Tradition and style go hand in hand. Weave into the restaurant and find whitewashed walls and wooden benches smartly upholstered in green tartan; double doors lead through to high ceilings and painted pine in the conservatory. Super food is served informally; expect to eat well, perhaps seafood chowder, haunch of venison, chocolate tart with blood orange jelly. Homely bedrooms tend to be big. You get walls of colour, crisp white linen, black and white bathrooms, the odd stone wall. Gleneagles is ten miles north, tee times can be arranged.

Price	£100. Singles £85. Lodge £150.
Rooms	13: 12 twins/doubles, 1 lodge for 4.
Meals	Lunch from £7.95.
	Dinner, 3 courses, from £24.95.
Closed	Never.
Directions	A9 north from Dunblane, then
	A823 south at Gleneagles.
	On left in village.

Roger & Bea McKie
Glendevon, Perthshire FK14 7JY

Tel	0845 371 1414
Email	info@anlochan.co.uk
Web	www.anlochan.co.uk

 Travel Club Offer: see page 367 for details.

Ethical Collection: Food.
See page 373 for details

Windlestraw Lodge

There are few better distractions in Scotland than following the river Tweed; fishing lines glisten in the sun, lambs bleat high on the hill, ospreys glide through the afternoon sky. This is the river which brought prosperity to Scotland, its mills a source of huge wealth in Victorian days. Windlestraw, a supremely comfortable country house, stands in evidence; it was built as a wedding gift for a mill owner and sits on the side of a hill with timeless views down the valley. Outside, a fine copper beech shades the lawn. Inside, a dazzling refurbishment has softened the grandness giving the feel of home. You get stripped floors, painted ceilings, roaring fires, a panelled dining room. Light pours in through windows at the front, gilt mirrors hang on walls, fat sofas encourage idleness. There are binoculars with which to scan the valley, a terrace for afternoon tea, a sitting room for a quiet snooze. Country-house bedrooms are fine or finer, two are sublime; all come with crisp linen, those at the front have super views. Don't miss Alan's fabulous food or a round of golf at Peebles. Brilliant.

Price	£130–£180. Singles from £80. Half-board from £105 p.p.
Rooms	6: 5 doubles, 1 twin.
Meals	Lunch by arrangement. Dinner, 4 courses, £40.
Closed	Rarely.
Directions	East from Peebles on A72. Into Walkerburn; house signed left on western flank of town.

 Travel Club Offer: see page 367 for details.

Julie & Alan Reid
Tweed Valley, Walkerburn,
Scottish Borders EH43 6AA
Tel	01896 870 636
Fax	01896 870404
Email	reception@windlestraw.co.uk
Web	www.windlestraw.co.uk

Ballochneck

Donnie and Fiona's magical pile stands one mile up a rutted drive, soundproofed by 175 acres of lush Stirlingshire country. Swans nest on the lake in spring, which doubles as a curling pond in winter (you can), while Suffolk sheep graze the fields and deer come to eat the rhododendrons. The house – still a home, albeit a grand one – dates to 1863 and was built for the Lord Provost of Glasgow. Inside you get all the aristocratic works – roaring fires, painted panelling, magical windows that bring in the view, wonderfully ornate ceilings – but Donnie and Fiona are the real stars; expect a little banter, a few good stories and a trip to the top of the house where a full-size snooker tables stands amid purple walls. Vast bedrooms at the front have huge views, beautiful beds and acres of crisp linen; one has an open fire, while a claw-foot bath next door comes with candles and views down the valley. Breakfast is a feast, and served in summer in a magnificent Victorian conservatory amid beds of lavender and wandering clematis. Stirling Castle and Loch Lomond are close. *Children over 12 welcome. Minimum stay two nights at weekends.*

Price	£145–£160.
	With interconnecting twin £215.
Rooms	3: 1 double en suite; 1 double with private bathroom; 1 interconnecting twin (let to same party only).
Meals	Dinner, 4 courses, £35.
Closed	Christmas & New Year.
Directions	M9 junc. 10; A84 west, B8075 south, then A811 for Buchlyvie. In village, right onto B835 for Aberfoyle. Over bridge, up to lodge house 200 yds on left. 1 mile up drive to house.

Donnie & Fiona Allan
Buchlyvie, Stirling FK8 3PA

Tel	01360 850216
Fax	01360 850376
Email	info@ballochneck.com
Web	www.ballochneck.com

Travel Club Offer: see page 367 for details.

Kilcamb Lodge

A stupendous setting, with Loch Sunart at the end of the garden and Glas Bheinn rising beyond. As for Kilcamb, it has all the ingredients of the perfect country house: a smart yellow drawing room with a roaring fire, a dining room that's won just about every award going and super-comfy bedrooms that don't stint on colour. The feel here is shipwreck-chic. There's a 12-acre garden with half a mile of shore, so follow paths to the water's edge and look for dolphins, otters and seals or watch duck and geese; if you're lucky, you may see eagles. Back inside you'll find stained-glass windows on the landing, a ship's bell in the bar, fresh flowers in the bedrooms. Come down at eight for a four-course dinner and feast on goat's cheese and chive mousse, cream of celery and stilton soup, roast venison with a juniper jus, then lemon curd crème brûlée. Warmly decorated bedrooms have all the trimmings: super king-size beds, padded headboards, big white towels, shiny bathrooms. Ardnamurchan Point is up the road and worth a visit: it's the most westerly point in mainland Britain. *Minumum stay two nights at weekends in May.*

Price	£130–£180. Suites £230. Singles from £95.
Rooms	10: 7 doubles, 3 suites.
Meals	Lunch from £7.50. Dinner, 4 courses, £48.
Closed	January. Limited opening November & February.
Directions	From Fort William, A82 south for 10 miles to Corran ferry, then A861 to Strontian. Hotel west of village on left, signed. A830 & A861 from Fort William takes an hour longer.

David & Sally Ruthven-Fox
Strontian, Argyll PH36 4HY

Tel	01967 402257
Fax	01967 402041
Email	enquiries@kilcamblodge.co.uk
Web	www.kilcamblodge.co.uk

Doune

You arrive by boat (there's no road in): a ferry across to Knoydart, the last great wilderness to survive in Britain. You'll find mountains, sea and beach — a thrilling wonderland of boundless peace. Guillemots race across the water, waves lap on the shore, the Sound of Sleat fuses with the sea and shoots across to Skye. Martin and Jane look after you with unpretentious generosity and are now part of the tiny community which rescued this land from ruin. The dining room is the hub, pine-clad from top-to-toe with a stove to keep you warm and a couple of guitars for the odd ceilidh; some of the staff are folk musicians and fiddles often fly. Food is delicious — crab from the bay, roast lamb from the hill, chocolate tart with homemade ice cream. Bedrooms along the veranda are as simple as they should be, three pine rooms with bunk galleries for children, hooks for clothes, easy chairs for watching the weather, small shower rooms. There's a lodge for groups with an open-plan layout. The walking is magnificent, the sunsets are breathtaking. Miss it at your peril. *Boat pick-up Tuesday & Saturday: minimum stay three nights.*

Price	Full-board £72 p.p. per night or £432 p.p. per week. Lodge: full-board from £55 p.p. or £330 per week. Discounts for children.
Rooms	4 + 1: 2 doubles, 1 twin (with mezzanine beds for children), 1 single. Catered lodge for 12.
Meals	Full-board (includes packed lunch).
Closed	October-Easter.
Directions	Park in Mallaig; the boat will collect you at an agreed time.

Martin & Jane Davies
Knoydart, Mallaig,
Inverness-shire PH41 4PL

Tel	01687 462667
Fax	08700 940428
Email	martin@doune-knoydart.co.uk
Web	www.doune-knoydart.co.uk

Tomdoun Hotel

A quirky little place wrapped up in the middle of nowhere: in good weather Reception moves onto the veranda and the dogs sunbathe on lilos. Below, the blissful river Garry jumps from one loch to another; beyond, Glas Bheinn rises from the forest. Interiors are stylishly unpretentious (posh, but old!) with piles of logs and vintage luggage in the hall, a country-house dining room for breakfasts, and a smouldering coal fire in the lively bar. Come to fish – the hotel has rights on the loch and river – and if you're lucky, they'll cook your catch for supper. If not, settle for langoustine and cockles from Skye, or halibut fresh from Lochinver. A Swiss filmmaker liked the place so much he returned to shoot a movie. Exquisite walking in the wild and peaceful glen, with Loch Hourn 20 miles upstream (where the road runs out). Bedrooms are simple, homely, nicely priced, full of colour; those at the front have huge Glengarry views. There's loads to do: 35 munros to climb, clay-pigeon shooting, white-water rafting, water-skiing, abseiling, mountain biking.

Price	£80–£110. Singles from £35.
Rooms	10: 3 doubles, 2 family, all en suite; 3 doubles, 1 twin, 1 single all sharing 2 baths.
Meals	Packed lunch £7.95. Bar meals from £9.95. Dinner, 3 courses, from £18.95.
Closed	Never.
Directions	A82 north from Fort William, then A87 west from Invergarry. After 5 miles, left for Glengarry. Hotel 6 miles up on right.

 Travel Club Offer: see page 367 for details.

Michael Pearson
Glengarry, Invergarry,
Inverness-shire PH35 4HS
Tel   01809 511218
Email   enquiries@tomdoun.com
Web   www.tomdoun.com

Entry 317   Map 8

Loch Ness Lodge

A super-smart country house built from scratch in 2006, it overlooks the famous loch so don't forget your telephoto lens. Inside, plush interiors are the order of the day: French oak floors, period colours, designer fabrics and fresh flowers everywhere. There's an open fire in the airy sitting room so grab the newspaper and sink into a sofa; red Zoffany wallpaper in the restaurant adds colour and style. Bedrooms are seriously indulging with huge beds dressed in Egyptian cotton and extravagant bathrooms that come in creamy sandstone hues. One room is a riot of red crushed velvet, another has armchairs in a turret. Five have sublime loch views, all have bathrobes, CD players and flat-screen TV/DVDs. Dinner is serious, a five-course feast, perhaps velouté of woodland mushrooms, carpaccio of short-horn beef, roasted breast of Gressingham duck, handmade oatcakes with a plate of cheese, Tia Maria panna cotta. There's loads to do – both coasts are equally accessible – and don't miss Glen Affric, one of Scotland's loveliest. There's a sauna, a hot tub and treatment room, too.

Price	£180–£230. Suites £280. Cottages £560–£930 per week.
Rooms	7 + 5: 3 twins/doubles, 2 doubles, 2 suites. 5 self-catering cottages (3 for 2, 2 for 4).
Meals	Dinner, 5 courses, £45. Lunch by arrangement.
Closed	3 January–end February.
Directions	A82 south from Inverness for 10 miles. On right after Clansman Hotel.

Scott Sutherland
Brachla, Loch Ness-side, Inverness,
Inverness-shire IV3 8LA

Tel   01456 459469
Fax   01456 459439
Email   escape@lodgeatlochness.com
Web   www.lodgeatlochness.co.uk

Glenmorangie, The Highland Home at Cadboll

Glenmorangie – glen of tranquillity. And so it is; this is heaven. Owned by the eponymous distillery, this 1700s farmhouse of thick walls and immaculate interiors stands in glorious country, with a tree-lined path down to the beach; see your supper landed by fishermen, or search for driftwood instead. A perfect place and a real find, with levels of service to surpass most others, where staff are attentive yet unobtrusive, and where the comforts seem unending. Bedrooms are exceptional: decanters of whisky, *fleur de lys* wallpaper, tartan blankets and country views. Rooms flood with light, there are bathrobes and piles of towels, the best linen and blankets, and the cottage suites are perfect for families. Downstairs, the portrait of the Sheriff of Cromarty hangs on the wall, a fire crackles between plump sofas in the drawing room, and views of the garden draw you out. The walled half-acre garden is both beautiful and productive, with much for your plate: superb dinners, five courses, are served in intimate dinner party style. All this, and golf at Royal Dornoch, Tain and Brora.

Price	Half-board £165–£195 p.p.
Rooms	9: 6 twins/doubles, 3 cottage suites.
Meals	Half-board only. Light lunch from £7. Dinner for non-residents, £45.
Closed	3–23 January.
Directions	A9 north from Inverness for 33 miles to Nigg r'bout. Right on B9175, for Nigg, over r'way crossing for 1.5 miles, then left, following signs to house.

	Martin Baxter
	Fearn, Tain, Ross-shire IV20 1XP
Tel	01862 871671
Fax	01862 871625
Email	relax@glenmorangieplc.co.uk
Web	www.theglenmorangiehouse.com

Mackay's Rooms

This is the north-west tip of Britain and it's utterly magnificent: huge skies, sandy beaches, aquamarine seas, cliffs and caves. You drive – or cycle – for mile upon mile with mountains soaring into the heavens and ridges sliding into the sea. If you like big, remote landscapes, you'll love it here; what's more, you'll have it mostly to yourself. Mackay's – they have the shop, the bunkhouse and the garage, too – is the only place to stay in town, its jaunty contemporary colours mixing with stone walls and stripped floors to great effect. Bedrooms are perfect – extremely comfy, warmly coloured, big wooden beds, crisp white linen – and Fiona, a textiles graduate, has a fine eye for lovely fabrics and upholstery. There are excellent bathrooms, flat-screen TVs, DVD players too. Breakfast sets you up for the day – grilled grapefruit, whisky porridge, venison sausages, local eggs – so head east to the beach at Ceannabeinne, west for golf on top of the cliffs or catch the ferry across to Cape Wrath and scan the sea for whales. There's surfing for the brave and the beautiful. Unbeatable.

Price	£100–£130. Singles from £90. Cottage £500–£950 per week.
Rooms	7 + 1: 5 doubles, 2 twins. 1 self-catering cottage for 6.
Meals	Lunch from £5. Dinner, 3 courses, £25–£30.
Closed	November–Easter.
Directions	A838 north from Rhiconich. After 19 miles enter Durness village. Mackay's is on right-hand side opposite memorial.

Fiona Mackay
Durness, Sutherland IV27 4PN

Tel	01971 511202
Fax	01971 511321
Email	fiona@visitmackays.com
Web	www.visitmackays.com

The Albannach

It may take a while to get here, but you won't regret it for a moment. The coast is magical, its glimmering seas, rugged mountains and empty roads a tonic for the soul. Add to this a night or two at the Albannach and you find paradise in the Highlands. Ostensibly this is a restaurant with rooms – Colin and Lesley's faultless food is worth the trip alone – but the house is no less alluring, so climb up to find fat white sofas in the conservatory, an open fire in the panelled snug, and cherry red walls in the baronial dining room. The house is one room deep with views from the front of water, village, mountain. Bedrooms are divine, big or bigger, all dressed in Sunday-best fabrics with Farrow & Ball colours, silky curtains, carafes of water and Bose sound systems. The suites are majestic with unbeatable bathrooms, and the simpler rooms are not simple at all; everything here is fantastic. As for the food, expect the best, perhaps duck with foie gras, red pepper soufflé, Lochinver halibut with a champagne sauce, sublime apple tart with calvados gelato. Walk, fish, some people swim. Heaven.

Price	Half-board £125-£170 p.p. Singles £200. Winter weekend breaks available.
Rooms	5: 2 doubles, 3 suites.
Meals	Half-board only. Lunch, by arrangement, from £12. Dinner, 5 courses, £50 for non-residents.
Closed	January & February.
Directions	North from Ullapool on A835, then A837 for Lochinver. In village, left, over bridge, for Baddidarrach. House signed left after half a mile.

Colin Craig & Lesley Crosfield
Baddidaroch, Lochinver,
Sutherland IV27 4LP

Tel	01571 844407
Email	info@thealbannach.co.uk
Web	www.thealbannach.co.uk

The Torridon

An 1887 shooting lodge built for the Earl of Lovelace with 58 acres of lawn and field racing down to the shores of Upper Loch Torridon. You're in the middle of nowhere, but you wouldn't be anywhere else. Mighty mountains rise around you, red deer, sea eagles and otters pass through. Inside, sparkling interiors thrill: a huge fire in the panelled hall, a zodiac ceiling in the plush drawing room, 300 malts in the pitch pine bar. Huge windows pull in the view, walkers pour off the hills to recover in luxury, there's a telescope with which to scan water and mountain. Bedrooms are a real treat, some big, others bigger, all packed with spoiling extras. Some rooms come in smart contemporary style (padded headboards, cool colours, silky throws, super bathrooms), others are deliciously traditional (country-house colours, warm florals, old armoires, a shower in a turret). The two-acre vegetable garden is a work of art in itself and provides much for the table, so feast on fresh food sublimely cooked. Cattle graze in the fields, magnificent Liathach waits to be climbed. There's an inn and a boathouse, too.

Price	Half-board £132.50-£237.50 p.p. Boathouse from £750 per week.
Rooms	19 + 1: 10 doubles, 1 twin, 1 single, 2 four-posters, 5 suites. Self-catering boathouse for 4.
Meals	Half-board only (except boathouse). Lunch from £5. Dinner, 5 courses, £40 for non-residents.
Closed	January.
Directions	A9 to Inverness, A835 to Garve, A832 to Kinlochewe, A896 to Annat (not Torridon). In village, right by sea.

Daniel & Rohaise Rose-Bristow
Torridon, Achnasheen,
Wester Ross IV22 2EY

Tel	01445 791242
Fax	01445 712253
Email	info@thetorridon.com
Web	www.thetorridon.com

Travel Club Offer: see page 367 for details.

Ethical Collection: Environment;
Community; Food. See page 373 for details

Tigh an Eilean

Tigh an Eilean is the Holy Grail of the West Coast – you arrive to realise it's what you've been looking for all these years. It's a perfect place in every respect, from its position by the sea in this very pretty village, to the magnificence of the Torridon mountains that rise around. Inside, smart country-house interiors are just the ticket: warmly stylish with pretty wallpaper, lovely fabrics, comfy sofas and wood-burners everywhere. There's an honesty bar, a couple of sitting rooms, and an award-winning restaurant that looks out to sea, but Cathryn and Christopher – ex-London lawyers who escaped the city ten years ago – refuse to stand still and have just re-built the pub, turning it into a lovely terraced bar with a restaurant above, where doors open onto a roof terrace; scoff the freshest seafood while gazing out to sea. Bedrooms (most have the view) come kitted out with colourful fabrics, crisp linen, fitted wardrobes, the odd antique. Delicious food flies from the kitchen and Shieldaig, a working fishing village, still gathers in the bar, to play its fiddles and sip the odd malt.

Price	£160. Singles from £75. Half-board from £115 p.p.
Rooms	11: 5 doubles, 3 twins, 3 singles.
Meals	Lunch & dinner in bar, £5–£25. Restaurant dinner £44. Packed lunches available.
Closed	November–March.
Directions	On loch front in centre of Shieldaig.

Christopher & Cathryn Field
Shieldaig, Loch Torridon, Ross-shire
IV54 8XN

Tel	01520 755251
Fax	01520 755321
Email	tighaneilean@keme.co.uk

Viewfield House

This old ancestral pile stands high above Portree Bay with fine views tumbling down to the Sound of Rassay below. Twenty acres of mature gardens and woodland wrap around you, with croquet on the lawn, paths that weave through pretty gardens and a hill to climb for 360° views of sea, ridge and peak. As for this Victorian factor's house, expect a few aristocratic fixtures and fittings: hunting trophies in the hall, cases filled with curios, a grand piano and open fire in the drawing room, vintage Sanderson wallpaper in the dining room. Family oils hang on the walls, you'll find wood carvings from distant lands and a flurry of antiques, all of which blend grandeur with touches of humour. Upstairs is a warren of bedrooms. Most are big, some are vast, all come in country-house style with traditional fabrics, crisply laundered sheets and sea views from those at the front. Dive into Skye – wildlife, mountains, sea lochs and castles all wait. Light suppers are on tap – salads, salmon, spotted dick; alternatively, dine out on Skye's natural larder. There's Highland porridge for breakfast, too.

Price	£80–£130. Singles £40–£65.
Rooms	12: 4 doubles, 3 twins/doubles, 2 twins, 2 singles all en suite. 1 double with separate bath.
Meals	Light supper £3–£14. Packed lunch £5.40.
Closed	Mid-October-Easter.
Directions	On A87, coming from south, driveway entrance on left just before the Portree National filling station.

Hugh Macdonald
Portree, Isle of Skye IV51 9EU

Tel	01478 612217
Fax	01478 613517
Email	info@viewfieldhouse.com
Web	www.viewfieldhouse.com

Travel Club Offer: see page 367 for details.

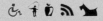

Greshornish House Hotel

A single-track road peters out at this supremely peaceful hotel, which stands in ten acres of woodland gardens with long views across Loch Greshornish to the Totternish peninsular. Inside, a slightly eccentric country house, with a grand piano in the snooker room and a sofa'd bar that doubles as reception. Neil and Rosemary are everywhere and run the place with infectious charm. Downstairs, an open fire glows in the half-panelled sitting room, afternoon tea is laid out in the conservatory and splendid local food is served in the dining room, where tables are smartly dressed with white cloths and fresh flowers. Bedrooms are mostly large and come in a warm traditional style. A couple at the front are huge and have fancy bathrooms; all have excellent views of the water or the gardens, expensive bed linen and deep peace. Outside, there's croquet on a sweeping lawn, a terrace for drinks before dinner and paths that lead down to the loch; porpoises, seals or otters all come through – and watch out for sheep on the road to get here.

Price	£110–£198.
Rooms	9: 4 doubles, 2 twins/doubles, 1 twin, 2 family.
Meals	Lunch £5.50–£22.50. Dinner, 3 courses, about £38. Packed lunch about £6.
Closed	Christmas. Occasionally in winter.
Directions	A87 through Portree then west on A850 for Dunvegan. Signed right after 10 miles. 2.5 miles down single track road to hotel.

Neil & Rosemary Colquhoun
Portree, Isle of Skye IV51 9PN

Tel	01470 582266
Fax	01470 582345
Email	info@greshornishhouse.com
Web	www.greshornishhouse.com

Stein Inn

A small inn down by the water where Angus cooks super food and refuses to put up his prices. The position is perfect, Skye at its loveliest. You're bang on the loch on a road that goes nowhere. Razorbills and guillemots fly low over the water, islands sparkle in the distance, fishermen land their catch on the jetty, sunsets streak the sky red. Inside, stone walls, smouldering fires, pine cladding and a bustling bar that's crammed with locals at weekends. There are maps on the walls, nautical curios, a pool table at the back. Bedrooms above fit the bill perfectly. They're spotless, colourful, nice and comfy, with a warm country style and an honest price. Some are big, some are small, compact bathrooms are more than sufficient. Back downstairs you can dig into impossibly fresh food from a menu that changes daily, perhaps carrot and sweet potato soup, whole Dover sole fresh from the loch, then homemade profiteroles and chocolate sauce. Corncrakes and sea eagles pass through, the northern lights sparkle in winter, Dunvegan Castle is worth a peek.

Price	£60–£90. Singles £35–£50.
Rooms	5: 2 doubles, 2 family, 1 single.
Meals	Lunch & dinner £3–£20.
Closed	Christmas Day & New Year's Day.
Directions	From Isle of Skye bridge, A850 to Portree. Follow sign to Uig for 4 miles, left on A850 for Dunvegan for 14 miles. Hard right turn to Waternish on B886. Stein 4.5 miles along loch side.

Angus & Teresa McGhie
Stein, Waternish,
Isle of Skye IV55 8GA

Tel	01470 592362
Fax	01470 592362
Email	angus.teresa@stein-inn.co.uk
Web	www.stein-inn.co.uk

Ullinish Country Lodge

A sparkling whitewashed Georgian farmhouse which stands on the west coast under a vast sky; mighty views stretch across Loch Harport to the Talisker distillery at Carbost. Samuel Johnson stayed on his famous tour, though you can bet your bottom dollar he didn't eat as well as you will. Pam and Brian came to add to Skye's gastronomic reputation and have done just that, serving up some of the best food on the island. Inside, a total refurbishment reveals warm interiors: tartan carpets in the hall, leather sofas in front of the fire, a telescope for a star gazing. Bedrooms upstairs are positively plush with huge mahogany beds, stately colours, silky crowns and watery views. There are decanters of sherry, claw-foot baths and flat-screen TVs. Head outside and discover the tidal island of Oronsay. Dolphins and whales pass, sea eagles patrol the skies, there are standing stones and iron age remains. As for dinner, expect the best, perhaps Dunvegan langoustine cooked five ways, loin of venison with a beetroot sorbet, wild strawberry soufflé with lime leaf ice cream.

Price	£120–£160. Singles from £90. Half-board from £135 p.p.
Rooms	6 doubles.
Meals	Light lunch from £12.90. Sunday lunch £16.95. Dinner, 4 courses, £45.
Closed	January & 1 week in November.
Directions	North from Skye bridge on A87, then A863 for Dunvegan. Thro' Bracadale and Struan signed left. House on right after 1 mile.

Travel Club Offer: see page 367 for details.

Brian & Pam Howard
Struan, Isle of Skye IV56 8FD
Tel   01470 572214
Email   enquiries@ullinish-country-lodge.co.uk
Web   www.theisleofskye.co.uk

Tigh Dearg

This far-flung island chain is worth every second it takes to get here. Come for huge skies, sweeping beaches, carpets of wild flowers in the machair in summer, stone circles, ancient burial chambers, white-tailed eagles and fabulous Hebridean light. It's hard to overstate the sheer wonder of these bleakly beautiful islands, five of which are connected by a causeway, so drop south to Benbecula (*Whisky Galore* was filmed here) or Eriskay (for the Prince's Strand, where Bonnie Prince Charlie landed). Up on North Uist you'll find 1,000 lochs, so climb North Lees for wonderful watery views, then tumble back down to the island sanctuary of Tigh Dearg. The house is a delight, immensely welcoming, full of colour, warmly contemporary, with windows that flood the place with light. Swanky bedrooms come with suede headboards, power showers, bathrobes and beach towels, bowls of fruit and crisp white linen. In the restaurant, lobster, crab, squid, sole all come straight from the water. Walk, ride, fish, canoe, then return and try the sauna. Come in November for the northern lights. Fabulous.

Price	£80–£145.
Rooms	8 twins/doubles.
Meals	Bar meals from £8.50.
	Dinner, 3 courses, £25–£30.
Closed	Never.
Directions	North into Lochmaddy. Left, signed
	Police Station. On left after 200 yds.

Iain MacLeod
Lochmaddy, North Uist,
Western Isles HS6 5AE

Tel	01876 500700
Fax	01876 500701
Email	info@tighdearghotel.co.uk
Web	www.tighdearghotel.co.uk

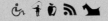

Scarista House

All you need to know is this: Harris is one of the most beautiful places anywhere in the world. Beaches of white sand that stretch for a mile or two are not uncommon. If you bump into another soul, it will be a delightful coincidence, but you should not count on it. The water is turquoise, and coconuts sometimes wash up on the beach. The view from Scarista is simple and magnificent: field, ridge, beach, water, sky. Patricia and Tim are the kindest people, quietly inspiring. Their home is island heaven: coal fires, rugs on painted wooden floors, books everywhere, old oak furniture, a first-floor drawing room, fresh flowers and fabulous Harris light. The golf club has left a set of clubs by the front door in case you wish to play (the view from the first tee is one of the best in the game). A corncrake occasionally visits the garden. There are walking sticks and Wellington boots to help you up the odd hill. Kind local staff may speak Gaelic. And the food is exceptional, maybe twice-baked crab soufflé, seared loin of Harris lamb, marmalade tart with plum compote. A perfect place.

Price	£175–£199. Singles from £120.
Rooms	5: 3 doubles, 2 twins.
Meals	Dinner, 3 courses, £39.50. Packed lunch £5.50.
Closed	Christmas & February.
Directions	From Tarbert, A859, signed Rodel. Scarista 15 miles on left, after golf course.

Patricia & Tim Martin
Isle of Harris, Western Isles HS3 3HX

Tel	01859 550238
Fax	01859 550277
Email	timandpatricia@scaristahouse.com
Web	www.scaristahouse.com

Becoming a member of Sawday's Travel Club opens up hundreds of discounts, treats and other offers at many of our Special Places to Stay in Britain and Ireland, as well as promotions on Sawday's books and other goodies.

Where you see the 💼 symbol in this book it means the place has a special offer for Club members. It may be money off your room price, a bottle of champagne or a day's trout fishing. The offers for each place are listed on the following pages. These were correct at the time of going to print, but owners reserve the right to change the listed offer. Latest offers for all places can be found on our website, www.sawdays.co.uk.

Membership is only £25 per year. To see membership extras and to register visit www.sawdays.co.uk/members. You can also call 01275 395433 to set up a direct debit.

The small print

You must mention that you are a Travel Club member when booking, and confirm that the offer is available. Your Travel Club card must be shown on arrival to claim the offer. Sawday's Travel Club cards are not transferable. If two cardholders share a room they can only claim the offer once. Offers for Sawday's Travel Club members are subject to availability. Alastair Sawday Publishing cannot accept any responsibility if places fail to honour offers; neither can we accept responsibility if a place changes hands and drops out of the Travel Club.

England

Bath & N.E. Somerset

2   Half bottle of champagne on arrival.
3   Glass of prosecco on arrival (not Christmas or bank holidays).

Berkshire

9   20% off room rate on Sunday nights. Drink at the bar on arrival.

Brighton & Hove

11   Bottle of house wine.
14   10% off room rate Sunday-Thursday (excluding bank holidays).

Cambridgeshire

20 10% off room rate Sunday-Thursday.

21 10% off room rate Monday-Thursday. Glass of champagne with dinner.

Cornwall

23 Cornish cream tea on arrival.

24 10% off room rate Monday-Thursday.

25 Bottle of house wine with dinner. Upgrade subject to availability.

26 Bottle of premier cru champagne on arrival.

27 Half bottle of champagne on arrival for stays of 2 nights or more.

28 Half bottle of champagne in room on arrival.

31 10% off room rate Sunday-Thursday.

32 Bottle of house wine with dinner on 1st night.

33 Free picnic & map for walkers, or bucket & spade for those off to beach.

38 Bottle of champagne on arrival (half-board only).

Cumbria

39 Bottle of house wine with dinner on 1st night.

41 10% off standard room rate.

43 Champagne afternoon tea on day of arrival.

44 Champagne & afternoon tea.

47 Bottle of Moët champagne for stays of 2+ nights.

Derbyshire

53 10% off room rate Monday-Thursday. Free entry to Haddon Hall.

Devon

57 Bottle of Michel Lafarge Bourgone Blanc on arrival.

61 10% off B&B or DBB Monday-Thursday.

62 Glass of of champagne before dinner.

65 £20 voucher to spend on Percy's lamb & pork.

66 Bottle of house wine. Fishermen receive a day of free trout fishing on the Tamar.

67 Cornish pasties & Devonshire chutney on arrival.

69 10% off room rate Monday-Thursday.

71 10% off room rate Monday-Thursday.

72 10% off room rate Monday-Thursday, or stay 4 nights & the last night is free.

74 Glass of champagne on arrival. Upgrade subject to availability.

75 Bottle of house wine with dinner on 1st night.

78 Bottle of house wine with dinner.

Dorset

87   Aperitif before dinner.

90   Glass of champagne on arrival.

93   Bottle of house wine with dinner.

Essex

96   Bottle of champagne on arrival. Upgrade subject to availability.

Gloucestershire

101   10% off room rate Monday-Thursday.

102   Stay midweek (Sunday-Thursday) & receive a bottle of champagne.

105   25% off room rate Monday-Thursday.

112   Afternoon tea on arrival. Room upgrade subject to availability.

113   Glass of champagne on arrival.

Hampshire

119   Glass of champagne on arrival.

120   10% off DBB Sunday-Thursday.

Herefordshire

123   10% off room rate Tuesday & Wednesday. Bottle of house wine.

124   10% off room rate Sunday-Thursday.

Isle of Wight

126   Glass of champagne for each guest before dinner.

Kent

130   Bottle of white wine.

132   Cream tea during stay.

136   Bottle of champagne in your room on arrival for stays of 2 days or more.

138   Drink from the honesty bar on arrival.

London

142   Bottle of house wine with dinner on 1st night.

145   Glass of champagne on arrival.

146   Bottle of wine.

Norfolk

150   Bottle of Norfolk wine with dinner on 1st night.

151   Bottle of house wine with dinner for 2.

154   Glass of champagne on arrival.
157   10% off room rate Monday-Thursday. Bottle of house wine with first dinner.
163   House cocktail each night.

Northumberland
168   Glass of house wine on arrival.

Nottinghamshire
170   10% off room rate Monday-Thursday.
171   Half bottle of champagne in your room on arrival.

Oxfordshire
173   Cocktail on arrival & goody bag of homemade treats.
178   Glass of champagne on arrival.

Shropshire
186   Bottle of champagne in your room on arrival.
187   10% off room rate Monday-Thursday.
188   10% off room rate Sunday-Thursday, 5% at weekends.

Somerset
189   Bottle of house wine with dinner.
192   Glass of champagne on arrival.
196   Bottle of wine with dinner on 1st night.
197   Cream tea on arrival.

Suffolk
200   Bowl of fresh fruit & decanter of sherry.
202   10% off room rate Sun-Thurs. Late checkout. Glass of champagne on arrival.
204   Half bottle of champagne in your room.
205   Copy of Ruth Watson's cookbook, *Fat Girl Slim*.
207   10% off room rate Monday-Thursday. Glass of champagne on arrival.
208   3 nights for price of 2, Sun-Thurs (not bank holidays). Upgrade subject to availability.

Sussex
211   10% off room rate Monday-Thursday (not mid-May to September).
213   10% off room rate Sunday-Thursday.
214   20% off room rate Sunday-Thursday, October-April (not Christmas).
215   Bottle of house wine with dinner on 1st night.
217   Glass of champagne on arrival.

219 Bottle of house wine with dinner.

221 Bag of home-toasted muesli.

Warwickshire

222 Afternoon tea 4pm-6pm, or a glass of house wine if you arrive later.

223 Half bottle of champagne in your room.

225 Bottle of house champagne with any booking Sunday-Thursday.

Wiltshire

228 10% off room rate Mon-Thurs. Late checkout. Glass of champagne on arrival.

229 Glass of champagne in bar on 1st night.

231 20% off lunch & dinner for stays of 2 nights or more.

Worcestershire

235 10% off room rate Sunday-Thursday.

Yorkshire

242 Late checkout (12.30pm). Upgrade to a suite, subject to availability.

253 Half bottle of champagne on arrival.

254 Champagne & canapés served in your room.

257 Bottle of wine with dinner.

Wales
Anglesey

259 Afternoon tea on arrival.

Cardiff

260 3-night stay (incl. Sat/Sun) half price; bottle of house wine for all 2-night stays.

Conwy

266 10% off room rate Sunday-Thursday for stays of 2 nights or more.

Denbighshire

267 20% off room rate Monday-Thursday.

Glamorgan

270 10% off spa treatments. Glass of champagne before dinner on 1st night.

Gwynedd

274 Afternoon tea on day of arrival.

Monmouthshire

278 10% off room rate Sunday-Thursday, or glass of champagne before dinner Friday-Sunday.

Powys

284 Take the tandem out for the day & get a free packed lunch.

285 Half bottle of champagne in room on arrival.

287 10% off DBB if you stay 2 nights, 15% for 3 nights or more.

289 Free entrance to spa & thermal suite.

Scotland

Argyll & Bute

293 Glass of champagne on arrival.

296 Bottle of house wine with dinner on 1st night.

Dumfries & Galloway

298 Half bottle of champagne on arrival.

299 10% off room rate Sunday-Thursday.

Isle of Colonsay

302 Pre-dinner glass of prosecco in the bar or restaurant.

Perth & Kinross

307 Canapés on arrival.

308 Book 2 nights gourmet DBB & take home a shoulder of local lamb & bottle of South African wine.

310 Afternoon tea with homemade shortbread on arrival.

311 10% off room rate Monday-Thursday. Glass of champagne on arrival.

312 Bottle of house wine with dinner.

Scottish Borders

313 15% off room rate for 2-night stays, Monday-Thursday.

Stirling

314 Tea & homemade cake on arrival.

The Highlands

317 10% off room rate Monday-Thursday.

322 Afternoon tea on arrival. Two tickets for Inverewe gardens.

324 Tea & scones every day 3pm-6pm.

327 Afternoon tea on arrival.

Many of you may want to stay in environmentally friendly places. You may be passionate about local, organic or home-grown food. Or perhaps you want to know that the place you are staying in contributes to the community? To help you we have launched our Ethical Collection, so you can find the right place to stay and also discover how each owner is addressing these issues.

The Collection is made up of places going the extra mile, and taking the steps that most people have not yet taken, in one or more of the following areas:

• **Environment** Those making great efforts to reduce the environmental impact of their Special Place. We expect more than energy-saving light bulbs and recycling – in this part of the Collection you will find owners who make their own natural cleaning products, properties with solar hot water and biomass boilers, the odd green roof and a good measure of green elbow grease.

• **Community** Given to owners who use their property to play a positive role in their local and wider community. For example, by making a contribution from every guest's bill to a local fund, or running pond-dipping courses for local school children on their farm.

• **Food** Awarded to owners who make a real effort to source local or organic food, or to grow their own. We look for those who have gone out of their way

to strike up relationships with local producers or to seek out organic suppliers. It is easier for an owner on a farm in rural Wales to produce their own eggs than for someone in central London, so we take this into account.

How it works

To become part of our Ethical Collection owners choose whether to apply in one, two or all three categories, and fill in a detailed questionnaire asking demanding questions about their activities in the chosen areas. You can download a full list of the questions at www.sawdays.co.uk/ethical_collection

We then review each questionnaire carefully before deciding whether or not to give the award(s). The final decision is

Photo: Strattons, entry 150

subjective; it is based not only on whether an owner ticks 'yes' to a question but also on the detailed explanation that accompanies each 'yes' or 'no' answer. For example, an owner who has tried as hard as possible to install solar water-heating panels, but has failed because of strict conservation planning laws, will be given some credit for their effort (as long as they are doing other things in this area).

We have tried to be as rigorous as possible and have made sure the questions are demanding. We have not checked out the claims of owners before making our decisions, but we do trust them to be honest. We are only human, as are they, so please let us know if you think we have made any mistakes.

The Ethical Collection is a new initiative for us, and we'd love to know what you think about it – email us at ethicalcollection@sawdays.co.uk or write to our Green Editor. And remember that because this is a new scheme some owners have not yet completed their questionnaires – we're sure other places in the guide are working just as hard in these areas, but we don't yet know the full details.

Ethical Collection in this book
On the entry page of all places in the Collection we show which awards have been given.

A list of the places in our Ethical Collection is shown below, by entry number.

Environment
27 • 51 • 121 • 150 • 164 • 167 • 284 • 322

Community
27 • 51 • 150 • 167 • 256 • 322

Food
27 • 51 • 121 • 150 • 164 • 167 • 256 • 284 • 312 • 322

Ethical Collection online
There will be stacks more information on our website, www.sawdays.co.uk. You will be able to read some of the answers each owner has given to our Ethical Collection questionnaire and get a more detailed idea of what they are doing in each area. You will also be able to search for properties that have particular awards.

Photo: An Lochan, entry 312

If you have any comments on entries in this guide, please tell us. If you have a favourite place or a new discovery, please let us know about it. You can return this form or visit www.sawdays.co.uk.

Existing entry

Property name: _____

Entry number: _____ Date of visit: _____

New recommendation

Property name: _____

Address: _____

_____

Tel/Email/Web: _____

Your comments

What did you like (or dislike) about this place? Were the people friendly? What was the location like? What sort of food did they serve?

_____

_____

_____

_____

_____

Your details

Name: _____

Address: _____

_____

_____ Postcode: _____

Tel: _____ Email: _____

Please send completed form to:
BH, Sawday's, The Old Farmyard, Yanley Lane, Long Ashton, Bristol BS41 9LR, UK

Have you enjoyed this book? Why not try one of the others in the Special Places to Stay series and get 35% discount on the RRP *

British Bed & Breakfast (Ed 13)	RRP £14.99	Offer price £9.75
British Bed & Breakfast for Garden Lovers (Ed 4)	RRP £14.99	Offer price £9.75
British Hotels & Inns (Ed 10)	RRP £14.99	Offer price £9.75
Devon & Cornwall (Ed 1)	RRP £ 9.99	Offer price £6.50
Scotland (Ed 1)	RRP £ 9.99	Offer price £6.50
Pubs & Inns of England & Wales (Ed 5)	RRP £14.99	Offer price £9.75
Ireland (Ed 6)	RRP £12.99	Offer price £8.45
French Bed & Breakfast (Ed 10)	RRP £15.99	Offer price £10.40
French Holiday Homes (Ed 4)	RRP £14.99	Offer price £9.75
French Hotels & Châteaux (Ed 5)	RRP £14.99	Offer price £9.75
Paris Hotels (Ed 6)	RRP £10.99	Offer price £7.15
Italy (Ed 5)	RRP £14.99	Offer price £9.75
Spain (Ed 7)	RRP £14.99	Offer price £9.75
Portugal (Ed 4)	RRP £11.99	Offer price £7.80
Croatia (Ed 1)	RRP £11.99	Offer price £7.80
Greece (Ed 1)	RRP £11.99	Offer price £7.80
Turkey (Ed 1)	RRP £11.99	Offer price £7.80
Morocco (Ed 2)	RRP £11.99	Offer price £7.80
India (Ed 2)	RRP £11.99	Offer price £7.80
Green Places to Stay (Ed 1)	RRP £13.99	Offer price £9.10
Go Slow England	RRP £19.99	Offer price £13.00

*postage and packing is added to each order

To order at the Reader's Discount price simply phone 01275 395431 and quote 'Reader Discount BH'.

Photo: The Lime Tree, entry 292

① Cornwall

② Hotel

③ **④** Primrose Valley Hotel

Roll out of bed, drop down for breakfast, slip off to the beach, stroll into town. If you want St Ives bang on your doorstep, you'll be hard pressed to find a better hotel; the sands are a 30-second stroll. Half the rooms have views across the bay, two have balconies for lazy afternoons. Inside, beautiful open-plan interiors revel in an earthy contemporary chic, with leather sofas, varnished floors, fresh flowers and glossy magazines. Bedrooms tend not to be huge, but you can't fault the price or style, so come for Hypnos beds, pastel colours, bespoke furniture and good bathrooms; the suite, with red leather sofa, hi-tech gadgetry and mind-blowing bathroom, is seriously fancy. Andrew and Sue are environmentally aware, committed to sustainable tourism and marine conservation. Their hugely popular breakfast is mostly sourced within the county; food providence is listed on the menu. There's a groovy bar with movie posters and leather sofas that's stocked with potions from far and wide. The New Tate and Barbara Hepworth's garden both wait. Great staff, too. *Minimum stay two nights at weekends.*

Price	£100–£155. Suite £175–£225. **⑤**
Rooms	9: 6 doubles, 2 twins, 1 suite. **⑥**
Meals	Platters £8. **⑦**
Closed	25-26 December & January. **⑧**
Directions	From A3074 Trelyon Avenue; **⑨** before hospital sign slow down, indicate right & turn down Primrose Valley; under bridge, left, then back under bridge; signs for hotel parking.

⑩ Travel Club Offer: see page 367 for details.

⑪ Ethical Collection: Environment; Food. See page 373 for details

Andrew & Sue Biss
Primrose Valley, Porthminster Beach,
St Ives, Cornwall TR26 2ED

Tel	01736 794939
Fax	01736 794939
Email	info@primroseonline.co.uk
Web	www.primroseonline.co.uk

⑫ Entry 27 Map 1

⑬